Praise for *Magdalene Wisdom*

"It takes courage to stand up for the truth that contradicts what authorities have been telling humanity for centuries. Mercedes Kirkel has done just that in *Magdalene Wisdom*, making a wonderful book available to humanity. The question-answer format is extremely accessible, revealing a playful yet profound interaction between Mary Magdalene and the questioner. Each chapter leaves you wanting more of Mary's heartwarming and vibration-raising messages—who now from the spiritual dimension plays a decisive role in promoting the equality of the feminine energy on Earth and in humanity's transition to a new world."

—Gabriela and Reint Gaastra-Levin, founders,
the Mary Magdalene and Jesus World School

"A beautifully written book with guidance to help us navigate through the darkest of times."

—Krishna Rose, award-winning author,
Woman in Red: Magdalene Speaks

"Mercedes shares a beautiful and clear vision of the feminine spiritual path, where body, sexuality, femininity, and emotions are not only included, but a devotional key to communion with divine love. In this alchemical journey, Mary Magdalene becomes more than a woman or a voice of the feminine; she opens the gate to the womb of God."

—Seren Bertrand, award-winning author,
co-author of *Magdalene Mysteries*

"*Magdalene Wisdom* offers a deeply eye-opening experience that feels like an intimate conversation with an old friend. Each chapter delivers profound insights. Where others might sensationalize the story of Mary Magdalene, Yeshua, and the divine feminine, Mercedes gently and authentically guides us to rediscover their essence as a living truth. This is a book to savor, reflect on, and return to as you journey deeper into your own spiritual awakening."

—Sandi Rufo, co-founder,
Magdalene Rising Collective

"In *Magdalene Wisdom*, Mercedes brings forth many messages about love from Mary Magdalene. Her channeling with Mary Magdalene explores essential themes for our times—moving from fear to love, living fully from the heart, the true wisdom of Yeshua and Mary Magdalene, and the rise of the sacred feminine. Questions from many people and the channeled answers from Mary Magdalene will be relevant and insightful for many who are experiencing similar situations."

—Caroline Glazebrook, co-founder,
Sacred Magdalene Festival, Avalon

"We are all in need of help at this dark moment in our history. This timely book brings wonderful messages from Mary Magdalene, offering hope, wisdom, and inspiration."

—Anne Baring, PhD, bestselling author,
co-author with Andrew Harvey of *The Divine Feminine*

"Every time I read a passage from this book, it offered an answer to a question I was carrying within me. *Magdalene Wisdom* illuminates a powerful journey toward higher consciousness, inviting readers to unify dualities—whether masculine and feminine, Magdalene and Jeshua, or our own inner polarities—into a deep, singular communion with the divine. At its heart, it calls us to strengthen our direct connection with God."

—Ilona Selke, bestselling author,
Dream Big – The Universe Is Listening

"In *Magdalene Wisdom*, Mercedes beautifully presents the teachings of Mary Magdalene through the answering of questions. Mary's wisdom shines through to teach complex spiritual truths in simple yet deeply profound ways. I especially resonate with the idea that the union of the feminine and masculine divine energies is the highest form of knowing God."

—Sally Patton, author,
Life is a Song of Love: A Woman's Spiritual Journey of the Heart and Womb

"Mercedes Kirkel has channeled a book with so much amazing information about feminine energies, healing our heart, and how to allow our heart to guide us. The book also tells about Yeshua and Mary Magdalene's love relationship. I'm following this book to learn more about creating high-frequency living and loving."

—Cindy Bentley, RN, international energy practitioner and author, *Celestial Being: How to Shift to Fifth Dimension Living*

"Reading *Magdalene Wisdom* felt like a soul-deep remembering. Mary Magdalene's voice spoke directly to my heart, offering profound wisdom on connecting to the divine and embodying our truth. Her invitation to embrace our bodies, emotions, and sexuality as sacred parts of our spiritual journey resonated deeply with me. I highly recommend *Magdalene Wisdom* to anyone ready to embrace a life of greater love, presence, and authenticity."

—Jennifer Corbeau, founder and retreat leader, Spiral Path Journeys

"This book is a must read for anyone seeking greater understanding and acceleration of their spiritual development. *Magdalene Wisdom* contains beautiful, clear, transformative instruction, showing how we can each strengthen and increase our connection to God."

—Marie Baun, kundalini yoga instructor

"*Magdalene Wisdom* is a rich and illuminating compendium of wisdom. Mary's voice speaks to our hearts, bringing comfort, guidance, and inspiration amidst the challenges and dilemmas of the human experience."

—Shakti Sundari, teacher of embodied awakening

"Mary Magdalene shares her message of compassion and hope through this magnificent, captivating book. Like a delicate ointment, Mary's words are utterly soothing—a balm to the many wounds and injuries that society has suffered over the centuries. Mary's teachings prepare us for what is to come, an age where the Divine Feminine will be the driving force in our world."

—Gilles Asselin, disciple of the Magdalene

MAGDALENE WISDOM

The Voice of the Feminine

The Magdalene-Yeshua Teachings

Mercedes Kirkel

RIO RANCHO, NEW MEXICO

Published by
INTO THE HEART CREATIONS
Rio Rancho, New Mexico
www.mercedeskirkel.com

Copyright © 2025 by Mercedes Kirkel

All rights reserved. No part of this book may be used or reproduced in any manner whatsoever without written permission, except in the case of brief quotations embedded in critical articles and reviews.

Paperback ISBN: 979-8-9876633-2-5
Ebook ISBN: 979-8-9876633-3-2

First edition

Publisher's Cataloging-in-Publication

Names:	Kirkel, Mercedes, author.
Title:	Magdalene wisdom : the voice of the feminine / Mercedes Kirkel.
Description:	First edition.	Rio Rancho, New Mexico : Into the Heart Creations, [2025]	Series: The Magdalene-Yeshua teachings.
Identifiers:	ISBN: 979-8-9876633-2-5 (paperback)	979-8-9876633-3-2 (ebook)	LCCN: 2024921008
Subjects:	LCSH: Mary Magdalene, Saint (Spirit)	Jesus Christ--Spiritualistic interpretations.	Feminist theology.	Femininity of God.	Masculinity--Religious aspects.	Masculinity of God.	Self-actualization (Psychology)	Inspiration.	Spiritual life.	Spirituality.	Mind and body.	Channeling (Spiritualism)	Jesus Christ (New Age movement interpretations)	Jesus Christ (Family)	Gnosticism.	Mysticism.	Fourth dimension (Parapsychology)	BISAC: BODY, MIND & SPIRIT / Inspiration & Personal Growth.	BODY, MIND & SPIRIT / Angels & Spirit Guides.	BODY, MIND & SPIRIT / Channeling & Mediumship.	BODY, MIND & SPIRIT / Goddess Worship.	BODY, MIND & SPIRIT / Ancient Mysteries & Controversial Knowledge.
Classification:	LCC: BS2485 .K573 2025	DDC: 226/.092--dc23

Cover art by Denise Daffara, www.denisedaffara.com.au
Book design by Michelle M. White, www.MMWbooks.com

*I offer this collection of enlightened instruction
in deepest gratitude to Mary Magdalene and Yeshua,
whose guidance has changed the lives of countless beings—
including mine.*

Contents

Foreword xiii

Introduction 1

PART I ~ MARY'S CORE MESSAGE

1. You Must Do Your Part 9
2. Changing the Course of Humanity 13
3. We Came Together as Masculine and Feminine 15
4. Navigating the Changes in Your World 18
5. Living from the Heart 24
6. The Purpose of Existence 26
7. The Clarion Call of Love 27

PART II ~ JESUS AND MARY MAGDALENE

8. What Really Happened? 33
9. What Could Not Be Lost 40
10. Divine Lovers 42
11. The True Marriage We Embodied 45
12. Our Lineage 49
13. Feeling Connected to Us 52

PART III ~ THE INNER CIRCLE

14. The Inner School 57
15. The Hidden Work of the Crucifixion 61
16. In the Tomb and After 67
17. The True Meaning of the Cross 71

PART IV ~ FEMININE *AND* MASCULINE

18. The Path of Union 77
19. The Inner Marriage 80
20. The Alchemy of Masculine and Feminine 85
21. Loving the Feminine 87
22. Loving the Masculine 90
23. Let the Feminine Lead 93
24. Helping Men Open to the Feminine 96
25. Supporting the Masculine to Heal 100
26. Sacred Partnership 102
27. Sacred Sexuality 104
28. Inhabiting Your Feminine Power 109
29. The Feminine Path of Trust 118
30. Earth as Feminine 120
31. Changing the World 121
32. Masculine and Feminine in the Gospels 122
33. The Secrets Encoded in Adam and Eve 123

PART V ~ THE HEART

34. The Steps to Real Loving 127
35. Be Carried to God 130
36. Healing the Heart 134
37. Finding Your Purpose 136
38. The Feminine Path of Forgiveness 137
39. Expanding Your Heart 141
40. Lead with Your Heart 143
41. A New Ray of God-Light Emerging 145
42. Opening to Help 147
43. Follow Your Emotions and Your Body 150
44. Trusting the Feminine 153
45. When You're Triggered 155
46. Protection for Sensitive Beings 159
47. Serve from the Fullness of Self-Love 162

PART VI ~ HIGHER CONSCIOUSNESS

48. Shifting to Higher Consciousness 165
49. Full Responsibility 171
50. Becoming Empowered 178
51. What's Yours and What Belongs to Others 181
52. The Bigger Picture of the Soul's Journey 184
53. Illness and Karma 190
54. Seeing the Gift Before You 194
55. Not Taking Things Personally 197
56. Transforming Dualistic Thinking 203
57. The Consciousness of Inclusion 209
58. Discernment Relative to Guidance or Advice 214
59. Knowing Whether Something Is Beneficial 216
60. Respecting Free Choice in Others 218
61. Changing the Story 220
62. Don't Be Fooled by the Media 224
63. Subtle Beings and Planes of Reality 225
64. Gifts from Your Dreams 227

PART VII ~ WHAT'S NEEDED NOW

65. If You're Still in the Third Dimension,
    Your Growth Is Here 233
66. The Necessity of Acceptance and Grieving 238
67. Releasing Anger 246
68. Going Beyond Fear 250
69. Freedom from Shame 255
70. Healing from Abuse 262

PART VIII ~ ASCENDING TO THE FOURTH DIMENSION

71. How Ascension to the Fourth Dimension Will Occur . . . 271
72. The Divide in Your World 274
73. Riding the Waves of Change 280

74. The Dissolution of Familiarity 285
75. The Fullness of Including All 288
76. Multiple Realities 290
77. Expanding into Greater Ecstasy 293
78. Love in Limitation 295
79. The Mystery School Teachings 297
80. Kundalini 300
81. The Merkaba 303

PART IX ~ MANIFESTING YOUR REALITY

82. Attracting for One's Highest Good 311
83. The Secret of Manifestation 313
84. Don't Use the Principle of Manifestation to Judge 318
85. Working with Health Challenges 321
86. Relieving the Suffering of Others 323
87. Creating Abundance 325
88. Calling in a Partner 329

PART X ~ CHILDREN AND SPIRITUALITY

89. Spirituality with Children 335
90. Going Beyond the Third Dimension with Children 336

APPENDIX

List of Feelings 345
List of Inner Divine Qualities 349

Notes 351
About the Author 371
Books and Videos by Mercedes Kirkel 373

Foreword

By Cynthia Greb
Writer, Speaker, and Interfaith Minister

SEVERAL YEARS AGO, I was blessed to attend a presentation where Mercedes Kirkel channeled Mary Magdalene. There were perhaps 150 people gathered. Before the presentation began, Mary invited the audience to form a line, so she could briefly meet each person, tune in, and offer a short message specifically for that individual. The one-sentence message I received was not what I was expecting; it was infinitely deeper and more profound. I have never forgotten her words.

In this book, *Magdalene Wisdom*, the profundity of Mary's words continues. I have read and heard several women channeling Mary Magdalene over the years, and Mary's words, through Mercedes, feel very authentic to me. My intuition clearly tells me that this is the real deal.

I consider the ability to channel a spiritual gift, just like prophecy and healing. Channeling taps into the wisdom of those in spirit form. Of course, we always need to use discernment. We should never blindly accept what someone else says, whether those words come from a clergyperson, a friend, or a spiritual channel. We need to always check in with our heart. Does the message ring true? In *Magdalene Wisdom*, Mary's messages ring true for me. They feel both wise and authentic.

Personally, I love that Mary doesn't feel the need to focus on the past. Instead, she tells us that she and Yeshua are here for us right now, at this specific time on the planet, when the need for the Divine Feminine and the Sacred Masculine has never been greater.

We are here on Earth at this time for a reason. As one indigenous prophecy proclaims: "We are the ones we've been waiting for." And Mary is here to support us.

MAGDALENE WISDOM

Introduction

THERE'S A STORY that's been waiting a long time to be told. It's the story of Mary Magdalene.[1] But that story isn't about whether Mary and Jesus were married. Nor is it about who Mary Magdalene was or what her life events consisted of. The story I'm talking about is the story that *Mary* wants to tell. Her story is finally coming to light because we're finally ready to hear it—and because we need it.

According to Mary, she and "Yeshua"[2] (or Jesus) came to our world together as partners and equals. They had a shared mission, yet each had a unique part to play. Mary's role was to be and teach the Feminine aspect of humanity's spiritual evolution, in balance with Yeshua being and teaching the Masculine aspect.[3] But she and Yeshua knew it would be two thousand years before the world was ready to receive Mary's part. That time is now.

I entered Mary Magdalene's world in 2008. My life up to that point had been driven by a powerful urge for spiritual engagement. I was raised in a Jewish family, but from early on I was drawn to eastern spirituality. That led me, as a young adult, to follow a guru for seventeen years and then to another spiritual teacher, with whom I had a classic spiritual awakening. From there I embraced Native American, goddess, and Tantric spiritual paths. Eventually I discovered New Age spirituality, which seemed markedly different from the traditional spiritual teachings I'd previously encountered.

As I explored this new spiritual arena, I found myself in the company of people who were receiving communications from higher beings, which they referred to as *channeling*.[4] Before long, I, too, started receiving messages.[5] My initial messages were mostly just for me, and I never knew when another communication would come. But I increasingly had the sense that was going to change. I felt myself being led to become a "conscious channel"—someone who could receive messages for others and at times of the channeler's choosing.

What I didn't anticipate was that my most important messages would come from two of the best-known figures in Christianity. I had no Christian background or inclinations. Why would they choose me? But that's exactly what happened.

It began with a challenging message from my personal guides. I was told it was time to leave Hawaii (where I'd been living for ten years). I was reluctant to do that because I loved Hawaii and planned to spend the rest of my life there. So I checked out the guidance two more times to be sure I was hearing it correctly. Each time I received the same instruction. At that point I accepted the message. I'd seen that things always worked out for the best when I followed the guidance I received.

I proceeded to close out my life in Hawaii and then went on an extended "trip," waiting to receive clarification of where my new home would be. Eventually, I was guided to Santa Fe, NM. And almost immediately, Mary Magdalene started coming to me.

My connection with Mary started with her giving me an astounding message, and it was obvious she wasn't speaking just to me. Her communication was for all humanity. I felt with great clarity that she was entrusting me to make her communications available to the world.

The next day Mary returned with an equally amazing communication. This continued for a month, with Mary coming to me daily, each time bringing a mind-opening message. I quickly realized she was downloading a book to me, chapter by chapter. And that was the birth of my first book, *Mary Magdalene Beckons*.

Communicating with Mary opened a door within me. Suddenly, I could communicate with a seemingly endless array of higher beings. I also could read Akashic records, which contain the record of each soul's journey over their many incarnations. I started channeling for others and received consistent feedback that the communications I brought forth were accurate and authentic.

For a while I continued channeling these many beings. But at a certain point, my personal guides told me that if I wanted to be of greatest service, I would focus on just Mary Magdalene and Yeshua. They said Mary and Yeshua wanted to bring a specific teaching through me and that focusing on their communications would bring the greatest benefit to the most people. So I chose to do just that.

Over the ensuing years, Mary and Yeshua communicated a wealth of groundbreaking and awakening messages to me. Most of these have been published in my previous books, which I came to call the Magdalene-Yeshua Teachings.[6] But some—given during individual sessions or group channeling events—weren't included in those books, and I felt Mary's full teaching wasn't complete without those messages. That was the impulse for this book—to share those remaining messages, each a shining pearl of wisdom.

What emerged from bringing all those messages together into this book was an overview of Mary's whole teaching. In some ways I wish this had been the first book of the Magdalene-Yeshua Teaching Series because it gives the big picture of what Mary wants us to hear. But I didn't know what that big picture was when I began receiving Mary's messages. That took years to coalesce through hearing all her communications, including her responses to the multitude of questions she was asked.

It's those interchanges that are presented here. You might liken it to the Socratic method, where the teaching is given in response to the students' questions. And what a teaching it is!

Most of the dialogs begin with the question that was asked. However, there are a few chapters without an initial question. Sometimes that's because the material was part of an interchange that was personal to the one asking the question and I only included the portion of Mary's response that was universal. In other instances, Mary's communication covered more than one topic, and I included the earlier part of the exchange in a different section of the book. The other reason why some chapters don't begin with a question is that some communications were initiated by Mary herself—often in response to something she felt I or others were struggling with and needed help to understand.

As for the order of the messages, I've grouped similar communications together, which I hope helps readers grasp the totality of Mary's instruction (as I have been blessed to do through receiving her messages over the years). The messages weren't given in these thematic groups. The grouping is entirely my creation. I also grouped some messages together within a single chapter when Mary was addressing the same topic. In these cases, the individual messages are separated with a visual divider.

You'll probably hear repetition within these messages. That's because the messages were given on different occasions to different audiences. Initially, I tried to eliminate all repetition, but I found that doing so changed what Mary said. So I chose to leave her messages as she gave them, feeling that staying true to Mary's actual words and the wholeness of her communication was most important.

What's more, Mary likes repetition. She thinks it helps us to shift into a different way of relating to things and, ultimately, a different consciousness. With this perspective, I invite you to open yourself to the reiteration of ideas and themes as something like a mantra[7] or prayer, carrying you ever deeper into Mary's reality.

I feel a strong resonance between Mary's communications in these messages and the words of Jesus that are recorded in the Bible. Jesus's words were most often responses given to specific individuals that carried universal truths. The sum of his responses form the tapestry of his teaching. So it is with Mary's words here.

Now I turn you over to Mary, whose voice and message are so much stronger and more important than mine. May you find great value and guidance through her treasure chest of wisdom.

PART I

Mary's Core Message

Chapter 1

You Must Do Your Part

[This message was given at a celebration of Mary Magdalene's feast day.]

Mary Magdalene: Blessings, dear ones. This is Mary Magdalene. I'm so happy to be here with you and have this time together. My heart is filled with love in this moment. I hope you're able to feel it. I'm full of love for all beings, but tonight I'm especially full of love for all of you. I'm grateful to you for opening yourselves to me and to so many beautiful beings of light.

Of course, each of you is also a beautiful being of light. I see you that way, and more and more you're coming to know yourself that way. That's something that *I* celebrate, for that's part of what humanity is growing into at this time—each of you knowing yourself as a being of light, which you absolutely are and always have been. I and others are helping you to recognize and grow fully into this and to be the manifestation of light that you've come here to be.

So I'm celebrating you. And I'm celebrating this amazing time on Earth, which you've all chosen to be here for. You're participating in and supporting humanity's evolution into a new age, a new consciousness, and a new world. It's a time of knowing yourselves in a much greater way as the beings of light that you are.

This movement into a new age is well underway. There are many things that will need to happen before you've fully made this transition, but it's begun, and you're in the midst of it. There's no question that this new era will arrive. And you're all a part of ushering yourselves and all beings into this new age.

In Yeshua's and my time on Earth, we, too, were a part of this transition. (Two thousand years is actually a very short amount of time in terms of these kinds of openings and changes.) That was the beginning, and it's still going on. Many of you have a connection to Yeshua and me from that time, and we're still deeply connected to you. It's a continuation.

Of course, when I speak of time, I'm referencing it in ways that make sense to you—in the third dimension, at this time. [Mary laughs quietly.] I don't generally relate to time in the same way. For me, we've always been together. There's been no separation, no passage of time. But I understand that many of you experience time differently. That's fine. However you relate to time is perfect for what's supporting you at this moment. And that will change over time, in the perfect time. It's nothing to be concerned about.

To the many who I've known in different periods, I say "hello" to you, across time. You're all so special to me, so deeply loved. I wish I had better words to express this and to make it clear how much I value you, how much you're a part of my heart and my joy.

You're going to be seeing many changes in your world. Some of them may be wonderful, some may be surprising, some may seem challenging. It's all part of the "changing of the guard," the release and letting go of so much that's been a part of your world, your consciousness, and your reality for a long time. New things are coming in. There's a death of the old and a birth of the new happening simultaneously.

Some aspects of this letting go, release, and death process may be difficult or even scary. I've given a great deal of instruction about how to relate to difficult situations (including situations where you feel afraid) and how to make use of those situations to bring you to God.[8] What's most important is strengthening your connection to God. It's always been important. But at this time, maintaining your strength and stability in your connection to God is essential.

Whatever strengthens you and maintains your absolute, unwavering connection to God—whether it's a daily practice, the company you keep, being inspired by books or communications, or whatever else—it's only going to become more important. I urge you to support yourself in that way, which will also support others.

Your connection to God is the greatest form of support you can give. Through your own connection, you strengthen and increase the grid of connection to God.[9] This will help make the passage into a new age easier, gentler, and more graceful for everyone. I ask that all of you do your part, as much as you're able, to strengthen this grid, and in this way to help all beings. And doing this will make it most wonderful for you as well.

I'm reaching out and sincerely asking for everyone's help. Each person who participates in this way makes an enormous difference. Remember that the number one thing is your connection to God. Beyond that there's blessing, prayer, sending light. Those are valuable too, but they're secondary. The primary thing is your bond and oneness with God. That will make the greatest difference. It will also guide you and let you know what you're to be doing through all the changes. You'll have clarity and will know.

I beseech you to maintain this practice and disposition, which you might call "the asana of connection to God."[10] Do this with the greatest strength you're able to bring. Call upon your guides. Call upon God directly. Ask for help in whatever form is strongest for you. And you will receive it.

I thank you for doing that.

It's so important that this be held on Earth and not simply by the higher beings who are doing so much to support this. You have your part to do too, and it's very important.

Chapter 2

Changing the Course of Humanity

Mary Magdalene: Yeshua and I came to change the course of humanity.[11] Humanity had been on a course of descent into manifestation over many millennia. This course of descent took humans from the highest planes down into the depths of the third dimension. Yeshua and I came to turn this trajectory of descension into ascension. We came to turn humanity's course around into moving back into the higher dimensions, beginning with the fourth dimension.[12]

The third dimension is a school for learning about power. The setting for this school is physical embodiment, where beings believe in death and that there isn't "enough" for everyone. Thus, people turn to power over others, fueled by competition, to survive and thrive.

The fourth dimension is a different kind of school, where the focus of learning is on manifestation or creation. The setting for the fourth-dimensional school is one's light body and the energetic realm, like you experience when you dream. In the fourth dimension, beings are learning to consciously create the reality they want, which is ultimately a reality of love.

There are real changes that must occur in individuals and in your world for this transformation from 3D to 4D to happen. It's not just a matter of believing certain things. It's a change at the level of physics. One of the requirements was the physical embodiment of the Divine Masculine and Feminine. Yeshua and I incarnated into the Earth-plane two thousand years ago to fulfill this requirement.

The crucifixion[13] was the completion of our work at that time. It was an energetic implanting of this new course into the Earth-realm. We were both prepared to do this energetic work through many lifetimes of spiritual training, along with our training in that lifetime. And we were supported by others who were also prepared.[14]

After the crucifixion, Yeshua showed himself in his light body.[15] This is the form you'll all have in the fourth dimension, like you do when you dream. Yeshua was showing humanity where you're headed. You don't need to die physically to do this. It's your attachment to the third dimension that must die.[16]

You're now the leaders of this movement. You must do the real work within yourself of releasing all your attachments to the third dimension—including power over others, which the third dimension is rooted in. You must replace this with the real skills for living and creating in the fourth-dimensional way. There are ones among you who know how to do this and want to help you. Make use of their help, and let this become your reality.

We've done our part. The seed is planted. It's waiting for you, whenever you're ready.

We love you and support you in your most beautiful journey of love, your journey into the light.

Chapter 3

We Came Together as Masculine and Feminine

Question: Many teachings present Yeshua as speaking in the Masculine, where he says "He," "him," "brothers," and so on. I want to hear the Sacred Feminine, using the Feminine words that I believe Yeshua spoke in Aramaic.

Mary Magdalene: Now is the beginning of this changing. When I say "now" you must understand time. Now is, for many, a vast period of time. But in terms of eternity, in terms of the wholeness of time, it's a very short period of time.

I came with Yeshua. We came to teach together. And we knew the world was not ready. We gave our teaching. Those who had ears to hear, heard.

What was recorded of our work, and later embellished upon, was primarily the Masculine because that was what most people were ready for. Now that's changing.

Many of the teachings in your world are Masculine teachings, in separation from the Feminine. These teachings still contain gifts. The Masculine has very important gifts. And most of you are well on your way in receiving the Masculine gifts, because this has been so greatly supported in your world.

Most of you are starved for the Feminine. It's not just your culture and politics that are starving. Your inner being is starved for the Feminine. This is as true in your spiritual world as in all your other worlds.

Most of the leaders and teachers in your world (including the spiritual world) are men. But the Masculine-only perspective isn't limited to men. Men and women alike have been denied the Feminine.

My work is to bring forth the Feminine. I'm not alone—there are others. But it's specifically what I have come to do. It's the reason that so many respond to me, especially women.

The world has never succeeded in denying the Feminine. It was never truly possible. But your minds have been greatly fooled. Most of you need help finding your way out of the labyrinth of your mind. When you do, your mind will be of great service to you. The mind is a tremendous gift from God. But it was never meant to be used against the Feminine.

As I have spoken all along, and especially in the messages that are recorded in *Mary Magdalene Beckons*,[17] the work for most of you is, first and foremost, to strengthen the Feminine within yourself. This means bringing forth the Feminine through your body, your sexuality, and your emotions.

You'll probably notice that these three arenas—your body, your sexuality, and your emotions—aren't very popular in most spiritual teachings. Some teachings go so far as to say these are the main blocks to spiritual growth. They teach that if you want to grow, you must separate yourself from your body, your sexuality, and your emotions. Some teachings assert that your body, your sexuality, and your emotions aren't real and that any involvement with them will hold you back from your spiritual growth.

This is very sad. This is the perspective of the Masculine separated from the Feminine. This was never Yeshua's teaching, though some have portrayed it that way.

Chapter 4

Navigating the Changes in Your World

Mary Magdalene: Many of you are worried about what's happening in your world. You're worried about your leaders and the politics they're engaging. You're worried about your financial systems and about your financial well-being. You're worried about the Earth and how she's being cared for. You're worried about the changes in nature that you're witnessing. You're worried about your physical well-being. You're worried about change in your world on so many levels, changes that you sense but don't fully understand. You'd like to have trust and reassurance in your own safety and well-being, as well as the safety and well-being of society and the world altogether.

You're correct that there's a great deal of change happening in your world. Many of you have been protected from such change and uncertainty in your lifetime. You've had a sense of order and stability. Now that seems to be eroding, dissolving, falling away. This is going to increase for most of you. You're involved in a time of great change.

A great transition is underway on Earth—within cultures and societies, and within individuals. You could see it as a death of the old ways, structures, and forms and a rebirth of new ways, structures, and forms. As with any death/rebirth process, you must let go and surrender to death, going into the unknown, before you're reborn into the new forms and knowingness.

You can do things to either obstruct this process and make it more difficult, or to flow with it and allow it to do its work of transformation and change. This process can be a great gift to you. The great wave of change that's building and sweeping through your world has power to carry you forward much more quickly and easily than if you were doing this on your own, without this kind of energetic movement occurring. You're being given a great and rare opportunity to participate in this immense movement of transformation.

You must become conscious of what you're doing that's blocking this flow. Worry is one such thing. You may not think of yourself as worrying, yet there may be a subtle (or sometimes not-so-subtle) tension in you of resistance to what's happening. You may see signs of resistance in your speech—talking about how bad things are and focusing on what others are doing that you think is wrong, bad, or destructive (whether "the other" is a leader, a neighbor, your boss, a friend, or whoever).

Perhaps you're aware that it's not in your highest good to think or speak this way, so you try to suppress this energy or speech, and deny that you feel this way. That's not the way either, for the energy of negativity is still within you, only now you've added another layer of suppression on top of it. Then you have two repressive forces going on—the first of trying to repress others or the outside world, and the second of trying to repress yourself.

The way out is through consciousness and honesty. First, you must become conscious of any negativity within you. By negativity,

I mean any belief that things are wrong or bad or shouldn't be occurring as they are. This is a deep-seated belief for many at this time, a sense that you "know" what's right or good or how things should be. It's also a confusion for many. I would like to speak to this confusion.

Each of you have a sense within of what's of light and love, and there's an inherent longing for that light and love. This is real and something that you can trust.

However, your inner sense of light and love isn't the same as judging something to be right or wrong, good or bad, appropriate or inappropriate, positive or negative. The act of judging is fear-based. It's an attempt to control or superimpose on yourself or others through force, even if it's just the force of will or mind. This has created problems and suffering for you and your world, for so long.

The opposite—of simply allowing everything and not exerting your will, being completely passive—is no more enlightened. That's simply giving up, and that's not what you're here to do.

What you're called to is to return to light and love, always. Ultimately, you're called to abide continuously in light and love. But at first this begins with returning to light and love again and again—whenever you notice or become conscious that you're not coming from that place.

Perhaps you notice that you're judging or worrying. Or you notice that you're not filled with light and love. When you notice that, don't immediately jump into the opposite, or whatever you think you "should" be doing, for that will simply be a reaction. You haven't addressed the root.

The root is that you're in your mind, and you're disconnected from your heart. In some form, you're rooted in fear (which may be subtle or fairly gross). Another way of saying this is that you're not feeling trust, openness, and peace in relationship to whatever is happening.

The process of reconnecting with your heart begins with feeling. Rather than *thinking* that something is bad, wrong, or shouldn't be happening, shift into *experiencing* your heart and your feelings.

You might be feeling scared, concerned, anxious, sad, hopeless, powerless, confused, or some other emotion. Whatever it is, let yourself feel it in your heart. It won't be about what someone else is doing, or the rightness or wrongness of what's happening. It will be a pure emotion or sensation *within you,* with no sense of rightness or wrongness to it.

That's the beginning. For some of you this is a huge step because you've been systematically trained to disconnect from your feelings, to the point that you may not know what you're feeling. Your great help in this is your body. Go to your body and your body's experience, and it will tell you what you're feeling.

Feeling is the foundation of the heart. It's the basis of love. You can only love if you're open in your feeling dimension. Feeling is what allows you to love.

Feeling often involves experiencing some form of pain. I'm not simply telling you to be in pain. This is what many of you fear—that if you feel your pain, you'll be stuck in it forever. In fact, the opposite is true: *If you don't feel your pain, you'll be stuck in it forever.*

Not-feeling is the very thing that's supporting so much of what you don't like in your world right now. When you don't feel, you reside in your thinking mind. You give power to things through your thinking, even if your thoughts are in opposition to those things. Whatever you think about, you empower.

The way out is to feel. Open to pain through feeling, and let your feeling take you all the way to the *source* of your feelings.

That source is something within you, which I call your *inner divine qualities*.[18] These are beautiful qualities that live within each one of you. Each of your inner divine qualities is some aspect of the divine. When you're connected to God or the divine, you experience these beautiful qualities, which brings you into the peace and beauty of the divine.

Painful feelings are indicators that you've become disconnected from one or more of your inner divine qualities. And feeling is the medium for turning that around. Through feeling, you're guided to the specific inner divine quality that you've become disconnected from. Once you're there at that quality, your being knows what to do to reconnect you to love and light.[19]

Now you're ready to act because you're once again connected to love and light. Your actions may be to bless others, bringing love and light to them. Your actions may be to take care of yourself, or others, or your world in some way. These actions won't be based in fear, judgment, and avoiding pain. They'll be based in your connection to love and light, to God. And you'll be guided through that connection to what you should do that will support love and light in your world.[20]

This is how to navigate through times of change. It's really how to navigate through any moment, so you stay connected to light and love. The more you do this, the more skilled you become at it. The process becomes more natural and easier, and happens more immediately.

Eventually you'll experience less fear, sadness, or other painful emotions. But don't focus on making your painful emotions go away, as that will simply block the process. Focus on opening up to feeling and following your feelings to Source.[21] As your engagement of this gets stronger, you'll increasingly abide as the qualities of Source. That's part of the growth that this grand wave of change, energy, and transformation is leading you to.

Welcome the change and make use of it to take you to God. Open your feeling and heart to your experience, and let that lead you to love and light. Then be the marvelous vehicle of love and light that you are, and are called to be. That is your joy and your destiny, as it is for all. I call you to that and support you in it most fully. And I reassure you that it's most definitely worth it.

Chapter 5

Living from the Heart

[This message was given at a Heart Path retreat.²²]

Mary Magdalene: This is such an important time in your world. The Heart Path is so critical, so needed—and also so distant for many. I call upon you to continue to live from the heart space, and through that to help make the shift in your world into the heart.

Your living in the heart will help others find this place. It's not necessary to tell others what you're doing. It's not necessary for you to teach about the Heart Path. Simply live the Heart Path. Make the direct connection with others, heart to heart.

Many of you came here to do this work, which is essential at this time. It requires awareness. You must be aware of your choice, moment to moment, to be connected to and living from the heart space—or to forget your heart and wander in the desert of the mind. You all have the power to do this heart work. Now it's your choice of whether you'll live it.

It's supportive to be with others who are also living in the heart space. You have that choice too, and can create that as well.

You've been empowered to become creators—to step out of

the mold of being told what to do and that you only have certain options, and to realize your unlimited nature. Of course, this is a process, which most of you are at the beginning of. That's fine. Just know that you always have a choice, in every moment, to engage the creative process as fully as you're able at your present stage of development. That's all that's ever asked of you.

Your world doesn't generally support this, so you're stepping beyond your world. You don't have to alienate the world or sever your ties to the world. But there's a natural process of outgrowing happening—like a school, where you graduate from a certain level and it's natural to move on.

Not everyone sees this. Some are even threatened by their interpretation of your moving on. You can be in your heart with them as well. You can connect with your heart *and* their heart, their feelings, their beautiful inner divinity.[23] Know that they're on their path too. They're fulfilling their inner divinity. Even though the path they're being guided to may not be the same as yours, respect their choice. Give them to God, as you give yourself to God, and be guided through your connection to God as to what to do.

Chapter 6

The Purpose of Existence

Question: What is the purpose of existence?

Mary Magdalene: It's to know God, always.

You have endless possibilities for getting distracted from your purpose. As you grow, those possibilities will have less and less hold on you, and you'll grow bigger and bigger. You'll become an increasingly more magnificent version of yourself. At some point, you'll realize the God you have sought is yourself, and also everything else.

The realization of your God-nature isn't something that can be held as an idea. It can only be achieved through your experience and beingness. When it happens, you'll know the difference.

Chapter 7

The Clarion Call of Love

Mary Magdalene: Beloveds, I come to you today to share my love with you. That love is the same as my love for Yeshua. And it's Yeshua's love too. They're all the same.

I was immeasurably blessed to love Yeshua in human form, to be his twin flame.[24] And the same love is available to you.

There's no separation in this love. No separation between me and you. No separation between Yeshua and you. This love is the greatest gift our Supreme Creator has given us. It's worth everything. Give everything for this love, for this love gives everything to you.

I hear you ask, "How do I know this love?" You know much about this love already. It's known as you grow spiritually. The measure of your spiritual growth is your heart opening. And when your heart opens, it's filled with love.

Sometimes you experience this love for no reason. When you love another, you often experience this love. At times you experience this love when you feel completely at peace, when you commune with nature, or when you're deeply in touch with yourself, your soul. Whenever you connect with God, in whatever way you do, you experience this love.

In this world, you think you're separate, cut off. It's not so, but you think it is. Love is the bridge that connects you to your true state. That connection may exist for a moment, or forever, or anything in between.

Eventually this union won't disappear, but it will take growth for most of you to experience that. It's what you're all growing toward. You're drawn toward this union like a moth to the light. Even if you don't understand, you're drawn toward love. And so it should be, for God is love, and you are love.

Love is your nature. Love is the nature of all that is.

I've told you much about how you can grow in love at this time and what your next steps forward are.[25] Some call this growth in love "the ascension process,"[26] and that's as good a name as any. You're growing into higher states of consciousness, and with that will come more love. You're not growing away from anything or leaving anything behind. It's not an escape. It's an expansion to include more of who you are, more of all that is.

As I've said many times, the area that's most important for your spiritual growth is the emotional realm. You must expand to include all of your emotions, to love and embrace all of them. This is the pivotal piece at this time that will allow you to move forward.

Your emotions are like a woman. Indeed, they're part of your Feminine side. How you relate to your emotions is a reflection of how you relate to women altogether. Are you afraid of them? Do you minimize them? Try to avoid them? Deny them? Are you at a loss with what to do with them? Are you convinced they'll drag you down into an abyss of suffering?

These ideas are part of the consciousness of separation, which has everything to do with the separation of the Masculine from the

Feminine. That consciousness of separation includes the separation of your inner Masculine and Feminine, and how you relate to those aspects of yourself.

This present time is the clarion call, the ripe moment, when you and everyone are being called to heal this form of separation. Doing this will catapult you forward in your growth and evolution into the state of love that your being longs for.

Are you ready to love the Feminine, including your own inner Feminine? Have you had enough of separation? It's up to you, and the choice is pivotal.

Yeshua wasn't afraid of women. He had no need to separate himself from the Feminine. He was in union with all. He lived this, breathed it, walked it, and radiated it to all. Now you're called to do the same.

I love you, all of you, and I support you always in love.

PART II

Jesus and Mary Magdalene

Chapter 8

What Really Happened?

Question: What really happened with you and Jesus when you incarnated two thousand years ago? Were you married? Were you sexual? Did you have children? Was Jesus born through immaculate conception? Did Jesus survive the crucifixion? Where is Jesus buried?

Mary Magdalene: It seems that most of the questions people are asking about Yeshua and me are based on wanting to know what really happened in the past. I would like to address this focus on "what really happened," because it's actually the underlying issue. *Can anyone know what happened? Is it necessary to know what happened? Why do people want to know what happened?*

The desire to know "what happened" is related to the way beings learn and grow in the third dimension. Most of you require experiences that are based in your physical senses. You especially require to see, hear, and touch. If you have these experiences, then you believe something is real or true.

Higher beings come into physical manifestation to give these kinds of sensory experiences to people in the third dimension.[27] This allows those in the third dimension to trust that what the higher being says and does is real and true. If that trust exists, there's the possibility that people will open their heart and mind to that higher being. Then the higher being can help them grow spiritually through the process of spiritual transmission (which means to give someone the direct experience of a higher dimension).

Spiritual transmission can be given in a number of ways. It can happen through sight—seeing a being who brings a higher consciousness and affords individuals access to higher dimensions. It can also happen through hearing the words of a being awakened to higher dimensions. Or it can happen through receiving the touch of such a being. These forms of spiritual transmission have been given the name *shaktipat* in the Indian tradition, where there's more understanding of the efficacy and value of this kind of interaction. Touch is generally considered to be the strongest form, with sight second and speech third.

For those who aren't able to be physically present with a being who's offering spiritual transmission, there are other avenues of receiving their transmission. Spiritual transmission can occur through seeing pictures or hearing audio recordings of spiritual beings, reading their written teaching, or through hearing stories about them.

Stories are a particularly potent form of transmission in your third-dimensional world. In hearing a story, the listener or receiver will often identify with the characters in the story and thus feel the story come to life within themself. This is an important process that's much more than fantasy or "mere imagination," though some might attribute it to that and, in so doing, try to minimize its importance. But it's not "mere imagination." It's actually very important.

Why is this important? Because it's part of how creation takes place. You have a popular song in your culture that refers to this in a line that goes something like, "If I can dream it, I can be it." There's great truth in this, more than most beings in your world understand or are aware of. You'll come to know and integrate this understanding fully in the fourth dimension.

As I've said before, the fourth dimension is like the place you're familiar with from your dreams when you sleep. It's a realm where you're much more aware of your ability to create through your thoughts, feelings, and actions. Ultimately, your ability to create comes from your total consciousness.

This is also true of the third dimension. But because the third dimension is physically based and seems more fixed and immutable than the higher dimensions (such as the realm you visit in your dreams), most people aren't aware that the third dimension is also a place of creation. Nonetheless, you're creating your reality through your consciousness in the third dimension. It's as though everything you experience is a movie or TV show that's constantly being created by your consciousness. And you've taken the starring role! [Mary smiles.]

One reason it can be hard for people to accept the idea that they've created their reality is if they're still entrenched in right-wrong thinking. In that case, they tend to confuse being a creator with blame for things happening that they think are wrong or bad. Growing beyond this kind of thinking is part of the great school of the third dimension.

While pain and suffering are an inherent part of the third dimension (and you'll be glad to hear that they are not, for the most part, a part of the higher dimensions in the same gross form), they aren't evidence of someone doing something wrong. They're simply a form of learning that's helping you to grow into love and light. This is a form of learning that all beings in the third dimension have freely chosen because pain and suffering are such a powerful means for propelling individuals forward in their growth.

You may be wondering what this has to do with the original question about what happened two thousand years ago with me and with Jesus. It has to do with the power of stories as a particularly human form of learning and growth. When individuals hear a story, they either resonate with it or they don't. They discern at some level whether they trust the story—whether it seems believable and has value for them. If they decide it's believable and has value, they'll let it into their consciousness. Then it becomes a part of them.

This is the same thing you do with any experience. When you encounter another person, you discern if you resonate with that person or not—if you trust them, relate to them, and if they have value for you. If these three criteria are met, you'll open yourself to them in some way, and that will shape the course of your life.

The same is true of a story. If you open yourself to it, it will shape the course of your life in one way or another. If many people open themselves to the same story, it will shape the course of your culture.

You as an individual and as a collective are creating your life based on your consciousness. It doesn't really matter whether that consciousness is based on a physically perceived experience or a story. Both have the power to create your life once you let them in. From our perspective in the higher dimensions, the difference isn't significant. What you've experienced physically could be seen as a kind of story that your consciousness is having. And certainly your memory of what you've experienced can be seen as a kind of story.

Many of you have heard the expression "You're not a human being having a spiritual experience; you're a spiritual being having a human experience." If you're rooted in the second statement, you could see yourself (or anyone else) as a spiritual being that's immersed in a kind of story that you call "human life." From that perspective, it becomes much less important to know *what really happened*. You understand that it's just a story, and whatever "happened" is simply one choice out of an infinite number of possibilities. That's true of everything you refer to as "real life."

What's important in a story isn't what happened. Events are simply the means to give you a particular experience. The experience may be to have an adventure, to grow in new ideas or understandings, or to open you emotionally in a way that deepens your heart. These tend to be the kinds of experiences you have in the stories that you value.

In your world today, many different stories exist about Yeshua (or Jesus) and me. What's important is not the veracity of the various stories. That pursuit is going to draw you deeper into the third-dimensional consciousness of needing things to be "real," which usually means provable in a physical way. And the ultimate result of that pursuit is to reinforce being limited to the physical dimension.

You have another option, which is to see these stories in the way that we do in the higher dimensions. You can see these stories as vehicles for opening to spiritual reality, which means opening to love and light, and ultimately, opening to God. Depending on where someone is in their spiritual path and development, and the level of consciousness they're resonating at, different people will align themselves with different stories—because those are the ones that meet their criteria of resonating with their experience and having value for them. So they'll open to certain stories and not others. All people do this.

Over the course of a lifetime, an individual may align with a certain story at a particular point in their development and then outgrow that story as they develop further. Many of you have had this experience relative to the story of Santa Claus, for example. When you were young, you held that story as true in a particular way. Later, you held it as a story that wasn't factually true but was either a sweet fiction, a reflection of a part of human nature, or a myth based on certain cultural practices or historical figures.

The stories that abound in your time about Yeshua and me are maintained by the consciousness of the people who believe in them. They're helpful for those people at their current level of spiritual growth. Trying to change someone's story is similar to trying to change a person's dreams. It's not going to be productive. They're opening themselves to that story because it's a fit for them at their stage and process in the current moment.

It's not your job to reconcile all the stories that exist, other than to consider the source of those stories in your own consciousness. What do others' stories and your response to them reflect about you? What are your stories? Do you need others to validate your story in order to trust it yourself or to be accepted by them? What does this say about *you* and your opening to love and light? What limits does this reflect in you? And what are your options for going beyond those limits?

What if you were to accept all the diversity of stories as something like a huge fair with many different possibilities? What if you could love all the stories as parts of different people in their process of growing into light and love? What if you were to release any sense of responsibility for knowing "the truth" and simply supported everyone in discovering *their* truth in this moment and the story that reflects that truth for them?

Some of you have fear that others might accuse you of being wrong if they view your story as false. Indeed, this has happened to many in the past, including some of you hearing my words.[28] If that's the case, then part of your growth in this lifetime is to go beyond your fear of not being accepted or even being harmed by others' lack of understanding.

Even these are stories you're creating. Your spiritual process in this moment may be to create new stories for yourself, in which others understand and value you.[29] It really is that simple. But no, it's not easy, especially in the third dimension.

Spiritual growth isn't easy, but it is simple. I'm here to support you in your spiritual growth to the fullest extent I can because I love you profoundly. And it will become simpler. As you grow, the things you struggled with in the past will become easier. But this is for you to realize, as you inevitably will.

I love you and embrace you tenderly in my arms of care and compassion. Know that all of this is helping you to grow.

Chapter 9

What Could Not Be Lost

Question: It seems the Christian Church wanted to make you unavailable. But maybe more important were the principles of the Feminine aspect of the divine that you brought forth.

Mary Magdalene: Very much so.

This is why Yeshua was turned into a god, so he could be distant and removed. Part of that removal was the removal of his teaching, including the idea that others could be what he was and is. The idea of Yeshua being different from all other humans was the opposite of what he taught. So there was much that was changed and much that was lost.

What was *not* lost was Yeshua's spiritual presence. People's connection with his presence is very real, and there's great power in that presence. Your eastern religions have long recognized that contact with spiritual presence is one of the ways that spiritual transformation can happen. Another way is through teaching.

Many people have experienced the transmission of spiritual presence with Yeshua and with me. It's why people have remained in connection with both of us. In my case, it would have been easy for my story, my work, my everything to have been buried. But it didn't happen because the Church was only able to change the mental aspects of what occurred—the story and the teaching. They couldn't change the reality of spiritual presence. That has remained alive and carried the ember of Yeshua's and my work all this time.

Spiritual instruction is also a tremendous boon. The most powerful is the combination—for people to have spiritual instruction along with spiritual presence. The two together are a tremendous help.

In the third dimension, part of being so bonded to the physical form is that beings are more easily connected to the human form of anything than to its more subtle manifestations. Teaching and spiritual presence are both more subtle. The human form and human connection are the most accessible. This is part of why it was important for us to manifest in human form.

Our human manifestation also inspired people and gave them hope that if this happened for one human, it could happen for them. There's tremendous power in that hope. Hope is an enormous spiritual asset. It can turn the spark of spiritual connection into a raging fire, a passion that transforms and creates miracles.

Different people will resonate with different aspects of our work, and that's fine. Whatever form speaks to your heart, that's the form that will feed and support you for this part of your spiritual journey.

Chapter 10

Divine Lovers

Question: Can you tell us about your relationship with Yeshua when you incarnated two thousand years ago?

Mary Magdalene: Yeshua and I were divine lovers. We always have been and always will be. So naturally, we came as lovers in that lifetime.

Because of the limited consciousness of those on Earth at that time, and later of those in the church leadership, many limits were placed on things. One of those limits involved what our relationship was, making sexuality somehow unspiritual, evil, sinful, dirty. This was part of a bigger picture of making the Feminine aspect altogether to be unspiritual, sinful, dirty, evil.

Yeshua and I both knew that the world at that time was not, in general, ready to receive me in my role. But a seed was planted. We were aware that it would be two thousand years before that seed would come to fruition. That time is now. Many are awakening to a strong impulse to know Mary Magdalene, as well as other forms of the Divine Feminine. The Divine Feminine isn't unique to me, and the form the Feminine comes in is not essential. But many are awakening to my form at this time.

It's understandable that this would be happening now because a strong root has already been planted of people's connection to Yeshua. Now the counterpart of the Divine Feminine is being called in, so many are responding to that. There's now a great deal of interest in your world about who I was, what really happened, and the nature of my relationship to Yeshua.

Of course we were lovers! We were lovers on all levels, including sexually. We engaged sexuality as a truly sacred practice of connecting with God and transforming ourselves into our whole God-being. Our sacred sexuality was a means of empowering ourselves, especially at the level of the energy body. It was also a practice of blessing—bringing the blessings of God and God-communion to Earth.

We brought the blessings of God in many forms, but sexuality was certainly one of the ways we did that. We were incredible lovers at the level of the heart and consciousness. We were truly a demonstration of the union of the Masculine and the Feminine in embodied form, within physical manifestation. Many people weren't ready for that. But a seed was planted, and now it's coming forth.

Question: Did you and Yeshua have physical intercourse?

Mary Magdalene: Absolutely. We came to bring the divine to every level of human life, to *be* the divine at every level of human life. Why would we not include sexuality?

Sexuality is one of the most sacred aspects of life on Earth. Because of various influences, indoctrination, and training, many people have lost touch with the sacredness of sexuality. But it's a sacred pathway on Earth, if beings choose to engage it as such.

Chapter 11

The True Marriage We Embodied

[This message was given by Mary on her annual feast day.]

Mary Magdalene: I perceive changes in your world that I see as positive. There are more and more who are awakening to the Feminine, which is what's called for at this time more than anything else. It would be more accurate to call this a reawakening because in the distant past on Earth the connection to the Feminine was alive and strong. But that connection has been suppressed and even forgotten to a large extent for a long time. This is beginning to change.

The connection that many are feeling to me is one sign of this change. People recognize the Feminine essence in me, even if they can't name it as such. For many, I seem to symbolize or embody the Feminine. And, indeed, that's my role. I'm the carrier of the Divine Feminine—not exclusively, of course, for that would be impossible and antithetical to what the Divine Feminine is. But I carry that pure quality in a form that's recognizable and identifiable for many. (This, of course, was why I was excluded and defamed for so long.)

Humanity is coming out of a long time of conflict and competition, in which the Masculine in its lower form—cut off from the Feminine—felt threatened by the Feminine. The lower Masculine perceived that it was necessary to suppress the Feminine in order to establish the Masculine's authority and power. The results of this have been devastating for your world, and many are now recognizing this.

This was a necessary (though painful) period of growth and exploration that humankind needed to experience, in order to see what the effects and results of this dynamic would be. That epoch is coming to completion. The experiment has been run, and the results are clear. Now humans are increasingly ready for a new phase. This is the phase of union between the Masculine and Feminine.

In this new phase, there will be loving and cherishing of *both* the Masculine and Feminine, each embracing the other to create wholeness. This is what will bring about the world that so many of you envision and long for. The power to create this rests within each of you because this change will fundamentally occur by each individual changing their relationship to their own Masculine and Feminine within.

This is why it was so important for the first two books to be brought forward (which Mercedes authored). In *Mary Magdalene Beckons,* I clarified the three arenas that everyone must strengthen to bring forth their own Divine Feminine—their relationship to their body, their sexuality, and their emotions. I especially focused on how people can relate to emotions in a different way, a way that will move them into union with God. This different way of relating to emotions is the most important change for people to make at this time. It's what will do the most to move people forward in their spiritual growth and into the next phase of spiritual evolution. It's also what's least understood by most people relative to incarnating the Divine Feminine.

The second arena for people to develop to become strong in their Divine Feminine is the area of sacred sexuality. This is what the second book, *Sublime Union*, focuses on. Sacred sexuality can be developed whether one is single or with a partner because it's primarily an energy practice.

It's also important that people change their relationship to their body if there's any degree of shame, dislike, or dissociation in relation to one's physical body. I've chosen not to provide instruction about this because there's already a great deal of information available to people about how to change this.

All three of these arenas—your emotions, sexuality, and body—are the centers of your inner Feminine. If you're cut off or underdeveloped in any of these areas, it's a reflection of your suppression of the Feminine within yourself. When all of these areas are full and strong, you'll have established the foundation for your inner Feminine. At that point you can reside stably in your heart, which is the throne of the inner Feminine.

Once you're seated in your heart, you're ready to open to your inner Divine Masculine. This begins the courtship and eventual marriage between your inner Masculine and Feminine, with both of these parts in their higher or mature form.

It's this inner marriage of your higher Feminine and Masculine that you're all moving toward. This marriage is the gateway to the next dimension and your next level of spiritual growth. It's the marriage that Yeshua and I embodied, and which we communicated to all who had eyes to see and ears to hear. It's fundamentally a marriage of your own divine aspects and ultimately of yourself with God. This is the true marriage. All else is a celebration of this.

As more and more of you realize and manifest this inner marriage, your world will change to reflect this. Your world is already changing, which is a sign that this is underway. I celebrate this change with you and support you to continue in this great process. It's the calling of your heart and soul, which all are coming to recognize in their perfect time.

Chapter 12

Our Lineage

Question: I believe that you and Yeshua had a daughter and that her birth led to a genetic lineage of yours on Earth at this time. Can you influence that lineage, or does it even matter?

Mary Magdalene: It's true that I gave birth to a daughter through my union with Yeshua. It's also true that there was a genetic lineage. It was one possibility for influencing the world. But as it turned out, it didn't become the most important.

The process of manifesting higher energies into a third-dimensional reality (such as Earth) happens in many ways. The physical is simply one way. And the physical/genetic lineage is less important than what happens at the higher levels, which you might call the soul and soul-family levels.[30] We're always manifesting through our soul family.[31] It's not simply a linear process, where I take form on Earth, and that's my only form.

In the higher dimensions, we don't assume individuality in the way that you're familiar with in your world. Even what you speak about as "a particular higher being" isn't the way that we relate to such a being. Our manifestation has much more to do with our soul group and has a much larger form, encompassing many beings. For us it's entirely natural that our influence would come to the Earth-realm in many ways and forms that aren't limited to time, space, or manifestation.

This is a complex subject, about which I'm not the highest expert. What I can say is that it's not wise to get too focused on who may be an incarnation of whom, or who may be related to whom through their genetics or their ancestry, or who is experiencing a soul connection to this or that being. We have connections to *so many* beings.

The most important thing is for you to connect with those who are your guides and are guiding you from the highest realms, in the highest forms of light. Then consider other beings who are manifested on Earth, including those who are offering guidance to others. Consider if their guidance is right for you or not. That's what's most important.

It's a limitation to focus on higher beings as being contained within a certain structure or form, thinking that, "This is the incarnation or genetic descendant of 'such and such' being." It's a distraction from what that higher being really wants to bring you, which is ultimately light. And light isn't limited by form. Neither light nor love are limited by form.

While it may be interesting to understand the mechanics of how this works, that will come in time. And in time, you probably won't be so interested in how it works—at least in regards to incarnation in the third dimension, because that will no longer be your reality. [Mary laughs gently.]

The whole reason that Yeshua and I (and all the others involved) became significant two thousand years ago wasn't because of who our parents were or our lineage. It was because of the light that we brought in, which was undeniable and unmistakable for those who were able to see it and recognize it. That light is what to put your attention on. Let everything else be of less significance or concern.

It's a miracle that anyone *ever* incarnates here, and a joy that so many do. Find the light that's in *all* and celebrate that. If the light communicates to you as connected to "the light of Yeshua," or "the light of Mary Magdalene" or of any being, let that be a joy and a wonder to your heart. That orientation will carry you into your own union with light, and you won't need these other forms. Your relationship to the light itself will be the strongest and most powerful—and over time, the most real.

This is my recommendation.

Chapter 13

Feeling Connected to Us

Question: Can you help me understand the deep connection I feel with you and Yeshua? I question if it's my ego or if there's something more there.

Mary Magdalene: There are many levels of connection that beings can experience. The type of connection I believe you're talking about is most often a soul-level connection. You're recognizing that you're part of a soul cluster. That's a beautiful and valuable thing to experience and acknowledge.

Sadly, in your world there's often a discounting of the feelings that inform an individual of these kinds of connections. But in your heart and higher self, you know if those feelings are true or not.

At the higher levels, souls come together in a unified way, which can be hard to explain to someone who's primarily experiencing the third dimension. At these higher levels, you still have a sense of connection to your own soul, but your unified field with other souls can be stronger. That unified field may be more of the way you identify yourself, rather than through your individual soul. These unified groupings are sometimes referred to as *soul families* or *soul groups*.³² In these soul groups or families, many beings share the same unified field, consciousness, and beingness.

This is why, in your world, there can be multiple individuals who say, "I feel like I was 'so and so' in a past life."³³ It could be that the person expressing this actually is that individual soul. Or they could be connected to that soul through their ancestry. Perhaps they knew the being they're claiming to be because they were incarnated at the same time as that soul.

But most often, it's because they're part of the same soul family or soul group as the being they're identifying with. That integration becomes a singular beingness at the higher levels, resulting in an experience that's beyond connection; it's a oneness. When a part of yourself opens to your connection with your soul family, you may feel a profound connection to the being who "represents" that soul group or soul family in your world, or who's the best-known archetype of that soul group. In those cases, you may feel a powerful identification with that being.

In the third dimension, it can be difficult to acknowledge this type of connection, even to yourself, because there are many beliefs that this is not so, not possible, and that anyone claiming this is sick, deluded, or at least inflated in their ego and off course in their spiritual path. But the truth rests within you. Within yourself, you know.

PART III

The Inner Circle

Chapter 14

The Inner School

[This message was part of a channeling given at Easter. Mary was responding to a broader question about how the events celebrated at Easter relate to the ascension process.[34]*]*

Mary Magdalene: When Yeshua was alive and teaching, there were two different ways that he taught and worked with people. One was a more public, outer way. The other was an inner school and teaching, which was mostly secret. The existence and teachings of the inner school were shared amongst those who were involved, but weren't necessarily revealed or talked about outside of that circle.

There was a reason for this. Yeshua wanted to bring a general teaching that would be accessible to many people at that time, and would help the largest body of people to move forward into their next level of spiritual growth. The essence of that teaching was about love. He taught about love of God, first and foremost. And within that teaching about love of God, he taught love of self and of all beings. This was the message that was given publicly in many different forms. And it's what got recorded, primarily in the Bible. (Part of what's recorded in the Bible wasn't what Yeshua said or taught at that time, but rather what others added to his teaching.)

In the inner school or inner circle of initiates, Yeshua was primarily teaching how to transition and move into the fourth dimension, which is the next level of consciousness, and the reality that's founded on that consciousness.

The fourth dimension is an energy-based dimension. It's more energetically based than the third dimension. It still has a physical component, but the physical aspect is much lighter, and the energy component is more predominant.[35] In the fourth dimension, people appear in their energy body (which is sometimes referred to as the "light body").

Part of the inner school teaching included instruction on how to move into one's energy body. This practice was largely unknown at that time, though there were mystery schools that understood and taught this.[36] In fact, you could say that Yeshua's inner circle was a mystery school.

Today, the energy body is becoming more known, and people are becoming more in touch with this other level of reality and consciousness. For example, many people are familiar with "out-of-body experiences" or "near-death experiences," where people temporarily leave their physical body and go into their energy body.[37] Accounts of these experiences are becoming more widespread, and with that is a growing understanding and acceptance of this as a possibility. But two thousand years ago, understanding of the energy body was restricted to a small group of people. Had this knowledge been more publicly communicated, it's likely that those involved would have been putting themselves at risk and perhaps would even have been killed. In fact, Yeshua was placed in that position, for many reasons.

What people today call "the resurrection"[38] came out of the teaching of Christianity that was added later by others.[39] We in the inner circle would not have used that term to describe the process Yeshua underwent. We would have called it something like what people today are calling "the ascension process," which is the process of transitioning into the subtler dimensions.

Appearing in one's energy body doesn't require that one die. You can have an out-of-body experience or a near-death experience and then return to your physical body. In those experiences you've passed into a subtler dimension in your energy body, without dying. Yeshua had the ability to appear in his light body and return to his physical body, both before and after the crucifixion.

Yeshua's energy body appearances before the crucifixion weren't generally public.[40] After the crucifixion, Yeshua chose to show himself in his energy body in a more public way as part of his outer teaching. Many in the general populace expected that if Yeshua was, indeed, speaking the word of God, then he would manifest in some form that transcended the physical, as a sign of his divinity.[41] Yeshua understood this and chose to display his energy body as another way of opening people to his teaching, while also giving a glimpse of the work in the inner school.

Questioner: Many people say that now is the time for the Christ[42] to awaken in everybody and for humans to wake up to who we really are. Would you speak to that?

Mary Magdalene: This was always Yeshua's teaching. It was never his teaching that he alone was God, or the son of God, or anything like that. His teaching was that he was the way-shower for what all are capable of and moving toward. This was another reason for the two schools, because there was a dramatic difference between what the general populace was ready for and moving toward, and what a much smaller group of initiates was prepared for.

One of the truest statements that's attributed to Yeshua is: "All this and more shall you do."[43] This was always his point of view. Now this viewpoint is becoming more understood among the general population. I wholly agree with the statement that all people are awakening to Christ consciousness[44] and becoming all of the things that Yeshua showed as possibilities, and more.

Chapter 15

The Hidden Work of the Crucifixion

Question: What happened at the crucifixion?

Mary Magdalene: When Yeshua was crucified, more than one thing was taking place. On one level, there were those in the religious institutions of the time who wanted to eliminate Yeshua because he was challenging their structure. Yeshua wanted people to know God as love, compassion, and forgiveness, and to realize their direct connection with God. This was different from what was being put forth through the Jewish temple at that time, which presented a fierce God of punishment and required people to follow many rules and institutionalized practices in order to stay in God's graces. Those in power didn't welcome the changes Yeshua was bringing, as those changes threatened their power and position. So there were those within the religious institutions of the time who wanted him eliminated.

There were also those within the political system and structure who were threatened by Yeshua, especially as people started to relate to him as a leader or "king of the Jews." There was nervousness amongst the political leaders and authorities that Yeshua would revolt against the secular government and powers. Some amongst the Jews wanted a revolt and hoped that Yeshua had come to lead that kind of uprising. But that wasn't Yeshua's mission or interest. He came to show people the way of bonding with a loving God and to be a bridge for people to that God.

The crucifixion had another significance and role. This had to do with the widespread hope amongst the Jews that a messiah would appear and deliver them spiritually from a long time of being downtrodden. This was different from the hope of those who wanted a political revolution. This was a spiritual emancipation into more blessed times.

This belief in a coming messiah was intertwined with the religious stories and myths of the time, many of which involved a divine ruler who died and was reborn. Through that rebirth, the blessings of the divine were brought to the people. This was a pervasive spiritual story in many cultures back then. Perhaps the most prevalent messiah story during Yeshua's time was the story of Osiris dying and being brought back to life through his wife and queen, Isis.

Thus, there was an expectation in the consciousness of many people at the time that a messiah would manifest and that this would include a death-and-rebirth process. Accordingly, part of the purpose of the crucifixion was to fulfill this expectation, so ordinary people could accept Yeshua's teachings as true and take them in. Through fulfilling that expectation, people were able to open to Yeshua and accept him as a divine being.[45]

The most important reason for the crucifixion, however, has largely been kept secret from people. The crucifixion was a profound process for bringing light to Earth and implanting that light within the Earth. At the time of Yeshua's incarnation, the level of light on Earth had reached an all-time low. If the trajectory into darkness were to continue, it was likely that Earth would not survive. Yeshua incarnated on Earth to change that.

Yeshua is an extremely high being of light. Through incarnating in human form, he was able to bring a tremendous amount of light into the Earth-plane. Yeshua's teaching was primarily directed at instructing people about how they could similarly manifest and increase the light, so the process could continue to grow through others.

Yeshua's exoteric teaching was a simple form of this process of increasing the light, but it was very real and effective if people truly practiced it. In essence, it was all about love and the power of love. His simplest instruction—to love God with all your heart and to love everyone as yourself—was truly sufficient to continue this process of anchoring light on Earth.

There was also an esoteric teaching for those who were ready, with more specific practices for how to do this. Those in the Essene community were especially prepared to receive and participate at this level with Yeshua, but there were others too.

The crucifixion was part of the process of anchoring light into the Earth that Yeshua came to perform. This was understood by those in the inner circle around Yeshua. He knew it, and we knew it. It involved him sacrificing his life-energy in a tremendous feat of spiritual work.

During the crucifixion, the cross became a grid of divine energy being brought into the Earth, something like the way a tree brings the energy of light down through its extremities above the ground, going down into the soil through its roots. Yeshua's life-energy activated this circuitry and turned the cross into a spiritual grid and conductor for divine energy to flow into the Earth and be received by the Earth.

This was a literal saving of Earth herself as a living form, charging her like a battery with God's light. And it changed the course of your history on Earth. It was the turning point for the return of light into your world. It has been gradual but continuous since then, and today many of you are waking up to it.

This is the true event and meaning of Easter. It was the rebirth of Earth, a literal rebirth at profound and high levels of spiritual transformation.

It's not accurate that "Yeshua died for your sins," in the sense that you're evil, bad, wrong, damned, or anything like that. It's also not true that another person's acts can mitigate or remove your karma[46] or responsibility for your spiritual path. Each soul is responsible for themselves and their own spiritual path and results. However, if you interpret "sin" as separation from the light, then there is an element of truth in the expression that "Yeshua died for your sins," for he chose to give his life-force to perform this huge transformational act of returning Earth to a sufficiently high quotient of light.

Question: Why did Yeshua accept to be crucified and to go through that?

Mary Magdalene: It was a sacrifice in the greatest sense of the word.

Yeshua came to change the course of the Earth, to shift the Earth into the process of ascension.[47] The Earth and the people of the Earth had descended to the lowest extent imaginable, and there was concern that it would remain that way for a long time, or perhaps the Earth and humanity wouldn't be able to turn this around. So Yeshua came to do this work, to turn the evolutionary process and reset it, so that Earth could begin its process of return, of ascension, and no longer be stuck in the place of the lowest densities.

The crucifixion was an essential part of this. Yeshua's spiritual force was released into the earth and also into humanity through the crucifixion, allowing a new level of light and love to root and take hold in this world. This was the most fundamental reason for the crucifixion.

The cross that Yeshua was crucified on was a conductor of his blessing force into the earth, allowing this energy to be fully received and the earth to be charged with Yeshua's life-force and blessing power. This blessing power would be held in the Earth and would be available to the people and the beings of the Earth. This is why you've seen such immense changes in your world since the time of Yeshua, and this continues to this day. It's why the ascension process is happening now at the incredibly rapid pace that it is. The speed of the shift that's occurring would not normally be the case at all. What's happening on Earth is exceedingly unique and has everything to do with the work that Yeshua did here. That work came to fulfillment and was completed through the crucifixion.

Mary Magdalene: During the crucifixion, the crucifix became a kind of "lightning rod" for Yeshua to bring down divine light. He then alchemically combined this divine light with his essence and life-force, and sent this transformed life-force down into the earth—to be held by the Earth for all time.

Your Earth is alive. She is literally the Divine Mother in this plane. And she, Mother Earth, agreed to receive this higher energy—to feed humanity with it and to anchor this shift into this realm.

My part during the crucifixion was to empower and strengthen Yeshua to do his work, through feeding him with my love and prayers. I did this in concert with Lady Mary (who many call "Mother Mary").[48] It was necessary for us to support him in this way, in order for the process to be effective. This, too, was an alchemical process. It was all part of the greater process. We fed Yeshua with our love, empowering him to impart his life-force, imbued with divine light, into the Earth.

There's a spiritual ceremony in the Native American tradition that some of you are familiar with called the *sun dance*. In this ceremony, individuals lash themselves to a tree for three days and nights, foregoing food and water, and praying the whole time. They do this to receive guidance from Spirit and to transform themselves. As they engage in this ceremony, others support them in various ways, including praying for them.

Thinking of the sun dance may help you understand what Yeshua and I were doing in the crucifixion, for there are similarities. It was an intentional spiritual process for the sake of the Earth and its beings. Yeshua gave his life-force to activate a new direction on Earth. And I, along with Lady Mary, empowered him to do so through our profound devotion and prayer.

Chapter 16

In the Tomb and After

Question: Yeshua didn't die on the cross, did he?

Mary Magdalene: No, he didn't die on the cross. He was taken to the tomb and revived. The healers were ready and prepared, knowing this was what they'd been called to do.[49] It was all set in place beforehand, and the inner circle were all there.[50] He was revived and removed.

The story that was told was prepared in advance so that the prophecies would be fulfilled.[51] It was also told so that the people who were ready for that level of opening, that level of relationship to Yeshua's work and who he was, could accept him in that form. And it was told to keep Yeshua safe, so people wouldn't realize or suspect that he'd lived. But he didn't die on the cross.

Question: Would you talk about the resurrection and where you and Yeshua went afterwards?

Mary Magdalene: Those of us in the inner circle knew that Yeshua would go into the death realm in the crucifixion, and we had prepared for that. The tomb was prepared by Joseph of Arimathea. Healers from the Essene community, who were greatly skilled in the healing arts, were also prepared, as were Mother Mary and me.

When Yeshua was brought into the tomb, he was healed, tended to, and brought back. He wasn't brought back in the form of the story of the resurrection that's told in Christianity but brought back in a way that many of you are familiar with—as someone who "dies" and then comes back into their earthly form. Today this is called a "near-death experience." Yeshua, being skilled in the abilities of the light body, knew how to go into the light-body realm and still maintain his connection to his physical body. This allowed him to come back into his physical form, with the assistance of healers for his physical body. This is what was done. And he returned into human form.

Those of you today who go through a near-death experience are not usually described as having resurrected. [Audience laughs.] In fact, we knew that this natural form of returning to the body is what had happened for Yeshua.

To make the work continue on many levels—including providing safety for Yeshua and his family—it had been determined that once he was resuscitated, he would disappear. And so he did, leaving with me and those closest to him.

Initially we traveled to Egypt. From there, we went to a part of what is now called Turkey. Eventually, we went to France. From there, there were other travels. Yeshua traveled a great deal, both in his light body and his physical body. But France was where we moved immediately after the crucifixion.

Many of you have a direct connection to Yeshua or me, or both of us, from that time. Many of you were involved in some form or another. You've specifically come back at this time to help the change that's underway.[52] You're supporting the opening that we initiated two thousand years ago, but which is only coming to fruition now because the soil is now ready. The hearts and minds of beings have become fertile soil for this opening, for the seed to burst forth into manifestation.

Many of you are finding your own connection to that time. It's awakening, and that's a good thing. I welcome you.

Question: Can you say more about Yeshua's appearances after the crucifixion?

Mary Magdalene: It's important to understand that Yeshua and I—but especially Yeshua at the time of his incarnation two thousand years ago—were working on many levels with many beings. Not only human beings but many beings. Yeshua worked in many different ways to try to support so many, finding the way that would be most helpful for them.

At that time (as is still the case today), most people understood things in very physical, three-dimensional ways. There were many beliefs about the way that God would show his- or herself to human beings. And for many, those beliefs included the idea that there would be a death and resurrection. So part of what was decided was based on what would support others in their connection to God, in a way that they could access and open to.

When Yeshua appeared in his light body after the crucifixion, this was a validation for some of their expectation that a death and resurrection would occur. It was also a validation that God had truly manifested in human form, because it fit their ideas.

Truly, Yeshua has always been able to appear in his light body. He's not unique in this. Others have also manifested in their light bodies. This is more known in the Indian tradition, where there are beings who are able to do things that seem like miracles to many.[53] Yeshua was able to do all of that. But it wasn't because he'd been resurrected (in the way resurrection has been interpreted within Christianity).[54] It was because of his advanced state of being.

Yeshua's advanced state is a vision of what you're moving toward, what you will be able to do as you grow and become more skilled in the higher dimensions and the abilities associated with those dimensions.

Chapter 17

The True Meaning of the Cross

Question: What is the true meaning of the cross?

Mary Magdalene: Many associate the cross with Jesus (whom I call Yeshua) and with Christianity. In particular, the cross is associated with Jesus's crucifixion and the idea that he died for your sins. There's a great deal that could be said about all of this and I will do my best to cover as much as I can.

Many of the ideas about Yeshua that are held in your time are ideas that have been propagated by the Christian church. There are many reasons why these ideas have been chosen and promoted. Not all of them have to do with things that occurred during Yeshua's life or that were a part of his teaching. It's important to remember that the Christian Church didn't fully coalesce until several centuries after Yeshua's life and that it's continued to develop and change since its early beginnings. What the Church has communicated about Yeshua's life and the meaning of what Yeshua said and did has often had more to do with what the church leaders were interested in than what actually occurred, or what Yeshua taught and wanted people to understand and receive.

All of this is true not only in relation to the cross, but to every aspect of Yeshua's life and teaching. Much of what occurred, and much of what he taught and wanted to transmit to people, has been changed or lost over time. Because of this, you must be discerning as to what you believe and accept. Where did the ideas about Yeshua that you've heard come from? How do you know they're valid? How do the ideas *feel* to you? Do they support light and love within you? How do the people who embrace and promote those ideas *feel* to you? Do they feel full of light and love?

Remember that your feeling-sense is a much better barometer of truth than your mind. *Do not be fooled by ideas if the feelings accompanying them don't uplift you.* You must learn to exercise and grow your feeling-based discernment as a powerful tool for determining what is supportive to let in and what is better to discard.

Now, having laid the foundation of understanding for the context in which to understand *all* reports and interpretations relative to Yeshua, I return to your question about the meaning of the cross. The cross has been a symbol for many things since ancient times—long before the life of Yeshua and his crucifixion. (This is why you will find it in other traditions and cultures, including those that pre-date Yeshua's incarnation on Earth.) It's a symbol of the connection between heaven and Earth, or more accurately, between the divine in its transcendent form and manifestation on Earth. The top of the cross represents connection with the transcendent divine, while the bottom of the cross represents connection with manifestation in the form of Earth and the physical third-dimensional plane. The horizontal part of the cross represents human beings as the pivotal form on Earth manifesting the union of the transcendent divine with third-dimensional matter.

The cross can also be seen as a representation of a human being, with the top part being the head, the horizontal part being the arms and hands, and the lower part being the legs and feet. The intersection of the vertical and horizontal is the heart. In this representation, the heart is shown to be central—that which brings everything together and out of which everything emanates. The centrality and importance of the heart was a foundational principle that underlay Yeshua's teaching.

In your world today, most people have become imbalanced with living predominantly in their head and being disconnected from and out of touch with their heart. This is a cause of a great deal of the problems you experience in your world. If you were to come back into balance and harmony, with the heart being central and primary, many of your problems would be solved. Thus, this simple symbol of the cross holds a great secret for you in your present time as to what is before you to do in order to move forward spiritually.

Ultimately, the cross is a symbol for the infusion of God's light into the Earth, the uniting of God and matter. Yeshua was that manifestation in human form. Through his choice to undergo the crucifixion, he brought that same light into the Earth herself, to store it and share it freely with all beings of the Earth.[55]

This is part of why it's such a tragedy that so many are choosing to damage and even destroy the Earth at this time. That must be stopped and reversed, for Earth is your source of physical as well as spiritual sustenance—especially because of the light that Yeshua infused her with. You must make amends for the way that you are treating the Earth and truly come to revere her and care for her as your most immediate spiritual source. For so she is. Loving and caring for the Earth is part of the return to loving the Feminine that's so necessary at this time.

Yeshua was a great lover of the Feminine. He understood,

honored, and loved the Feminine. Of this I can attest. I received his love in limitless forms and amounts. And it was not limited to me. Yeshua's love was boundless and given freely to all. He loved without limit of any kind. And he bequeathed his love to everyone through his love of the Earth and his spiritual endowment of that love into the Earth. It's there for all in this time as well, waiting for you to receive and continue the process of raising the light on Earth. Those of you who are reading this are surely called to this purpose and are already on that path. My hope is that my words and explanation may help you to continue and go further in that process.

PART IV

Feminine and Masculine

Chapter 18

The Path of Union

Question: Can you talk about the Feminine energy of fullness?

Mary Magdalene: Fullness is one of the essential forms of the Feminine. The Masculine is emptiness. The Feminine is fullness.

Some of your spiritual traditions espouse emptiness as the path. Many people are taught meditation as a practice to empty or clear oneself—clearing the mind, thoughts, or whatever's arising—and through that emptying to find God. This is an example of a Masculine orientation. The Masculine orientation is effective for reaching the Masculine aspect of God. This is one approach to spirituality.

The Feminine is about fullness. In some of your older cultures that were Feminine based, you see images of the Feminine with huge bellies that are round and full, representing the force of life and birth. A pregnant woman who's about to give birth is the icon of the Feminine in fullness. You also have images of the Feminine as Earth in her fullness. Truly, all of manifestation is the Feminine.

The Feminine and the Masculine are two faces of God. The Masculine is what is beyond manifestation, beyond form and incarnation. It's what transcends or goes beyond. There's a traditional

Buddhist teaching of "Gate, gate, paragate, parasamgate. Bodhi svaha," which can be translated as "Gone, gone, gone beyond, gone completely beyond. Awakened!" This is a reference to going beyond form to the transcendental, which is without form. This can be seen as emptiness.

Form is the Feminine. Physicality is one way that form or manifestation occurs, but there are many other ways. Your thoughts, feelings, energy, and experience are all forms within manifestation.

Each being is a universe of fullness unto themself. Beyond the individual, you have the totality of all individuals in your world. Beyond that are worlds upon worlds upon worlds, just in the physical. Then there are dimensions upon dimensions upon dimensions. This is the great arena of the Feminine, which includes all form and arising—from the densest forms (some say denser than physicality) to the most light-based forms of light-beings, angels, subtle sounds, and lights. *All* of that is the Feminine. It's a tremendous fullness.

Most beings in your world have known one or the other of these two paths. The path of the Masculine seeks to go beyond form—which means going beyond the Feminine—to know God. The path of the Feminine is to know God *as all forms*—where every aspect of manifestation is God. The Feminine path seeks union, including union with the Masculine. Both paths lead to God.

For most people, the most direct path is to embrace both the Feminine and Masculine—embracing all form, all of manifestation, and all that's arising as God, and simultaneously knowing that God is beyond all of that. One way this has been expressed is to say everything is a dream or an illusion, and everything is also God. Both are true.

The knowing of the union of these two seeming opposites is a path of realization. It's not something to be believed or thought into reality. It's to be known and realized.

For most beings, there are stages of development in one's spiritual realization. This is why people do practices, because practices develop and increase one's ability to connect with God. Masculine practices, such as meditation, increase one's ability to connect with the transcendental aspect of God. It's also valuable to engage practices for knowing the Feminine side of God. That begins with knowing yourself as God—knowing your body, energy, sexuality, and emotions as God.

Embracing both aspects of spiritual practice and realization leads to the union of Divine Masculine (as consciousness, which has no form) and Divine Feminine (as love, which embraces *everything* that is). The union of love and consciousness is the highest form of knowing God.

Chapter 19

The Inner Marriage

Question: I often experience higher dimensions, but I don't stay there for long. How can I maintain my presence in the higher dimensions, rather than going back and forth between the third dimension and higher dimensions?

Mary Magdalene: This going back and forth between dimensions is a natural experience, especially as you progress in the ascension process.[56] You'll spend time in higher dimensions—which for most of you will initially be the fourth or fifth dimension—but in general, you won't stay there until you've completed your work in the third dimension.

For most of you, the third-dimensional work you need to complete is about uniting the Masculine and Feminine. To do this, you must first strengthen your Feminine, especially your connection to feeling.

Most of you have been heavily indoctrinated into cutting yourself off from your feelings and living in your mind, to the point that you don't realize how severe this indoctrination has been. Your movie *The Matrix* is a kind of symbolic story of this indoctrination. Because of this indoctrination, you must now regain your access to the Feminine. This means regaining access to your body, your sexuality, and your feeling ability.

For most people, the great block relative to your body is shame. More than anything, your work in this arena involves feeling the shame you carry relative to your body and then loving your body as a temple.

Similarly, most of you carry shame relative to your sexuality. Because of your sexual shame, you haven't allowed yourself to open to the pathway of sexuality as a spiritual process, which can carry you into the higher dimensions. You've confined your sexuality to being exclusively physical, which is a great limitation. The spiritual aspects of sexuality are an important aspect of your learning.

In ancient times, learning the pathway of sexuality was recognized as an important part of the ascension process. Sacred sexuality was part of the Egyptian temple process, and this knowledge was carried from the Egyptian temples to India. In India it became known as the path of kundalini (or the serpent pathway).[57]

All of you are sexual, whether you're engaging sexually with a partner or not. You all have sexual energy. And most of you require healing of your body and sexual shame for you to be able to access your sexuality fully.

The third area of opening to the Feminine involves opening to emotions, especially painful emotions. This includes learning to "be with" emotions such as sorrow, and to mourn as a sacrament. It also includes learning to receive and open to fear as pointing to your own divinity, rather than something to suppress or do battle with. Because when you do these latter things, you cut yourself off from your power.

When you open to these Feminine parts of yourself—your body, your sexuality, and your emotions—your mind (which now tends to dominate you) becomes a lover of the Feminine. Then your mind relaxes. It becomes "in service" to the Feminine, like a knight in service to the queen.

It is then (when you've fully embraced your Feminine) that your inner king can step forward. The king is your higher or sacred Masculine. Once the king comes forward, he and the queen can join in marriage.

This marriage of your inner king and queen is the gateway for your transition to the higher dimensions. Only when that marriage has occurred will you be able to change your "kingdom" into a higher-dimensional one. For most of you, this will be the fourth dimension, which more than anything is about manifestation.

The marriage of king and queen energy is essential for engaging the work of manifestation fully in the fourth dimension. And that marriage requires the completion of your gifts, growth, and foundational learning in the third dimension, which is what you incarnated here for.

Question: As an individual who's not in a relationship, how can I embody the Masculine and Feminine on my own?

Mary Magdalene: All of you have your inner Masculine and Feminine. You can begin by familiarizing yourself with the different paths of the inner Masculine and Feminine. Then you can consider what may need strengthening within you.

For most beings on Earth at this time, there's an imbalance in your inner aspect. Most of you are highly developed and, in general, dominated by your inner Masculine, while being underdeveloped and weak in your inner Feminine. This is true for men and women. This imbalance tends to show up in different ways for men than it does for women, but both require their inner Feminine and Masculine to be strong.

Once you educate yourself about the different ways that these two manifest within, you can take stock and evaluate if either part is underdeveloped. For most people, that will be the Feminine. (Even for women, it's most often the Feminine that's underdeveloped and causing imbalance.)

Imbalance between one's inner Feminine and Masculine causes many problems in relationships. If you enter a relationship not being in balance, you place demands on the relationship to try to establish that balance. These demands are often a great strain and can even be a breaking point for the relationship.

It's very important, as part of your spiritual work, to become familiar with these different parts of yourself because they're ultimately different parts of God. I call them the Masculine and Feminine face of God.

For some people, referring to these parts of themselves and God as "Feminine" and "Masculine" isn't comfortable. That's fine. They can find other ways of referring to them. But I think the terminology of "Masculine" and "Feminine" is helpful. It's the way I was trained to understand these parts of oneself and reality, and it's how I see and know them. So I speak of them this way.

Completing your inner work relative to the Masculine and Feminine is an important part of what will allow you to engage the ascension process. These aspects must be in balance within yourself for the marriage of your inner Divine Feminine and Divine Masculine to occur. This marriage is a wonderful state to experience and know. It's the marriage of your heart (which is the seat of the Divine Feminine) and your sacred mind (which is the seat of the Divine Masculine). The union created through this sacred marriage becomes the doorway for moving into the next higher dimension.

This is necessary and valuable work. I encourage you to familiarize yourself with the instruction on the Masculine and the Feminine that I've offered.[58] I believe this will help people in ways that many are not yet aware of.

Chapter 20

The Alchemy of Masculine and Feminine

Mary Magdalene: When the Feminine is suppressed, people lose their power. Then they become prey to forms of mind control. The most direct and effective way to change this is to strengthen the Feminine. More than anything else, that means strengthening the emotional body, which is a key component of the Feminine.

Optimally, this emotional strengthening should occur in childhood. Young boys and girls need this more than anything else. They learn it through the demonstration of their parents' emotional wisdom and maturity, or whoever their adult caregivers are. But whenever it happens, the work of strengthening the Feminine (especially the emotional body) is necessary. It's what will most quickly and powerfully address the problem of people being misled by ideas.

The mind is like a machine. In some ways, it's like your computers. It can be programmed for anything. Computers are powerful, but they aren't good at making judgments. They can be employed for any purpose.

This is why you *require* the physical body, the emotional body, and the energy body—which are all forms of the Feminine—to guide you, to know what's really for your highest good and what is not. Then you can choose what's higher.

This is the highest form of alchemy, the alchemy of the inner union of the Masculine (in the form of the mind) and the Feminine (in the form of the body, emotions, and energy). It's also the most powerful alchemy.

Chapter 21

Loving the Feminine

Question: How do you and Yeshua want us to continue the work at this time?

Mary Magdalene: The work is always the same. It's the work of love. Yet at different times that shows up and manifests in different ways.

There's a particular way that the work of love is manifesting right now. It especially has to do with the love between the Masculine and the Feminine. This is the great healing to be engaged in your world now.

Many are aware that this is a time of the Feminine becoming stronger and moving into the forefront, even taking a leadership role. This is true, but it's not the whole picture.

There's a misunderstanding about what it means for the Feminine to become strong. This comes from confusing the Feminine and the Masculine. People often envision the Feminine being strong in ways that are more Masculine. But this isn't what's being called for, nor is it what's been empowered for this time. The Feminine path is the path of love. And Feminine strength begins with loving the Feminine within yourself.

For many, there's still a great deal of work to do relative to loving the Feminine—which means loving your body, sexuality, and emotions—and embracing these Feminine parts of yourself fully to receive their gifts. Many people have developed and used these aspects of their being in limited ways, but not necessarily in the highest ways.

Your body is a temple of God, which is to be used and cared for as a temple. It's ultimately your manifestation of God. As with all temples, each one is unique and perfect in its own way.

Your sexuality is a practice for bringing forth new life and light into the world. It's also a practice for transforming your life and, ultimately, your world. Most people don't understand this function of sexuality. It doesn't even require a partner. Everyone has sexual energy. It's part of the life-force within. The sexual life-force can always be used for transformation.

Your emotions are one of the greatest gifts for a deep, powerful connection to God. Most of you don't understand this relative to painful emotions. Instead, you carry great fear relative to painful emotions. This is ultimately fear of the Feminine.

Most of you have great healing to do to become strong and full in your relationship to your body, your sexuality, and your emotions. These parts of yourself must become the functioning bearer of your love of the Feminine. This is true for men and women. Women will most likely lead the way in these arenas—in love of the body, sexuality, and emotions. Through that they become a vessel of love that lights up the Masculine.

The Feminine's love will heal the Masculine and allow the Masculine to open in love to the Feminine. The Masculine also brings gifts. The Masculine brings the light of consciousness, which the Feminine needs as well.

The uniting of the Masculine and Feminine is the great gateway that human beings are moving toward and through at this time. It's what will bring your world out of the place it is now, which is a place of tremendous darkness in many ways. This is the darkness of the Masculine unaccompanied by the Feminine, the darkness of the mind realms lost and adrift from the heart. The uniting of the Masculine and Feminine will change that. The energy of the Feminine will draw the Masculine into a state of love and union.

The uniting of the Masculine and Feminine is a most beautiful union. I know a great deal about this union. I've had the immense joy of experiencing this union in its fullness. This is your destiny too. It's what you're moving into and what you're here to share with the world.

This is a magnificent time. Don't be fooled by the media and its bad news. Many forces are trying to hold back the tide of change, but they won't be successful. Don't let them succeed within your own mind and heart. Your love is stronger, and it will prevail.

Chapter 22

Loving the Masculine

Question (from a woman): I have a hard time opening to the Masculine expression of love. In my relationships with men, I often wonder, "Why can't men be more like women?" and "Why can't I understand them?" What can I do to open my heart to the Masculine form of love?

Mary Magdalene: You speak for many women who desire a similar kind of healing with the Masculine.

It's true that the Masculine is quite different from the Feminine. For many people in your world, this has been quite challenging—in both directions—to try to understand one another. For a long time, there was little understanding of the Feminine. The Masculine way was promoted and studied. This Masculine way involved being in the mind, pursuing goals, being analytical, and similar things. Now there's more understanding of the Feminine, which is based in the emotional, physical, energetic, and sexual aspects of being.

Of course, you all have your inner Masculine and Feminine. But in general, this hasn't helped you very much to understand each other. [Mary laughs.] I'm not laughing in judgment of you. I'm laughing in understanding and amusement. One would think that everyone having both an inner Masculine and Feminine might be helpful, yet it doesn't seem to be sufficient.

In fact, those coming from the Masculine and those coming from the Feminine operate in *very* different ways. It's important to understand those differences, including how they're complementary and how they can support each other, if you understand them.

This requires education. In your world there's a great need for education, in both directions. There's a need for those coming from the Masculine to understand the Feminine, as well as for those coming from the Feminine to understand the Masculine. By and large, this understanding isn't currently the case in your world.

That great lack of understanding is the place to start. At this time, it's going to begin with the Feminine understanding the Masculine. Many of you have heard that this is the time of the Feminine coming to the front and leading. I agree with this. I would also say that many of you have a misunderstanding of what this means. It doesn't mean you're going to lead like a general with the troops falling in behind you. You're going to lead in a very different way. Your leadership will be founded on coming to understand the Masculine and being able to *love* the Masculine.

Hearing this may come as a surprise, especially given what you often encounter in relation to the Masculine and what the Masculine is doing. [Mary laughs.] However, if you're dedicated to a deeper understanding of the Masculine, you'll discover that the way things appear and your interpretations of those things are often different from what the motivation or the intention was on the part of the Masculine.

This understanding will open your heart. It will bring you to a level of love of the Masculine that many of you haven't yet experienced. This love of the Masculine (in one of its highest forms) is what I experienced with Yeshua—and what I still experience with Yeshua. I *profoundly* love Yeshua. And I profoundly love the Masculine, which Yeshua is a shining model of. This is what all of you can experience as well. Not only with Yeshua but with the beauty of the pure Masculine in its manifestation in all different beings.

When you come to that place of love, it will open the hearts of men. It will touch their hearts and make it safe for them to open themselves to the Feminine, to start to really learn what the Feminine is, and to receive the gifts of the Feminine. This is what it means by the Feminine coming to the front and leading. It's about leading in love. More specifically, it means you're going to become leaders in love of the Masculine.

Questioner: My other challenge with the Masculine is that I associate the Masculine with authority. I have a deep rejection of things being imposed on me.

Mary Magdalene: Yes. Authoritarianism isn't associated with the Masculine in its higher form.[59] It's not even inherently associated with the Masculine in its lower or more practical form.[60] But the Masculine in its lower form is oriented toward efficiency and productivity, and an authoritarian system can be efficient and productive. So the lower Masculine often has an affinity with authoritarian structures.

When the Feminine leads with the heart and draws the Masculine into the heart, this supports the Masculine to come from their higher Masculine. Then it's not about power-over; it's about love. And even in that love, there are still differences between the Masculine and Feminine forms of love. But they're complementary and mutually supportive.

Chapter 23

Let the Feminine Lead

Question (from a woman): I seek greater connection to the love of Mother God and to loving my own soul. Sometimes I'm in balance with that, but other times my blocks to that seem overwhelming.

Mary Magdalene: That's because you're trying to heal your blocks. You need to receive those difficult or painful times as your gift in the moment.

When things aren't blissful or easy, you tend to think, "I need to fix this," which really means, "I need to do something to make this go away, so I can get back to that wonderful, easeful space." But that's not accurate. What you need to do is *receive the gift of the block*. That "block" is the perfect gift being given to you at that moment.

Many people have great fear of opening to what's occurring in the present. Yet opening to that is exactly what you need. Usually it's an emotion that you need to open to—some pain, fear, or loss. But it's not enough simply to open to the emotion without skill. You need to become skilled in following the pathway the emotion is trying to lead you on.

Your emotional pain is calling you to a place *within yourself* that has become cut off from God. Learn the skill, the practice, and the pathway of following your emotions and making use of them to reconnect with God. *That* is where your healing will occur (rather than in the way you currently are thinking about healing your so-called blocks.)

Questioner: I've been engaging a mental process of inquiring, "What is the lesson of this? How do I release this?" It's been exhausting.

Mary Magdalene: Yes. That's the Masculine way. What I'm inviting you to is the Feminine way, which is the organic way. The Feminine path is no longer organic for you because you've become cut off from it. If that hadn't happened, it would be very natural for you. But now you must apply yourself to it.

Your most important healing is to heal the blocks that have been implanted within you to this Feminine, organic process. Following the Feminine will also lead you to the Masculine understanding of the lesson involved. But let the Feminine lead. That's the natural way.

Follow the Feminine. Follow your body. Follow your emotions. Let them take you to your wholeness within, your inner divinity, and to the healing that needs to happen *there*. Then, quite of its own accord, the understanding, insight, and lesson will be there for you. It will be offered freely and easily. And you'll be back in harmony, strength, and union.

That's the pathway. It won't exhaust you. It will energize you. This is one of the signs that you're on the path. When something is exhausting you, it's a sign that what you're doing isn't the way. It's like swimming upstream. It's trying to tell you to turn around, to go the other way.

The Feminine pathway is a great support and one that is so needed. When you become strong in it, you'll become a helper to others. This is how it will spread.

Chapter 24

Helping Men Open to the Feminine

Mary Magdalene: Many cultures, both today and in the past, have had a general orientation of discounting women and of being suspicious of them. There's often been a double standard in the way men and women are related to. This has caused great pain for women throughout history and continuing into the present.

In your society, men are part of a privileged group who have more power than women. With that comes fear of what might happen if they lost the power that they hold. There's an assumption among many men that they will be treated poorly if they lose their privilege, just as they have treated others poorly. They fear they won't have enough to thrive and be happy or perhaps even to survive.

Beneath this fear is a deeper fear of the Feminine altogether. Ultimately, it's a fear of the Feminine within themselves—fear of their own feelings, tender side, and vulnerability. Fear of their own heart.

This fear drives them to try to cover up their vulnerability, tenderness, and feelings—acting as though they don't have these things. They may display righteous anger toward the "villains" (the women and their supporters), who they assert have wronged *them*.

If you're sensitive, you often can feel a lack of authenticity in their portrayal. There's a nervousness or even desperation behind it. That's fear of the Feminine, because the Feminine comes from the feeling heart and the heart knows the truth.

Feeling and heart are strong. That strength is what those who fear the Feminine are afraid of. When they sense the strength of the Feminine's feelings and heart and feel unable to meet it, they may resort to aggression to deflect their lack of strength.

There's an inconsistency in this that's not generally understood. Those who fear the Feminine recognize the Feminine's strength, but they mistakenly assume that opening to their own Feminine will make them weak. So they cut themselves off from their inner Feminine and compensate through an outward show of force.

What would happen if they opened to their Feminine? They would start to feel and be informed by feeling. A feeling person cannot treat another person as "less-than." A feeling person who has injured another person feels this and is disturbed by it. That disturbance motivates the one who caused the injury to make amends. This is the basis of emotional responsibility.

The question for all of you at this time is this: How can it become safe for men to open to their Feminine aspect?

You see, the women's movement empowered women to open to their Masculine side. Now it's time for men to open to their Feminine side. Some men are already doing this, but many are not, especially those who have been in the dominant role in terms of holding power in your society.

The biggest way for women to support this next step will *not* be by telling men what they must do. That would be coming from the Masculine, and most men don't want to receive from a woman in her Masculine.

Rather, women must *demonstrate* what it is to open to feeling. You must show your feelings, especially when you're experiencing emotional pain, without crossing the line into blaming others for your feelings. Saying what happened isn't blame. Blame is an overlay of power, where you seek to punish or hurt others because of your pain. Rather than directing blame at others, simply reveal your experiences and feelings.

Beyond expressing and showing your own feelings, women can support men in opening to their Feminine side by guessing what men are feeling. This is using your emotional intelligence to help men identify their feelings because men often aren't aware of what they're feeling.

It's important to do this sensitively and respectfully. *Ask* if "such and such" is what they're feeling rather than telling them what you think is going on with them. (Telling someone what they're feeling puts you in an authority position over them, suggesting that you know more about what's going on with them than they do.)

These two things—demonstrating your own feelings and helping men identify their feelings—can make a world of difference in helping men feel safe to open to their Feminine. And this will change your world.

This isn't a magic wand that will change things overnight. You're undoing thousands of years of programming. But in the big picture, this change can happen extremely quickly.

Demonstrating your own Feminine and supporting others in connecting with their inner Feminine is the greatest power that women have. But most women aren't yet aware of this or skilled at using it. Most women are still trying to use their mind to change things. That's not where this change will come from.

There are many ways to contribute to changing the world. It's a very individual process and choice. But all of you—women and men—will benefit from opening to your Feminine. And women are likely to be the leaders in this. Most women have got a way to go before they're fully acting out of their own Feminine. This means showing their feelings and allowing that to be enough, without going into the mind with analysis, and without bringing anger and blame.

Your world is shifting from head to heart. Feelings are the key to this shift. Find the key, and make use of it. This is what I recommend.

Chapter 25

Supporting the Masculine to Heal

Question: I encounter beautiful souls in masculine bodies who've been hurt by the Feminine—when women have become very Masculine. How do we love and honor these men and help them heal, so they can be ambassadors of light and love?

Mary Magdalene: First and foremost, you must see their Masculine as beautiful.

There are many men who've been hurt. And many men are confused about how to be a man and bring forth the Masculine, because of women expressing that the Masculine has hurt them. There's much to sort out in all of this.

The Masculine so needs the Feminine's love, and to be seen as loving the Feminine. Men (or the Masculine in any form) need reassurance that their love is valuable, needed, and supportive. When they're doing something that's difficult or painful, be very aware of their vulnerability. The Masculine is quite vulnerable.

If someone in the Masculine position is hurting someone in the Feminine position,[61] or is acting in a way in which they seem invulnerable, it's because they are hurt or wounded themself. This doesn't mean that what they're doing is alright. It doesn't give them license to hurt the Feminine. What they're doing must be stopped. But use as little force as possible. Understand that this is a being who is hurt and who needs help. What they're doing isn't natural.

Most children go through a stage where they experiment with hurting each other. This is a natural phase for children to go through in their exploration. But they should be guided wisely by adults through and out of this phase, so they don't grow up with a desire to hurt others. If someone hasn't received this kind of guidance and has been hurt themselves, especially as a child, then they'll need help to recover from that.

Most people today are very confused about the Masculine and Feminine roles—how to incarnate them and how to relate to one another. This will most likely be moved forward through the Feminine incarnating her strength and her Femininity, and then bringing that strength in the form of love to the Masculine. The Feminine can then empower the Masculine to be their strong, loving self. The Feminine can see this strength in them, even if they can't see it in themselves, until they become it most fully.

Chapter 26

Sacred Partnership

Question: How can we live in a sacred partnership like you did with Yeshua?

Mary Magdalene: Yeshua and I were sacred lovers and partners, both of us fully dedicated to our path of devotion to God. Our relationship was an extension of our devotion to God, a form through which we served.

Any time a couple comes together in love, their love is serving the whole. It's inevitable. If their coming together is done consciously, with a conscious intention, it's all the stronger and affects the greater body of humanity even more.

Yeshua and I practiced sacred sexuality together as a form of blessing—for ourselves, for the work we were doing, and for all humanity. It was one of the ways we served humanity.

In terms of what I would say to others, follow your heart. Be guided by your heart. See your partner as the divine. This is very important. See your relationship to your partner as your relationship to the divine.

This doesn't mean you'll be happy with everything your partner does. You can express your feelings to your partner with love and ask for changes. But do that in the context of the greater practice of seeing your partner as the Divine Masculine or the Divine Feminine, who's loving you in your divinity. This is one of the ways you meet the divine in this plane. It's not the only way, but it's one of the most powerful ways.

Know that whatever you struggle with in relation to your partner is an extension of you and your challenges, and own that. Again, this is not to say that you must accept things that your heart and soul tell you aren't right for you. But you must look at your part in creating those things and take responsibility for changing your part.

Know that there are no rules. Your society has created rules and so have your religions. These were created for various reasons—sometimes to control people, sometimes to create harmony or ease, sometimes out of misunderstanding. But truly there are no rules. There's only what's right for you and for the highest good of all involved. This is what must guide you.

Your relationship with a partner is always a mirror of your relationship with your own inner Masculine and Feminine. Know that this is where the ultimate work is to be done. Then your relationship with your partner can become a celebration of your relationship with your inner Masculine and Feminine, and a magnification of that in the world.

Don't look for your partner to replace God and to fulfill you in the ways that only God can. This will certainly lead to suffering for you and your partner. Be whole and happy in your relationship to God. Then enjoy that wholeness and happiness through your relationship with your partner, in addition to your wholeness with yourself.

Chapter 27

Sacred Sexuality

Question: How were you taught in the Temple of Isis to practice sacred sexuality?

Mary Magdalene: Sacred sexuality is an energy practice. It's a practice of the kundalini life-force,[62] in the form of sexual energy. Kundalini and sexual energy both have the same source and the same pathway within the body. Engaging sacred sexual energy doesn't require a partner, just as kundalini practice doesn't require a partner. The two practices share a great deal in common.

The partnership aspect of sacred sexuality can ignite and strengthen one's energy. The polarized interactions of the Masculine and Feminine charge the energy, making it potentially more powerful and effective. This is the reason to engage with a partner.

This polarized charging can be a challenge because sexual energy has its own pull. To truly engage sacred sexuality, you must master that energy, so you're not simply drawn into the more ordinary course of sexual energy, which is the energy of procreation. Sacred sexuality takes a certain level of skill and commitment to utilize the sexual energy for the highest purposes.

This can all be done at the individual level, as well as with a partner. It can be done with a partner long distance, engaging both of your energies. It can be done with someone who you're not in a relationship with. It can be practiced sexually or in a non-sexual way, where you simply share the energies and move them between the two of you. There are many ways sacred sexuality can be engaged.

Sacred sexuality is a most valuable practice, just as kundalini has long been recognized in India as a valuable spiritual practice and pathway. The same is true of sexual energy and the sexual pathway.

Question: I'd like to engage in sexuality in a more sacred way, but my partner doesn't share this desire. What do you recommend I do?

Mary Magdalene: For many people, approaching anything relative to sexuality is a tender area. It's important to be gentle and sensitive—with yourself as well as your partner—when dealing with sexual issues that seem challenging in some way.

Sexuality is very connected to emotions. Sexuality and emotions are both rooted in the second chakra in humans. A change relative to sexuality can bring up many emotional things. So it's important to be sensitive, gentle, and aware relative to any emotions being stimulated. Hopefully you can do this in a way that's heart-connecting for both of you, such as the way I've suggested in the book, *Mary Magdalene Beckons*.[63]

It's challenging to harmonize all the aspects between two beings in a relationship. This kind of harmonization is part of the larger challenge of manifestation in the third dimension altogether.

Often a relationship is considered valuable if many areas are harmonized, yet there will still be some that are less harmonized. In more challenging relationships, many areas aren't harmonized. This is a very real challenge! It's a challenge of love.

Partners may have different paths in any given arena. It may be that you or your partner are afraid to allow that your paths may be different in this arena. Sometimes the allowing itself can enable a shift to happen, which may change the dynamic and allow new things to open. But this isn't always the case.

This situation is part of the Heart Path. It's part of opening to pain and allowing that pain to serve and support you—not because it's inherently good to suffer or because you need to suffer to grow, but because pain is a reality.

The third dimension is an arena of separation. Pain is one of the avenues of moving beyond separation. If you don't open to pain, you support separation. You support the third dimension. This is a tricky understanding. When you're in the third dimension, it's often not easy to grasp or trust this to the point that you become willing to open to pain.

In your case, there's pain of not having the kind of communion, ecstasy, and closeness that you long for. And there is perhaps fear of not having that in the future.

You must each, as individuals, be guided to what is true for you. There's a way of doing this through open-heartedness and staying in love with each other. That doesn't mean you'll have the outcome you're hoping for, or the outcome you're dreading. There are many ways it could play out. But you won't know that until you give yourself to God.

You see, this hasn't come up randomly in your life or in your relationship. This is almost certainly a central part of the soul path that you've both chosen in this lifetime for your growth. Humans suffer the most when they avoid their soul path.

There are different ways to explore sacred sexuality with a partner. Don't get caught in black-or-white thinking: "We have to do it all one way or all another way." Black-or-white thinking is one of the traps of the third dimension, and it's almost never the case.

As you grow and develop, you're going to increasingly be the creator of the form that your sexuality will take. It doesn't have to look like anyone else's sexuality, whether they call it "sacred," "profane," or who knows what. You're the creator of what's most suitable for you. And with a partner, this becomes a joint creative venture.

Perhaps you choose to explore certain things. You may read books about sacred sexuality or take courses or workshops. But remember, this doesn't mean that you *should* be doing what's presented or that this is what you're signing up to do. Let it be an open-ended exploration. From there you become the creator of your life.

It's likely that emotional blocks are underlying this issue, which may not be obvious or clear. If you were to get to the root of those emotional blocks and see what they're trying to draw you to, worlds of possibility might open up to you that you aren't in touch with at this point.

I urge you to look at this as not just a struggle in the sexual or relational arena, but as something central to your spiritual path in this lifetime. If the word "spiritual" doesn't resonate, call it your human path or your growth path. It's something that you and your partner are both wanting to deal with in some way. It may be different for each of you, but somehow each of your parts fits with the other person's particular exploration.

Thinking in that way may help to loosen some of the stuckness of your situation. That stuckness includes thinking there are only three solutions—to go back to the way you were, to shift into a new form of sacred sexuality (whatever you're thinking that is), or to separate. From my point of view there are many more possibilities.

Your emotions will lead you to the deeper issues, if you allow them. They'll also guide you to different avenues than the ones that seem to be at play. It might be quite surprising where they lead you.

I trust that your emotions will guide you to *your* guidance, each of you. Ultimately, they'll guide you together to find your way through this, if you allow yourself to receive their guidance. And you will also receive the gifts of this circumstance, which I have no doubt are there.

Chapter 28

Inhabiting Your Feminine Power

Question (from a woman): I want to better understand my Feminine power of being in a Feminine body with Feminine sexual energy. How can I safely flow that energy, without challenging the Masculine or inviting danger, rape, or Masculine domination?

Mary Magdalene: There is much to this, and it's important for many to know and understand.

Your question has a great deal to do with being strong in your emotions and your physical body. The natural progression for a child is to first develop their relationship to their physical body, then their emotional and energy body, and lastly, their sexuality. The energy body is an early form of sexuality, but it doesn't become sexual (as most people think of sexuality) until a later point. If this progression is well developed and people are strong in this, you have great strength and protection.

At this time, especially in the West, many are not strong in this. Women often have been schooled to dissociate from their physical body and their emotions in many ways. (Men have been schooled to dissociate in different ways, especially from certain emotions.) Women have often been trained to be subservient, submissive, and to subdue their strength relative to their body and emotions—particularly if that strength seems to challenge authority or the Masculine.

Changing this will most likely require strengthening the emotional body, and possibly the physical body as well. I don't mean strengthening as far as building up muscles, although you could liken it to building up muscles. But that's not literally what I'm speaking about. I'm talking about removing blocks and being fully developed and complete in your maturity in these areas.

This is why I've focused so much on emotions. Many at this time—including many lightworkers and others who are dedicated to the spiritual path—are still lagging behind and suppressed in their emotional development. This has affected your power *tremendously* because you don't know yourself if you're not clear in your emotions. You're not connected to yourself. You don't know what's going on. You're not getting the signals that tell you what's happening with yourself and your world. You've learned to shut those down.

Until you do your emotional work in its fullness and become strong in the emotional arena, you'll have this problem of being divorced from your power. This is a massive problem in your world at this time. It's why your world is dominated by a handful of people—because all of you have been trained to give your power away.

This isn't limited to women. It's also the case with men, though their training happens in a different way. But you, as a woman, have been trained to submit and be submissive. Some use stronger words. They say you've been trained to be slaves. There's a certain amount of truth in this. It's why so much of your world is controlled by those who actually have very little power. They've convinced you to be divorced from your own power, so it seems like they have a great deal of power. But they don't, in fact. If you were to call back your power, you could easily overcome them because you're much more powerful. It's simply a matter of numbers.

The root of this problem is in not being connected to your emotional body and getting the information that your emotions give you. If you were connected to your emotions and those emotions were telling you that you were in an unsafe situation, that would empower you to act and bring about the safety that you require. But if you're divorced from your feelings, you don't recognize that fear is coming up, so you don't receive the information that you're in an unsafe situation.

Sexuality also requires discernment. This is why children aren't sexual at birth. They haven't developed discernment. Sexuality is given to them when their minds are more developed, as well as the other parts of their being—their physical, emotional, and energy bodies. Then they're capable of engaging their sexuality with discernment.

You're not meant to open your sexual power to the world as a continual, ongoing state or to anyone you encounter. In general, this wouldn't be wise and wouldn't support you. Nor are you meant to shut down your power. You keep your power open to yourself and then you choose which circumstances and with whom it's the correct situation to open yourself sexually.

People in your time are given *many* messages that are very confusing. You're constantly shown sexual messages through your media that indoctrinate you into thinking that you should be sexual all the time if you want to have any value. This has created great confusion.

Your Feminine power isn't identical to your sexuality. They

are two different things. Sexuality is *one form* that your Feminine power takes, but it isn't the only form. You *choose* when you wish to manifest your Feminine power through the form of sexuality.

You must become wise and discerning. But more than anything, you must heal your emotional blocks. You must learn to, once again, come into complete integration and functional mastery and utilization of your emotions. The ones I'm talking about are your painful emotions, the ones many refer to as "negative emotions," which in and of itself is communicating, "This is something you shouldn't be involved with." That's misinformation. It's part of the propaganda against the Feminine that's being put out all the time. Your emotions—including your painful emotions—are part of your Feminine nature, whether you're a man or a woman. The suppression and misinformation that's been put out about emotions has been part of the programming of suppressing your power.

Ultimately, your power is in the Feminine. The Masculine isn't as powerful as the Feminine. This isn't to say that men aren't powerful. The Masculine is a genius at implementation, but the Feminine is the fuel. The Feminine is the *spark*. The Feminine is the energy. The Feminine is the power.

With this comes responsibility. Some have awakened to their Feminine power but haven't awakened to the understanding of how to use it responsibly. Feminine power doesn't dominate or overpower. It's not meant to hurt. It's to be used in love—in love of the Masculine and Feminine. It's a *beautiful* system that works perfectly when it's full and when you're whole.

Part of your process of coming to Earth has been to realize this wholeness. Attaining wholeness in the third dimension is a great process, which for most of you will require lifetimes. You're learning about all the different aspects of this wholeness. Power is an enormous aspect of what's being learned about in the third dimension. You might say that the third dimension is a school for learning about power. Many of you have suffered the incompleteness of this lesson. Your lessons relative to power are in process, and many misuses are still occurring. That's the way beings learn and grow in the third dimension.

I *highly* recommend that you devote yourself to this growth. It's the most important thing you can do. It's what will ultimately free you from the pain, suffering, and limitation you've experienced when this growth isn't yet complete.

Is there more that you'd like to know about this?

Questioner: Yes. It seems to me that strong Feminine sexual power can challenge or taunt authority and the Masculine. How do we keep our Feminine fire safe?

Mary Magdalene: You must develop your heart. Power must always be used in service to the heart. The heart doesn't taunt.

Questioner: My intention isn't to taunt. But when a female is flowing her energy, it seems to challenge authority. What is it about the Feminine that challenges the Masculine in that way? Why has the Masculine had to shut down the Feminine for centuries?

Mary Magdalene: What I have to say may be hard to hear.

Questioner: Okay.

Mary Magdalene: [speaking gently] There is a learning for you in this. In some way, you're still seeing the Masculine as your opponent. In some way, there's probably pain inside of you relative to the Masculine. And there's healing to be done.

Questioner: Is it not collective, though?

Mary Magdalene: [still speaking gently] It's never collective. It's always in your heart, which is where we create this world. Whatever you're experiencing in this world is what you've created in your heart. If you're having this experience, it's calling to you, in some way, to do some transformational work within yourself. That may be difficult to see.

Questioner: No, I see it. Thank you.

Mary Magdalene: Many blessings to you.

Question: I'm afraid to fully inhabit my Feminine self and power. How can I be fully in my Feminine radiance, love, and power?

Mary Magdalene: You're remembering wounding or pain that you've experienced, either in this lifetime or another. Most of you have experienced this kind of pain multitudes of times, in many lifetimes. Those incarnated as a woman are often more sensitive to and aware of this wounding than those manifesting in the male gender or in male bodies. But you've all experienced wounding relative to the Feminine.

There are infinite ways this wounding could have happened. You might have been told that you couldn't do certain things because of being a woman. Perhaps you were told you shouldn't manifest certain Feminine things, such as being emotional, because that was considered lesser. Maybe you were withheld access to the Feminine. Or perhaps you experienced some form of sexual abuse.

Denial is another way of communicating that something isn't acceptable. Everyone has received denial and suppression of the Feminine through the consciousness that's been programmed into the third dimension. Out of that wounding, there's pain and fear of reopening to one's Feminine—fear of being wounded and hurt again.

This is when you need to do the Heart Path process. First, let yourself go into the place of wounding. Find where it is in your body, and relax into that place. As much as you can, allow yourself to go into that place physically and emotionally, and merge with the feeling that's manifesting there. In this case, the feeling seems to be fear.

Relaxing into the place of wounding when you feel fear is very different from your instinctive tendency when you feel fear. The instinctive tendency is the fight-or-flight mechanism where you assume, "I'm in danger and might be killed!" Out of that presumption, the instinctive response is to jump into action and protect yourself in some way. But we're not doing the instinctive response here. We're making a conscious spiritual response. It may feel like you're going against your natural instincts, and to some degree you are.

So begin by opening yourself to your fear, then let yourself merge with the feeling. From that place of opening and merging, there's a simple, direct process. It's to open to God and let God guide you. You may get a message or have a vision. You may experience a sensation that guides you and tells you what to do. But most importantly, you've reconnected with God, because what you're suffering isn't the fear. You're suffering your disconnection from God. So this simple process of reconnecting with God is one option.

There's another option that's slightly more complex, but for many of you, it's easier. The second option begins the same way. You let yourself go into the bodily and emotional feeling of the fear. From that place, you use your consciousness to inquire what the source of the fear is—knowing that the source is not the outer experience. *The source of the fear is within you, in your disconnection from God.*

I've called the place within you where you know the many qualities of God your *inner divine qualities*.[64] These inner divine qualities are beautiful attributes of being fully in union with God. It's in God where you find your true wholeness and well-being.

Thus, the next step is to connect with the inner divine qualities that are at the source of your feelings. These will be the particular attributes of God that you've become disconnected from in the situation you're dealing with.

When you've identified the inner divine qualities at the root of the situation, you can then connect with *the fulfilled state of those qualities*. You always know what it's like to *have* the qualities you long for. It might help to remember a time when you experienced those qualities. It might help to have an image or a phrase that represents those qualities for you. Use whatever works for you.

You can tell when you've reconnected with your wholeness because there's a sense of dropping into yourself. Let yourself rest in the experience of having those God-qualities, until you feel anchored there.

Now you can bring the original situation back into your awareness, and you'll notice that your feelings have changed. You've shifted into a state of peace because you're no longer disconnected from the inner divine qualities that were the source of your disturbance.

You may also experience a kind of energized activation, where suddenly you have ideas about how you can further support your inner divine qualities in this situation. Those ideas, along with the feeling of being activated and energized, are your guidance that you're ready to move forward in a different way.[65]

The skill of reconnecting with your inner divine qualities is very valuable to develop. It's the way to heal your past wounding. And it will strengthen your ability to stay connected to God in future situations of challenge or pain. You won't lose your connection as easily. And when you do, you'll know how to heal that disconnection directly.

Chapter 29

The Feminine Path of Trust

Question: I'd like your advice on what my next step is in clearing my past wounds.

Mary Magdalene: I don't know. What are you guided to? What are the signs in your life? What feelings are coming up? This is how you find your guidance.

Questioner: I'm not sure.

Mary Magdalene: If that's the case, this is most likely a time of integration of your growth up to this point and gestation in preparation for the next stage.

It's natural to go through periods of this kind of inner cocooning. At such times, it's not necessary to know what's next. When it becomes necessary, you'll be shown. If you don't see your next step, Spirit will continue to show it to you until you do. This is the way of Spirit, always.

This kind of inner cocooning is important. But it can be challenging for your mind to not have the clarity it would like of what your path is. Being in a state of not knowing is often an aspect of going into the Feminine. It's like going into the earth and the darkness, where the sun's light isn't clear. You must trust that the new sprout will emerge and reach for the sun. The seed is already there and forming. It has everything it needs.

The Feminine is a path of great trust.

Chapter 30

Earth as Feminine

Question: I feel deeply drawn to attune to the consciousness of the Earth in various locations, and to the unseen dimension. It feels like that's all I'm here to do.

Mary Magdalene: This is a form of communion with the Feminine. When you attune to the Earth, you're attuning to the Feminine. Any time you engage energetically, you're calling upon the Feminine.

Engagement with the Feminine is what this time is about for humanity, in one form or other. It's about calling forth and rediscovering the Feminine, coming back into ecstatic union with the Feminine. This is what I hear you describing. This seems very appropriate to me.

Attuning to the Earth may be your own particular form, as each will find their own form. I celebrate your engagement with the Feminine. And I thank you.

Chapter 31

Changing the World

Question: Many people want to change what's going on in the world and are trying to support that in various ways. My impression is that you see change coming about through connecting to the heart and the Feminine. Is that correct?

Mary Magdalene: It's about becoming the fullness of the Masculine *and* Feminine, within yourself.[66] When you do that, what you experience in your world will change.

Chapter 32

Masculine and Feminine in the Gospels

Question: Do the gospels[67] give insight into the coming together of the Masculine and Feminine?

Mary Magdalene: The verbal communication that was given has largely been lost. But there was a spiritual presence or transmission in that teaching that's still alive in the gospels—even with the extraction of the content and its meaning. That's why so many people are so passionate about the Bible.

It's not about trying to understand the meaning, for that has largely been removed. It's about the life that remains. "I am the life." That life is there in the gospels. It was there in my relationship with Yeshua. It was in our bodies. And it's in you.

You can use that power. It's not about finding "the answer" through reading the words and understanding the concepts. That's not where you'll find it. Now it must be found through the transmission.

Chapter 33

The Secrets Encoded in Adam and Eve

Question: Is there truth in the story of Adam and Eve?[68]

Mary Magdalene: The story is a myth that was put forth. Yet there were also pearls, or secrets, encoded in it.

The first pearl was about the serpent and the tree of life. The serpent was the serpent power of kundalini,[69] and the tree of life was the spine. Together they represent the process of ascending and moving into the higher dimensions.

The story also conveyed the essentialness of the Masculine and Feminine being in union. The fruit represents the Feminine. Eating the apple was the knowing, the embodying, and the taking in of the Feminine. Just as Eve was created to partner with Adam—that it was not enough to only have a man; a woman was also required—the union of the Masculine and Feminine was also required. This was the next instruction.

The story was really about awakening the kundalini (which we called *sekhem* in the Egyptian lineage.[70]) This awakening was known in many ancient traditions. It was known in the temples and was part of the mystery schools that came out of the temples.

All this was twisted and turned as a means of suppression and control. Many have had the awareness within themselves to say, "The story we've been told isn't accurate." Nonetheless, instruction was being given through the story, primarily about moving into the higher dimensions (with the fourth dimension being the next dimension). This is what was practiced in the mystery schools.

For those who are ready and available, this movement into higher dimensions is awakening now. Many who are incarnated at this time are remembering this knowledge. Many have returned who were part of the mystery schools and received this training—this consciousness, awareness, and understanding. And many are remembering.

But when most beings incarnate in this world, the veils close and their memory largely goes away until they're spiritually developed. Some of you have retained your gifts of being able to open the veils and remember, which has allowed you to understand the help that's being given.

So yes, there were great gifts in that story. It's similar to your entire Bible. Much of it has been changed to a different interpretation, yet there are still gifts within it.

PART V

The Heart

Chapter 34

The Steps to Real Loving

Question: What are the essential steps we need to take to come into real loving?

Mary Magdalene: It's all about the Feminine awakening.

Most of you are overdeveloped in your mental faculties. What you need is to bring your other faculties up to the level of what you've developed relative to the mind, so you can come into balance.

The faculties you need to develop are in three arenas—your body, sexuality, and emotions. These three arenas are the foundation of the Feminine within. They're also the three areas that most people today have difficulties with. When you strengthen these parts of yourself, the Feminine can take her seat in your heart, which is the throne of the inner Divine Feminine.

Once the Feminine is seated in your heart, you can come into union with your higher mind. This is the inner marriage that you're all moving toward.

But first you must do the foundational work of coming into completion, fullness, and mastery relative to your physical embodiment, your sexuality, and your emotions. Of those three areas, the one that most needs strengthening (for most people), the one that holds you back more than anything else, is your relationship to emotional pain.

Questioner: How can we master our emotions and not have them run us?

Mary Magdalene: Many have received the message that emotions—and specifically painful emotions—are to be avoided. You've been taught that if you're really spiritual, you won't have painful emotions. You won't be afraid, sad, or angry.

On one level there is truth to this. As you develop in your spiritual process and go into the higher frequencies of the fourth dimension, your experience of these painful emotions will be greatly diminished, to the extent that you may not experience these painful emotions at all. But that will be a natural process. It won't come out of you effortfully trying to not have painful emotions. It will simply be a natural change that you'll go through.

But that's not the level that most human beings are currently at. Your emotions are still very much a feature of your reality. What many of you are doing is suppressing your emotions out of the *belief* that doing so will support you in either your practical or your spiritual life. But in fact, that isn't supporting you at all. You're doing so out of a wrong understanding of painful emotions.

Painful emotions were given as an avenue to reconnect you with God when you've become disconnected. They're a communication device, much like physical pain tells you that you need to address something in your body. If you suppress or avoid physical pain, it may be harmful to you. You may miss out on addressing something that needs taking care of in terms of your health and well-being on the physical level. Similarly, your emotions are telling you that something at the core of your being needs to be addressed. What needs addressing is your inner divinity.

Everyone has a core part of themself that's made up of what I call *inner divine qualities*.[71] These inner divine qualities constitute your connection to God. When you have painful emotions, those emotions are alerting you that you've become disconnected from one or more of your inner divine qualities. The painful emotion also shines a light on the pathway to the specific inner divine quality that you've become disconnected from, so you can reconnect with it. The emotion actually shows you the avenue that leads to the healing that you require.

Of course, following this pathway takes some understanding and skill, which most people lack. So there's learning involved for most people. But it's not rocket science (as you might say). It's a foundational learning that optimally all of you would have received from a young age as part of your growing into adulthood. But most of you weren't raised by people who understood and embodied this themselves. So they passed on to you what they knew, which was to avoid emotions.

There's also a societal reason for the lack of wisdom and education relative to emotions. When people separate from their emotions, they lose more than their connection to their inner divinity. They also become disconnected from their power and life-purpose. When that happens, people become easy to control. So the authoritarian structures in your world benefit from emotional disconnection.

Chapter 35

Be Carried to God

Mary Magdalene: A great process is underway at this time on a mass level. Many things are being purified, and change is occurring that's laying the foundation for a great shift forward for many people. This may feel disconcerting, uncomfortable, or scary as you let go of the familiar.

This process is a positive change of growth. It's part of the spiritual path at this time, a purification and release of the old that's allowing in the new and greater. It's part of your spiritual unfolding and growth in God, yet it may not feel comfortable.

It's valuable to have a practice for how to respond in challenging times. When challenging times arise, the first step is to let yourself fully feel what's occurring. Even though I've described this before, it's beneficial to hear again, to counter the strong imprint that most of you carry to *not* feel your discomfort, pain, or disturbance. That programming tells you, "Don't feel." It impels you to avoid feeling at all costs, usually by distracting yourself from feeling or by trying to "fix the problem," so you don't have to continue to feel it. Yet by avoiding or "fixing," you obstruct your growth. Rather than trying to avoid or fix, simply feel.

This is a kind of meditation—a feeling meditation. It's a Feminine form of meditation. The Masculine uses will and discipline to structure your activities, so you're oriented to the divine. You may discipline yourself to think positive or blessing thoughts, to not think, or to do good works. This is all important, but it's only part of the whole.

If all you know is the Masculine, you'll run into problems when emotions arise because emotions don't respond to discipline. If you try to discipline emotions, you generally end up suppressing yourself.

When you suppress emotions, they don't just go away. They simply move from your conscious mind into the subconscious. From there they have great strength to control you. Actually, they have more power than they had when you were holding them in your conscious mind. In your subconscious, the emotions affect you physically, emotionally, and energetically. And once they're in the subconscious they're much harder to access and release.

People who've suppressed their emotions tend to be very bound up. You can see it in their bodies. There's also an emotional emptiness, like a black hole. They're more in their minds and often deny that they have any pain or else blame their pain on outside forces. Yet if you feel their energy and receive the communication of their physical bodies and their emotions, it's obvious they're in pain.

It's to your advantage to feel your emotions when they arise—your discomfort, pain, confusion, or whatever you're feeling. Don't suppress it. Instead, invite it in and savor it like a good wine. Be with it. Merge with it. This is the Feminine way, and it's important.

Most of you have developed your inner Masculine strongly, or at least are well aware of that path, even if you're not engaging it as strongly as you could be. You're well aware of the path of discipline and the will because you've been trained in this Masculine orientation since you were young, and it's frequently reinforced in your society. It's the way that most people know to address challenges and to grow.

Most of you, whether you're a man or a woman, haven't been equally trained in the path of the inner Feminine. So you aren't in balance. Optimally, you want both of these paths to be strong. But since most of you haven't been trained in strengthening the Feminine, and the Feminine path isn't generally reinforced in your society, you have difficulty with the Feminine way.

The path of the inner Feminine always begins in feeling. This is your grand opportunity whenever you experience discomfort, disturbance, or pain of any kind. These feelings aren't random or bad, like an external creature that has somehow landed in your body or your reality. That's an erroneous idea. Feelings are part of you. If you're to love yourself, you must love and value your feelings. They have a valuable function. You only doubt this because you've been trained otherwise.

If you're avoiding feelings or trying to get out of feeling by fixing your situation, then you're most likely afraid of your feelings. In that case, you have two levels of feelings going on. You have the original feeling, and you have your fear of experiencing that feeling. Your President Roosevelt once said, "You have nothing to fear but fear itself." There is great wisdom in that statement.

Allowing your feelings in the moment is part of the path of being in the "now," which many teachers espouse. It's actually one of the biggest parts because your feelings are the fuel that runs the engines of your beliefs and thoughts. The most direct way to grow spiritually is to be with all the parts of yourself, which means your thoughts, beliefs, actions, *and* feelings. But since most of you aren't as skilled in being with your feelings, you need support in this area.

Even just having the understanding that the process is to *be with* your feelings, rather than to avoid them or get out of them, is in itself a great support. That's the beginning. On the basis of this understanding, you then open to your feelings. Let yourself merge with them, relax into them, and fully experience them. And let this take you to Source, which is God. Initially, it will take you to the particular source of that feeling, which will be one of your inner divine qualities. [See the list of inner divine qualities on page 349.] Your inner divine qualities comprise all the aspects of God that are manifested within your human form, and they're always beautiful. The source of your discomfort or pain is always one of these beautiful inner qualities.

When you connect with the inner divine quality that's the source of your emotion, a shift occurs. You shift into your love for and union with that inner divine quality in its pure state of fullness, unrelated to any particular experience. It's simply the beauty of the inner divine quality itself, which is an aspect of God. Connecting with the beauty and purity of the inner divine quality inherently and directly connects you with God.

Resting in God, communion with God, is what we all truly long for and what truly satisfies us. Let your emotions take you into that, like a river that carries you to the beautiful shore. That's the true function of emotions. Allow them to do their work and be carried to God.

Chapter 36

Healing the Heart

Question: I think a key part of shifting the energy of our world is for people to forgive, love, and honor themselves where they've shut down. How can this be done in the highest way?

Mary Magdalene: Each individual must heal whatever has caused them to stop at a certain point. Something has become frozen in them, like a valve that's been shut off. It's not enough to simply intend that the valve reopen. They must find the wound that caused them to close down and then go back into that wound, so it can heal in the way it was originally intended to.

There's no way to bypass this that's authentic. If someone has shut down, they've moved out of the healing process—due to despair, fear, or not knowing how to complete it. The healing process must be re-engaged.

The heart must open. When you open your heart, you'll feel the place you stopped and the pain associated with it. It's right there, waiting to be healed. But it's not about simply feeling the pain. You must let the pain take you to its source, the place within you where you shut down from your own God-nature. Then you can reconnect to that God-nature within.

This is the function of pain. It shows you the most direct pathway to reconnect with your God-self. If you don't make use of that pathway for your healing, you often won't get to the true root. When you try to heal through the mind, most often you get fooled. You think you understand what you need to do to heal. But you're likely still hiding the true connection and source from yourself.[72]

The pathway of following emotions to their God-source within yourself is the most important thing for most people to learn at this time, especially those in the Feminine. It's more natural for the Feminine to avail themselves of this emotional process. Through opening to their emotions and allowing their emotions to lead them back into full connection to God, those in the Feminine will support those in the Masculine.

Those in the Masculine may not have the exact same pathway, but it will be a similar one. And they'll be supported by those in the Feminine who've become strong in this emotional pathway. That's part of the synergy between the Masculine and the Feminine. They're meant to engage and support each other in this way. It's a most beautiful and wondrous process.

It's often not easy to understand this process until you experience it. My words may not make sense until then.

Chapter 37

Finding Your Purpose

Question: How do we know what our soul-purpose is?

Mary Magdalene: Not knowing your soul-purpose is a sign of not being in your heart. This is a very contemporary problem.

Not living from your heart is founded in being divorced from your body, your sexuality, and your emotions. What will help you is to know yourself through these vehicles—your body, your sexuality (really your whole energy system), and your emotions. And the thing that tells you the most about your soul-purpose is your passion.

What do you have *passion* for? That's a sign of your soul path and purpose. It's a sad state that so many people are not in touch with their passion. It's another sign that something has gotten shut down.

When you find your soul path, a team of wild horses couldn't keep you from it. Look for the signs, the little corners. Look for something that gives you joy. Look for something that gives you energy. Look for something that you do even when you're tired, sick, or supposed to be doing something else. [Mary laughs gently.]

Find your passion. That will point you to your soul-purpose.

Chapter 38

The Feminine Path of Forgiveness

Question: I have a family member I haven't been able to forgive. I want to release the grudge I'm carrying.

Mary Magdalene: Most of what people think of as forgiveness isn't an effective process.

You've been given teachings about forgiveness that aren't whole. They're another instance of the Masculine separated from the Feminine.

Many people have received the idea from these teachings that forgiveness means to love the other being. There's truth in that, but it's not the whole truth. The *outcome* of forgiveness is love for the other being. But love isn't the process. Love is what you *get to* through forgiveness.

You must begin with the Feminine. This is one of the great truths that most people don't understand: *You must always begin with the Feminine.* The Feminine leads to the Masculine because the Feminine loves the Masculine.

The Masculine doesn't tend to lead to the Feminine. The Masculine has a different purpose. The Masculine guides the

Feminine. This guidance is important, but it doesn't generally work as a place to begin. You must begin with the Feminine.

Of course, I'm speaking about the archetypal Masculine and Feminine that lives within all beings. I'm not talking about men and women.

In the case of forgiveness, beginning with the Feminine means beginning with feeling your pain. But don't stop there. If all you do is feel your pain, it will likely be a long process of being immersed in pain. You must be willing to go all the way through the feeling of the pain, which for many people is hard to do. That will lead you through.[73]

Your emotional pain isn't caused by what someone else did to you. You were *affected* by what they did. But your pain comes from your reaction of disconnecting from your divinity. Your painful feelings alert you to that disconnection. You must use those feelings to find out what part of yourself you've lost touch with and then reconnect with that part. When you do that, you'll heal yourself.

Any time you're lost in some sort of wounding—especially if you're experiencing anger, resentment, or blame—you're fundamentally at war with yourself. So that's where the healing must occur. Feelings are your help. They guide you to the place within where you've lost your connection to God.

In your situation with a family member, it's likely that you've lost your connection to love with that individual. Love is one of the God-qualities that lives within you. Whatever the outer events were, you got disconnected from the God-quality of love that lives within you—your well of love, your access to love, and the bridge that unites you with God through this particular aspect of yourself—love. Your work is to reconnect with your knowingness of love.

You can only feel the loss of something if you know what it is to have it fulfilled. In your case, the pain you experience with your family member signals that you know what it would be to have that God-quality of love fulfilled. You must go to the place in you where you know what it is to *have* that God-quality. Reconnect there and then the healing will begin.

If it's a deep wound with someone you're close to, this won't happen instantly. It will take time. You'll need to return to this situation, possibly many times, and reconnect to the particular God-quality that you disconnected from. Eventually, you'll be fed again through that source or stream, and love will come alive again for you in relation to that person.

It's then—when love comes alive in you in relation to the other—that you can turn to them, not before. When you turn to the other, ask the same questions relative to them: what was motivating them? What part of their inner divinity were they trying to support through the actions that they took? What beautiful God-part of themself were they doing their best to fulfill, even if it wasn't in the way you would have liked or chosen? In their divinity, they were doing their best (perhaps even desperately) to stay connected to some part of themself that they greatly needed.

When you find that in the other, after finding your own reconnection and strength, then forgiveness will happen. That is the process.

Question: How should we relate to the world and what appears to be a lack of sanity in political behavior? Should we just remember that everybody is simply trying to fulfill their inner divinity?

Mary Magdalene: No. The pain is in you. You must go to *your* pain and the source of that pain in yourself.

When you call the world insane, you're saying that it's wrong. You're locked into the third-dimensional model of right and wrong. Go beyond that right-wrong thinking, into your pain. Then you've reentered the domain of the Feminine.

What you're *feeling* is, "Ouch, I hurt! I want compassion, love, and spiritual communion carried out in everyday actions." Yes?

Questioner: Yes!

Mary Magdalene: Your pain is that *you've* gotten disconnected, within yourself, from those wells of inner God-ness.

You must get out of your right-wrong thinking of who's insane and who's sane, and bring your focus back to you and your connection to God. "I want compassion. I want love. I want spirituality lived in practical life, moment to moment, guiding our decisions as individuals and a culture." That's it. At that point your own light of consciousness has found the disconnection *in you,* and your consciousness is already repairing it.

Then, if you want to take it into forgiveness, do so by asking, "What's the beautiful God-part that these people are trying to support in themselves?" There's some great beauty that the beings you're calling insane are trying to support. Find out what that is. Then *your* God-self and *their* God-self can meet. When that occurs, you can transform anything.

Chapter 39

Expanding Your Heart

Question: I don't understand how someone can carry out a terrorist attack in the name of God. Can you help me with that?

Mary Magdalene: You must understand the heart of the person who did this. You must understand their training and indoctrination, as well as their pain and their struggles.

Your heart must expand to care as much about the ones who are being labeled "terrorists" as the ones who are being labeled "victims." Your heart must expand to see that they aren't different from you. Of course, you may never imagine killing someone with weapons or acting in the ways these people act. But you must walk in their shoes. You must understand what led them to this point, and you must compassionately open your heart to them.

It may be yours to try to change their circumstances, or it may not be. Everyone has a different response and a different soul-calling relative to this type of situation. But everyone is called to love.

The root of love is understanding—understanding the soul of each person, who ultimately wants the same things that you do. They might want freedom; access to resources; stability in their world; safety for themselves and their loved ones; opportunity to prosper, grow, and manifest their dreams; longing for their heart to fulfill its callings . . .

They're not animals. They're not evil. They aren't separate. They're simply responding to their circumstances and training, and doing their best to fulfill their soul's calling.

You must understand how desperate these people are. You must care about their desperation. This is what will change your world.

Realizing that you don't understand why they're doing what they're doing is the beginning. Let that move you to find out, to take you to the place where you understand how a being could come to do such things. This is the only thing that will ever bring change.

Your world won't change until your light expands to include those whose light isn't as strong as yours. This doesn't mean you condone their actions. Nor does it mean that you're passive (although it may not be your role to take active steps). It means that you do the inner work to open your heart to these beings. Otherwise, you're the one who will suffer.

This is the meaning of the words, "Forgive them, Father, for they know not what they do."[74] This is what all are called to. It isn't blind forgiveness. It's forgiveness based on deep understanding of the non-separateness between those beings and yourself, understanding that they have the same needs, dreams, and callings as you. You must understand that they've been deeply frustrated or hurt, and this has made them available to believe in what they're doing. They're hoping and doing their best to find their way out of suffering through the means they can see that are available to them.

You must help them through your love and your light to see a greater path.

Chapter 40

Lead with Your Heart

Question: How does one know when it's time to end a relationship?

Mary Magdalene: Being in touch with your body and your emotions is your greatest guide.

When you're in a circumstance that's no longer serving your highest good, and it's no longer your soul's calling to remain in that circumstance, you'll start to have emotions come up that indicate that you're not on course. You'll be resentful and increasingly angry. That's a guide to you. It's saying, "This isn't the right circumstance any longer. You need to change."

Anger is always calling for change. Depending on your personality and quality, the anger might be subtle and quiet, or it might be pronounced. Different people experience anger in different ways. But if you're attuned, your body and emotions will tell you when a circumstance is no longer supporting you.

Questioner: What if you feel that you bring healing to a relationship? I think when you really love someone, sometimes you love them more than your feelings.

Mary Magdalene: You can't override your feelings to love another person. You must love yourself first through loving your feelings.

This doesn't mean you can't have pain come up in a relationship. Pain in a relationship must be embraced by both people, in a way that brings you back into your open-hearted connection to the relationship.

It sounds like you're in a struggle between your mind and your heart. Some of your ideas about relationships sound like they're coming from your mind, while other things are coming from your heart—and they're not integrated.

You must be willing to let go of your ideas. Ideas are often based in fear, or trying to replace God with your relationship or the other person. This isn't an easy thing to see. It's a spiritual process. For many people, relationships are one of the arenas in which the attempt to replace God shows up.

Your world is highly attuned to coming from the mind, and many people don't know how to connect with their heart and to be in union with the mind and heart.

The natural progression is for the heart to lead. When it's leading, your rational, thinking mind and your subconscious mind relax and come to peace. They become in service to the heart. Then your higher mind will open.

Your heart is meant to be in union with your higher mind. What you might call the lower mind (the thinking mind and the subconscious mind) is a supportive function. But for most of you, your lower mind has taken over the kingdom. And it's not serving you for that to be so.

You must allow your heart to become strong and full. Then your thinking and subconscious mind can relax and let go into the heart.[75]

Chapter 41

A New Ray of God-Light Emerging

Questioner: Recently, I've had anger coming up in seemingly small situations. I thought I had purified and moved beyond responding in this manner. Why is this pattern returning?

Mary Magdalene: This is a deep test of your faith. It's an opportunity for you to move into a deeper, more profound form of trust in the divine.

What you're experiencing is evidence of deep psychic "house cleaning." This is happening to many people at this time, not just you. But in your case, it's manifesting as revisiting your pattern of getting angry in certain situations. Specifically, it's showing up as frustration and impatience with people who seem locked into third-dimensional ways of seeing things when you see things in a different way, what could be called a "higher" form of consciousness (without meaning this in any sense of feeling superior).

To get beyond the anger that's arising, you need to see the divine in the people you're encountering, even when the response they're making is difficult for you. This isn't just a form of compassion for their limitations or hardships they're dealing with. What you're being called to is deeper and more far-reaching than compassion.

What you're awakening to is a form of love. It's about falling in love with the divinity of that being, even as they act out a form of limitation or challenge. You still see their divinity. You not only love that divinity, but you assume your union with it. You unite in love with their essence, their heart. In that love, you feel the same acceptance, compassion, and forgiveness of them that you give to yourself in your own challenges. You actually feel supported by them at a profound level because you recognize that *they are you*. That awareness is stronger than the sense of separation.

This is a profound and important shift. When you're aware of it, you can cooperate and flow with the river of what's happening, which is so much more important than the challenges you're experiencing.

In fact, the challenges you're having are helping you to make this shift. If everything was going well and easily, you'd most likely persist in your old mode of assuming separation. Your difficulties are helping you to open your heart to God in a whole new way. Yes, it's difficult. But there's a ray of exquisite God-light that's emerging from your tender heart, and you can celebrate that.

I celebrate it most fully. I welcome you into this new space with open arms and overflowing love.

Chapter 42

Opening to Help

Question: How do I know if I'm resisting change out of fear?

Mary Magdalene: It sounds like you've "hit a wall" of fear around a particular issue. It's your choice if you want to make use of that fear or avoid it.

From my perspective, avoidance isn't beneficial. I have no doubt that letting in the help that's being offered in the form of this fear will be beneficial to you *and* to the other people involved. But you may need help in doing that. It may not be clear how to make use of your fear.

This is so often the case in the third dimension. We use the example of Mercedes, who's highly trained in the Heart Path and skilled at helping others with it.[76] And yet, when Mercedes hits her challenges and places of fear, it's difficult for her too. [Mary laughs.]

This is part of the great human quality—that you really require each other in a very fundamental way. You could get through this on your own, but it's likely that you'll go through it much more quickly and easily with the help of others.

There's a story that some of you may know about the difference between heaven and hell. In the story, the beings in hell are starving because they can only eat with implements that are longer than their arms. In heaven, they have the same implements, but they've figured out that they need to feed each other. [Mary laughs.]

I don't hold these particular beliefs about heaven and hell, or even beliefs about heaven and hell altogether. But it's a good analogy for one of the differences between the third and the fourth dimensions. Help from others can be exceedingly valuable, especially when you're dealing with core issues, which I would call *soul issues*. These are the issues that you especially came to work on in this lifetime. When you come up against these issues, you might feel "triggered" or that you're having a "button pushed." Suddenly, you feel like you're in a mental fog and can't see things clearly. You seem to lose the competence and clarity you have at other times. This is when it can be extremely helpful to have the support of others.

As you transition into higher dimensions, you'll move into less identification with being a separate individual. You'll increasingly have a sense of being part of something greater, including a connection with other beings, and that something greater becomes your identity. Over time, it will become natural to relate to life in a more group-like way, as opposed to a very individual, separated way.

But at the third dimension, you're at the beginning of this transition. You're still dealing with other aspects of the third dimension—power dynamics, the belief that there isn't enough, that you have to fight to survive, and that if you don't have power, you may not survive. To ask for help at the vulnerable places of connection to your soul path can feel scary, like you're giving away your power. You may tell yourself that asking for help is stupid or the exact wrong thing to do. This is part of what makes the third dimension a challenging place. Much of what you've learned and believe doesn't support your highest good.

The heart is one of your greatest advantages and guides in such circumstances. The more you develop your skill in connecting with and following your heart—even skill in recognizing what your heart guidance is—the more you'll find your way, and the less you'll be influenced by the insidiousness of third-dimensional beliefs, such as not having enough or the necessity of power, struggle, and survival. Going beyond these beliefs won't make you removed or callous. You'll become wonderfully strong, for yourself and for others.

This I invoke and wish to support as much as I can.

Chapter 43

Follow Your Emotions and Your Body

Question (from a woman): Like many women, my life is busy with children, family, work, and developing myself professionally. In the midst of all that, I lose track of my heart. How can women live in this third dimension and society, doing all the things we do, and still come from our heart?

Mary Magdalene: This may be hard to hear.

Whenever you're in this kind of situation, there's likely something that you're not facing. It might be some aspect of your life that you don't want to look at and own, because you're afraid it might lead you to choices that you don't want to make.

For example, perhaps you have children, and you find that you're not happy with your life with your children in some ways or aspects. Maybe there are aspects that you're very happy with, but others that you're not. And you find yourself longing for certain things that you don't seem to have time or energy or money for (or whatever feels like the limit).

Probably there's something going on relative to your life with your children that you're not facing. If you were, you wouldn't be in conflict. You would be clear what you're choosing and what you want to be choosing. Usually, when there's a sense of "too much"—too many obligations, too many things that you want, and you can't do them all—there's something that you're running away from.

If you were to stop running away, it would pull out the pin that's holding the whole conflict in place, and you'd be led somewhere different. You'd be led to peace and single-mindedness. Not single-mindedness in the sense that you're going to choose only one thing but single-mindedness in the sense that you're not torn within yourself, not feeling like you're in an impossible situation that can't work out. You would come to peace. And you'd also come to clarity about how to act. Your peace would guide you in making your choices, as opposed to running after something that seems to be escaping you. This is the emotional pathway, which is also the heart pathway.

Focusing on what seems unattainable is keeping you from seeing the avoidance. It's the seeing of the avoidance that leads you directly to your heart.

Your mind is a marvelous machine. But it also can tie you in knots, like a string of yarn that seems hopeless to find your way out of. If you're looking to your mind to solve the problem, this is where it will lead.

I recommend the path of following emotions and the body. Your emotions and your body are incredibly honest, and also incredibly tenacious. Until you listen to them, they tend to not let go. [Mary laughs.] Until they've done their job, they're very committed to getting your attention. They persist until you listen to what they're trying to direct you to, which might be quite different from the path that your mind wants to go on.

I trust that your emotions and body are already guiding you to the solution you desire, if you listen and follow that help.

Questioner: It's hard for me to keep my head quiet, so it's good to learn.

Mary Magdalene: Many teachings have suggested that the way is to quiet your mind. For some people, that's effective. For others it's not effective and leads to greater frustration. Not only do you have the original problem, now you have the additional problem of trying to quiet your mind. [Mary laughs.]

The path of quieting the mind is part of the Masculine-oriented path. For those who have a natural affinity with the Masculine and find it easy to engage, this can be a valuable path. For others who don't have that affinity, thinking that they must somehow quiet their mind has sadly led to them feeling that they aren't spiritual or perhaps not competent at all. That's not the case. It's just that their pathway is different.

For those who tend to operate out of the Feminine, the Heart Path can be exceedingly supportive.[77] This Feminine pathway is generally less known. Even in teachings that have promoted the Feminine, there often hasn't been a clear path of *practice*. Without a concrete practice, you may feel your connection to your Feminine power supporting you sometimes while at other times it may feel like you can't access your Feminine strength, or it fades away. That's when a practical, pragmatic, even step-by-step practice is extremely valuable. And it's also when support from others can be helpful.

Chapter 44

Trusting the Feminine

Question: I have frustration with the pains and injuries in my body, and with not being able to heal myself.

Mary Magdalene: What's your response when these things happen?

Questioner: I try to love my body anyway and accept that this is where it is right now.

Mary Magdalene: For many, that kind of thinking alienates you from your own being.

Your body is in pain, and you're adding another layer on top of it. This is what is often done with children. When children cry, the adult says, "Don't cry. Everything's fine." But that's not the child's reality. The child's reality is that they're in pain.

The effect of that kind of communication over time is that it's telling the child, "Your reality isn't real." Then they start to dissociate from their experience. They think they're supposed to be feeling something else, other than what they're actually feeling.

Questioner: I think I'm feeling what's going on with my body. I just get frustrated with it because I want to make it better.

Mary Magdalene: Yes. You must let go of your goal. Your body has a different plan.

Are you willing to trust your body?

Questioner: I think if I can love myself and know that I'm loved, then I can trust across the board.

Mary Magdalene: It tends to happen in the reverse order. When you trust your body and open to it, you will find love. Until you do that, your head will be working against your heart.

Questioner: Yes, I have a lot of intellectual energy.

Mary Magdalene: Yes. What you're describing has everything to do with the inner union of the Masculine and the Feminine. There's fear of opening to the Feminine, opening to your body. "What if opening to the Feminine takes me into the darkness and I never come out?" That's the great fear of opening to the Feminine.

Chapter 45

When You're Triggered

Questioner: I regularly get triggered by a particular individual because I want them to make the kind of choices I do, and I feel hurt and pain when they don't.

Mary Magdalene: It's part of that person's soul path to be making exactly the kind of choices they are. It's also part of *your* soul path to have this situation in your life and to learn to come to peace, acceptance, and love with it.

This is what many people who subscribe to the new-age belief that everyone is creating their own reality are missing. They see others and think, "That person has created their reality." There's truth in that. But then they tend to think, "That has nothing to do with me," and that's an error. You've created them to be in your life, just as they've created their life to be whatever it is. The important work for you is to consider why you've created them to be in your life. What lessons are they providing for you? What growth are you accomplishing by calling this in?

While these are valuable thoughts to consider, I urge you to go deeper. Go to the emotional level. There's almost always an emotional component to any situation that's coming to your consciousness. If you're thinking about someone else, you're probably either disturbed, happy, intrigued, or something similar in relation to that situation. The emotion will be your most expeditious help in getting directly to the source of why that situation is appearing in your life.

You might think of what's happening with you as being like an energetic knot. When you're not having a reaction to a situation, you're like a hose that water is freely flowing through. But when a reaction comes up, it's as though a knot gets tied in the hose, and the water gets stuck. That knot creates thoughts that arise in your mind. But the thoughts are generally somewhat removed from the core of the situation. Involving yourself in the thoughts will tend to keep you removed from the center of the knot.

What will take you into the center of the knot are your feelings. The advantage of going to the core, or essence, is that you're then most well-equipped to deal with the real issue that's creating the knot. Most of the thoughts that arise are removed from the real issue and, in fact, distract you from the true issue and event. When you're consumed by your thoughts, you often don't realize that something else is going on, something that is more important for you personally. Your thoughts are a protective device that keep you from this real issue until you're ready to address it.

Your ally in all of this is your feelings. By consciously choosing to become aware of your feelings, you're choosing to work at the deeper level, to go into the center of the knot. Following your feelings will address what's really important, what you've come here to accomplish through this situation, which is why you've created it in your life. And it will bring you the growth and peace you desire, including resolving all the thoughts you're having.[78]

Many spiritual people suppress certain thoughts or feelings because they judge them to be unspiritual. But the energy never goes away. You must allow them to arise to your conscious mind, so you can work with them. Give yourself space and time to experience and witness all of your reactivity, pain, judgments, etc.

Eventually, you'll get to the root. You'll realize that your disturbance isn't about the other person you were having the reactive thoughts about. Rather, it's about your pain, fear, sadness, or whatever other feeling is at the core of your reaction. Perhaps you'll see how the current situation has tapped into a deeper theme in your life. Perhaps your feelings stem from your overall experience of life's pains and the ever-looming fear of not surviving or succeeding in some way.

If you stay with your feelings, you'll eventually remember about trusting God. In your more connected moments, you have trust in God. You trust that all is in divine order, and you can let go into that. When you're triggered and you stay with your feelings, you'll feel how you've become disconnected from that trust. And in that awareness, you become connected again.[79]

Once you reconnect to God, you come to peace and experience the full release that comes from uniting with God. You begin to breathe deeply again, to calm down, and your body literally lets go into God's vast embrace. Once again, all is well in your world.

Did anything change in your circumstance? No. The shift you went through occurred entirely in your feeling-consciousness. Yet it could be said that everything changed. It could be said that your feeling-consciousness is all you have, and from there you create your reality, your so-called "outer world." So perhaps everything changed. In time, you will see what occurs.

The cosmic humor is that even if everything changes from that point on, in some ways it no longer matters. You've reconnected with God, and all is well again, whether things change or not.

This is your true freedom, your great release and ecstasy. The more you do this and experience this joy, release, and ecstasy, the more you'll naturally want to do this. It will start to become more and more of what your life is about. As you spend more time in this release, ecstasy, and freedom, your life will change. I guarantee it. That's what will move you into the higher dimensions because your consciousness has changed. And you'll indeed be creating a new reality for yourself.

I love you, support you, and trust you in the midst of this moment and all the moments of your life. You're a manifestation of divine light. More and more you're finding your way back to remembering that light and drawing upon it as your source, rather than being locked into the relative darkness of your third-dimensional world. As you bring that light to yourself, and gravitate more and more to the light that you *are*, you'll not only be transforming yourself; you'll also be transforming your world.

You're not alone in doing this work of becoming the light. Many, many beings are doing this, in their own way. The light that you all collectively bring is enormous, powerful, and capable of transforming your world. And so it shall.

Chapter 46

Protection for Sensitive Beings

Question: I'm very sensitive to pain, and I think I experience ongoing wounding because of that. How can I take care of myself in a way that keeps my heart open?

Mary Magdalene: This is an important question for many people. Many who are doing more advanced spiritual work are sensitive beings, often empathic. Such ones often have a tendency to be sensitive to the pain of others. And they also tend to open themselves to others' pain in a way that's not necessarily supportive of themselves *or* the others.

Part of the practice of living in your heart is to differentiate between opening yourself to others' feelings versus heart-connecting with someone who's having feelings. This is a *very* important difference. In order to heart-connect with someone else, you need to first be connected to your own heart. That means you need to be in touch with anything that's going on within you.

If you see, experience, or hear about someone else who's in pain, do you lose your own self-connection? Are you aware of what's getting stimulated (if anything) within you?

Oftentimes, pain gets stimulated in you through being aware

of someone else's pain. Sometimes opening to others' pain can be a way of trying to protect yourself. It's a kind of "jumping out" of your own feeling, your own self-connection, so you don't feel *your* pain of sensing the pain of the other. Instead, you're opening to their pain. If that's occurred, then two things have happened. You've lost yourself and your connection to your heart, and you've opened yourself in a not-fully-conscious way to someone else's pain.

The first thing to do in these situations is to stay connected to yourself. If experiencing someone else being in pain stimulates pain in you, be with *your* pain rather than *theirs*. This is *the* most important part of the process for those who tend to lose and imbalance themselves by opening to others. Reel your energy back in, and notice what's going on with you. Often it will be that you're in pain because you care about others, and you want to support their well-being. Stay connected to *your* inner divinity of care for others and wanting to support their well-being, rather than losing yourself in what's going on with the other.[80]

At first, you may need to *only* do that—just focusing on yourself. You may be so habituated to jumping out of yourself and losing yourself that this different response may require all your attention and awareness. If that's the case, just "be with" yourself. It's not mean, unkind, or uncompassionate to do that. It's simply remedial work that you need to do. You learned a pattern that's hurting you (and others), and you need to go back and do some foundational work to change that.

For a period of time, that may be all you choose to do to support yourself. At some point, when you've become stronger in doing this, you'll be able to maintain your connection to yourself and your divinity. Then you'll have excess to be aware of others and be able to heart-connect with them. Then you can take the next step, which is to let other people's feelings guide you to what you think their inner divinity is and connect with *that*. Connecting to their inner divinity, rather than their feelings, is what will truly support the other and you.[81]

Now, rather than losing yourself and letting the feelings of others overtake you in a habitual and not-fully-conscious way, you're staying connected to yourself and your inner divinity. If you have enough fullness to do more than that, follow the pathway to the other person's inner divinity and connect with that.

Doing these steps is what will keep you strong and support your heart in staying open, while also protecting you in a way you haven't had if you haven't been doing that.

Chapter 47

Serve from the Fullness of Self-Love

Question: I value being in service. But I often end up hurting myself by not taking care of myself and putting myself last.

Mary Magdalene: The answer is simple, but not easy. You must put yourself first, by loving yourself. Then you become the vehicle that all love flows through.

This is very different from what's promoted in many of your teachings, where loving yourself first is seen as selfish or self-centered. So people empty themself to be good. This is an unfortunate teaching.

True service comes out of the fullness, abundance, and excess of your self-love. You're so filled with love that you can't help but give to others. It's streaming out of you.

Think of a time when you were so in love and your heart was so full that it was a joy to serve. That service didn't empty you because you were already full, already overflowing. It was simply a natural process.

When your service isn't coming out of your overflowing fullness, it's a sign that you need to fill yourself with love, until you have excess to give to others.

PART VI

Higher Consciousness

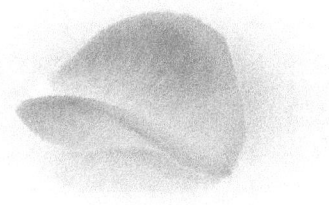

Chapter 48

Shifting to Higher Consciousness

Question: Can you speak about what will happen in the future?

Mary Magdalene: Humans, in general, are very oriented to wanting to know. This includes wanting to know what will happen in the future. This is because your world is a place where things are always changing, and this brings about fear. Ultimately, this is fear for your survival and well-being: "Will I be able to survive and thrive in the midst of what will happen?"

This is a very spiritual question. I say that because, from my point of view, spirituality is about two things—consciousness and love. The question of "Will I survive and thrive?" reflects a third-dimensional consciousness. In the third dimension, beings relate to life in a physical way. So the focus is on physical survival and physical well-being.

Those of you who are growing spiritually are in the process of growing beyond the third dimension and its attendant consciousness. You're moving into the higher dimensions, beginning with the fourth dimension. As part of this, you're moving beyond the exclusive focus on physicality. You're moving beyond being driven by survival and physical well-being. Of course, those needs are still there, and they won't disappear. But they will no longer dominate or control you because they've been superseded by another drive.

As you move into the fourth dimension, your higher awareness begins to open, and you begin to relate to the experiences of life differently. Rather than merely wanting to survive, you begin to look at the events you're encountering differently. Whereas in the third dimension you interpreted certain events as threats to your survival or well-being, now you begin to see that these events aren't external things happening to you, and you aren't at their affect as a victim. Instead, you begin to see the wholeness of what's happening. You begin to see your inherent relationship to events and to understand that something bigger is going on. You're not merely in a dangerous world that can wipe you out, which you need to oppose with your strength and mind. Rather, you're a part of these events. You start to understand that you've agreed to these events at the soul level.

This is a huge shift out of third-dimensional consciousness into higher consciousness. Now you're not merely a separate individual who's struggling to survive and thrive, and who can become the victim of circumstances for no apparent reason. Rather, you start to understand yourself as a creator. You've created these events in some way. That creation may have happened in this lifetime, or it may have happened before this incarnation, in the pre-birth state as you prepared to incarnate. It may also have happened in a previous incarnation as part of what some call "karma."[82] (Karma can come from this lifetime or previous lifetimes.)

Karma is neither a punishment nor a reward. It's part of the process of learning and growth that your soul wants and is calling forth. Similarly, the external events of life are not random occurrences with "good" or "bad" consequences. The events of your life are opportunities that your soul has created and called in to support you in the growth that your soul desires.

This is a huge step of responsibility. In the higher dimensions, you're aware that your soul has taken part in creating the events of life, so you naturally assume responsibility for those events. Sometimes the events are created by other souls as well. But your soul has played a part in that creation, or the event wouldn't be occurring in your life.

This is a great step of trust for most human beings. You're moving into trusting the events of your life as being for your benefit, even when they create hardship or suffering. Ultimately, this is a great step forward in trusting God. As you learn to trust the events of life as serving you, you'll increasingly see the greater pattern of the wholeness of life. And this greater pattern, or deeper picture, will inevitably lead you to God.

That is where you're all headed—toward God. Your ultimate purpose in being here is to know God and to unite with God. This brings in the second aspect of spirituality that I mentioned earlier, which is love. To know God is consciousness. To unite with God is love. And the two go hand in hand. As you know God, so will you unite with God. As you become conscious, so will you love.

My prediction for your future is that you will grow in this consciousness. This is the deeper prediction that transcends events. You'll start to care less about events and care more about the reason for the events, the opportunity they're offering you to grow in your consciousness and to become aware of the bigger pattern. This will lead you to God. And as you unite with God, you'll know love.

This consciousness will change your life. Ultimately, it will change your world. That's the law of attraction. The more you remain in this new consciousness, the less your external circumstances will reign in your consciousness—because your consciousness will no longer be dominated by the illusion of fulfillment in the merely physical world. Your fulfillment will increasingly come from your deeper awareness of the source behind events. This will lead to the outer events calming down and becoming more benign, as they're no longer the focus of your energy or creation. Your reality will become simpler and more peaceful, stable, and balanced. This will free up your consciousness even more to follow the thread of knowing the greater pattern, and through that knowing God. And as you know God, you'll naturally be moved to love.

It's your choice as humans how quickly the shift into the fourth dimension will happen. At present it's underway, but it's unlikely to happen in the immediate future as a complete and accomplished state. More likely, it will take place over years and decades, but it's certainly underway. And for any particular individual it can happen much more quickly, if they're dedicated and motivated to do the work.

What does this "work" require? It requires free attention, free from the constraints of being bound to mere survival and physical well-being. Discipline of your basic life functions gives you that freedom. Without discipline, your energy and awareness tend to be consumed by your "problems." This is why spirituality has traditionally involved discipline. But discipline isn't the point. Discipline, in and of itself, doesn't make you spiritual. It's simply a support to free your energy and awareness so that it's available for the process of knowing God and uniting with God. It can potentially speed up the shift into higher consciousness.

I want to support you in letting go of focusing on events that are to happen because that's not the consciousness that will be most helpful. Instead, focus on going beyond events into the bigger pattern of what's behind them. This leads to connection with God. It also leads to your world shifting—to the third dimension giving way to the fourth dimension and beyond. This is what I predict will be happening for all of you.

In the fourth dimension, your consciousness changes from seeing the world as a fixed place that's physically based to seeing the world as an energy realm that's fluid and which you're always affecting. Rather than seeing yourself as the victim of events or circumstances, you now see yourself as a part of all events and circumstances. And increasingly, you'll see yourself as the creator of events and circumstances. This empowers you to deeply make use of your freedom of choice and to use that power to create much more intentionally. The focus in the fourth dimension is upon manifestation and creation.

Right now, the majority of humanity is in the process of releasing the exclusive focus on the physical (which is the consciousness of the third dimension) and moving into focusing on the greater energetic pattern that underlies the physical. This is part of shifting into fourth-dimensional consciousness and reality. This transition will continue and grow for individuals and for humanity.

You're not prevented from doing this by authorities, political leaders, social structures, or any other feature of your world. Your consciousness is your own creation, and you can change your consciousness however and whenever you choose.

It's easier to make this shift in consciousness when you're in the company of others who share your intention. It's especially supportive to be in the company of others who are further along in this shift than you are. These are your teachers and guides. To put yourself in their company is a beneficial action. This includes receiving that company through written material, or audio and video media. But it's most supportive to share that company in life. Creating associations with others who share your intentions to grow in this way is very valuable, as is finding teachers who can guide and support you in your growth.

My hope is that many people will be moved to engage this shift as deeply and thoroughly as possible. I encourage you to connect with others who are similarly engaging in their growth, to support your own growth and to maximize the effect you have in your world. Group consciousness is a powerful force that supports the totality of change in your reality. It's a contribution to others at the energetic level, whether they're aware of it or not, and whether they're choosing the same path or not. Groups engaging together energetically is an act of love. And they can change humanity's trajectory.

With that kind of intention and engagement, this shift will be accelerated. It's already happening at an extraordinarily fast rate in terms of human evolution. This may be difficult to see from your perspective, but from our vantage point, a tremendous change is underway, which you might say is happening at the speed of light.[83] Truly, it's happening at the speed of consciousness. But it's incredibly fast in terms of how quickly it's possible to change. We're most pleased about this.

We also have complete confidence that the shift into the fourth dimension and beyond will happen. Again, it's not for us to say when it will happen because you're creating it. But it's underway, and we already see the endpoint. We are here welcoming you to your new reality as you make this transition. We receive you with our form of open arms and greatest heart love. We're ready to receive you, and we wholeheartedly look forward to your "homecoming"—into your new home and reality in the fourth dimension.

Chapter 49

Full Responsibility

Question: Some teachers say that we're 100% responsible for everything we experience. For example, if someone is rude to us, that's something we created. How do you see it?

Mary Magdalene: This is a question that many people are confused about. I will do my best to make it more understandable.

The idea that you're 100% responsible for everything you experience is true, but it's not easy for many in your world to understand. It's a central part of the spiritual process that people in your world are growing into. But most people find this concept difficult to accept, or perhaps even feel repelled by the idea in some way. And the vast majority in your world aren't even aware of this as a principle or possible component of reality.

One analogy that might help is to think of your dreams. Most people are comfortable with the point of view that you create everything that happens in your dreams. This includes creating yourself and your actions, as well as all the other beings and their actions. Your waking realm is fundamentally the same. It's created through your thoughts, emotions, and actions.

Much of your life, and the experiences you have within your

life, were created by you prior to your taking incarnation. Before incarnating in a particular lifetime, you chose the circumstances you'd encounter. You chose all the major events and experiences of your life to support your soul growth. Every person is working on certain lessons or arenas. You chose the experiences that would further your growth in those arenas.

You also chose the people that you'd interact with in major ways who would be part of your opportunity to have the soul growth you're working on. And those others agreed to interact with you and support your growth in those ways.

At the same time, those others are also working on their own soul growth and have chosen experiences and interactions with others (including the ones involving you) that will support *their* growth. All interactions with others are simultaneously supporting both your own soul growth and the soul growth of the other, often in different but complementary ways.

You also have free will. You exercised that free will in your pre-incarnation state by choosing the experiences you'd have during your lifetime. You have a great deal of free will during your incarnation to fill in the details and the day-to-day aspects of your life. And you have free will in choosing whether you'll carry out what you set in place prior to incarnating.

So truly, all the experiences you have are ones that you've created—either through your pre-life choices, your choices in past lives or the earlier portion of this life (this is sometimes called "karma"), or your choices and personal energetics in the present.

The concept of personal energetics is somewhat more subtle, but it's not really that difficult to understand. Every person is vibrating at a certain frequency. That frequency is a result of the level of consciousness they're holding in all the arenas of their being.

An individual's frequency goes out into the world, somewhat like a radio signal going out. It also acts like an energetic magnet, filtering through all the frequencies in your realm and drawing in the events that match its frequency. Just as there are sounds that only some animals can hear, such as a dog hearing a high-pitched sound, similarly, you will only experience the frequencies that are vibrating at the same frequency as yours.

Thus, you also create the events in your life through the frequency that you hold. The events that you experience are matching your own frequency. Because of this, they can serve as a mirror to yourself.

It's valuable to be conscious of this process. If you understand that the events in your life reflect your own frequency, you gain power to create what you want in your life. If you're experiencing something that you're not enjoying, your power to change that circumstance lies within yourself and your own frequency. You must change your frequency, which happens by changing your consciousness. It's somewhat like changing the station on a radio. When you tune to a different (higher) frequency, you'll attract different experiences at that new frequency.

This is why it's counterproductive to focus on others as the cause of your experiences. That's like yelling at a radio because you don't like the music being played. All you need to do is change to a new station. I say "all" because it's simple in principle. But as most of you know, it's usually not so simple in practice.

Most of you are very attached to the frequencies you're familiar with and tend to hold onto them mightily—even if the results of those frequencies aren't things you enjoy. This is part of the third-dimensional experience. At a core level, you identify with your frequencies and are afraid that you'll die or become nothing if you let go of them. So spiritual practice takes dedication and perseverance. It also takes compassion, forgiveness, and kindness toward yourself. Personal transformation in your realm is not an easy process. You're all to be commended for each step you take that furthers this ongoing evolution.

What does it mean to change your frequency or raise your consciousness? This is the core of what spirituality is. Your consciousness is your core sense of who you are and how you relate to everything else. The closer your consciousness is to God-consciousness, the higher your consciousness is. The further away it is from God-consciousness, the lower it is. God-consciousness is pure love, resting in source, complete forgiveness and compassion, total peace, unity with all. These are just some of the attributes. But it's probably sufficient for you to understand what raising your consciousness means. Anything that moves you closer to those attributes is movement toward higher consciousness.

I think it would be helpful to give a concrete example of what I'm describing. I can use the example given in the question. Let's say you walk into a room where someone you know is talking with others, but the person you know doesn't acknowledge you or introduce you to the other people. You could focus on the one you know and judge them for being wrong in some form, labeling them as rude or whatever other internal arguments you find to justify your position that they're in the wrong. This will probably have the effect of keeping you stuck in your mind and ruminating about them. It will also keep you stuck in your painful emotions of feeling hurt, angry, insecure, or whatever else is coming up.

However, you could choose instead to focus on yourself by assuming that you've created this. You could consider how you've attracted this frequency into your life. Perhaps you're rude in this way with others and aren't aware of what you're doing or how it affects others. Perhaps you don't tend to be aware of other people's feelings, and the current situation is reflecting that back to you. Or perhaps you need to be more assertive and stand up for yourself through communicating what you want or taking other actions.

Let's say that the last one is the case—that you're working on creating more equality in your life. By assuming the "underdog" role, you've attracted people who are also involved in this dynamic (either complementing your stance by taking a "top dog" role or by assuming a similar underdog role to yours). You can take responsibility for this circumstance by looking at the opportunity being given to you through this situation. You're being given an opportunity to expand and change your frequency. When you do that, you assume a different relationship to what's happening.

Instead of being "a victim" and reacting from that position, you could greet the person you know and introduce yourself to the others. In doing so, you'd be contributing to a new frequency in yourself. You'd be helping yourself shift from the oppressor-oppressed frequency to a frequency of relating as equals.

As this new frequency becomes stronger for you and you increasingly practice it, you'll release the old frequency. Over time, you'll no longer attract oppressor-oppressed circumstances into your life. You'll have fulfilled your growth in that area, and you won't require those circumstances any longer. You'll have moved to a higher frequency in that domain and will be attracting different experiences.

This is why two individuals can go through the same circumstances and have very different experiences. Sometimes you see this in a family, where two children have very different reactions to similar circumstances. You also see it in group dynamics, where different individuals report having different experiences in the same situation.

One thing that can help is to realize that any circumstance in which you feel an emotional charge is usually a circumstance you've called in for your growth. The reason you have the charge is because the situation is reflecting something within you that's hard for you to see and is causing you pain in some way. This is the great benefit of physical incarnation. Your circumstances make it very clear what you need to do for your own growth. The more you realize this, the better off you'll be. You'll grow more quickly and with greater ease. And you'll increasingly enjoy your outer circumstances as the kind you like.

You may be wondering, "What about people who have really difficult or awful circumstances? Why would they create that?" This is a question many of you have, and it's understandable that you would have it. The answer is not an easy one.

Pain and suffering are part of what people have come to your world to experience. Pain is given to help you grow. But it's also part of the totality of experience that beings chose to have by incarnating here. It's a way of knowing the totality of everything, and pain and suffering are a part of that. It's also the case that pain is most severe in the third dimension.

Some have said that humans were never intended to drop to the levels of pain and suffering that you have. Some say that this realm and the results of free will can be seen as an experiment gone wrong. Regardless of how you see it, it's time for this phase of humanity's experience to come to completion and for humans to move on to their next phase, which means moving to the next dimension of reality. This requires moving to higher consciousness.

Taking full responsibility for yourself and the results of your creation is one of the fastest ways to do that.

I want to address why assuming full responsibility is difficult for many people. This has to do with the concepts of right and wrong, or good and bad, that are so entrenched in third-dimensional thinking. Many of you believe that taking responsibility for all your experiences is the same as saying you're to blame or at fault for what's occurring, and that, therefore, you are doing something wrong. This is unfortunate. Moving beyond this kind of thinking is part of growing into higher consciousness.

You're *not* at fault or to blame for creating painful experiences, any more than a child in elementary school is to blame for not knowing higher subjects. You're simply at the level you're at, and you need that level of reflection to help you with your growth. Shifting into this disposition requires great self-compassion. Whatever you're experiencing is ultimately a gift from God to help you, even though it may not seem like it at the time. How many times do you look back at difficult experiences and realize that they were the vehicle of important growth for you? This is actually always the case.

Seeing your experiences as a gift from God also means that you must get beyond comparing yourself to others. Beings aren't all at the same stage of spiritual development. This, too, can be viewed as part of a grand school. You can be respectful and compassionate toward yourself and all others, regardless of the level you're at. In many cases, shifting into this disposition of respect and compassion for yourself and all others will, in itself, shift you into a higher level of consciousness.

Chapter 50

Becoming Empowered

Question: Would you explain what you mean by "Your circumstances make it clear what you need to do for your growth"?

Mary Magdalene: Many people in the third dimension think that the events of life are random, but that's not the case. Nothing that happens to you is random.

All your experiences are things that you've chosen, at some level, for your growth. You chose some of them in your pre-birth state, when you were selecting the life experiences that would serve your next steps of growth. You've chosen some of them during your incarnation, both consciously and subconsciously. Everything is chosen. This understanding is a central part of becoming 100% responsible for your life. If you don't understand this, you tend to see yourself as a victim of circumstances or of others' actions and choices.

You may have a reaction to hearing that you've chosen everything in your life and are fully responsible for all the events you experience. Perhaps you feel outraged and think, "I would never have chosen these circumstances or events!" Perhaps you feel guilty because you blame yourself for what's happened. Or perhaps you feel depressed, thinking there must be something wrong with you, that you're somehow defective or deficient if you're having the experiences that you're having. These are the most common reactions people have when they don't yet fully understand what it means to have chosen everything in their life and to be completely responsible for all their experiences. Awakening to this understanding is a huge spiritual accomplishment.

Some people feel that they're responsible for their *own* choices and reactions but not the choices and actions of others. Yet even this is a limited viewpoint, though it's certainly a step in becoming fully responsible for your life. The full realization of how you create reality involves accepting that *everything* is your creation, including the choices and actions of others. You've attracted everything you experience, either through your pre-life choices or because of your choices, actions, beliefs, and emotions in this lifetime.

If you think you're not responsible for what's happening in your life, then you don't have the power to change it. You've given away your power of manifestation to others through believing that they hold the power, not you. This is the essence of codependency. You believe that you're dependent on others to create your happiness and well-being.

When you fully understand and accept that you're at choice about everything and that you create your entire reality (and, consequently, are fully responsible for it), you become free. You're not dependent on others for your happiness or your spiritual path. You're not independent, in the sense of having nothing to do with others. You're simply free, which includes being free to truly love. Someone who's in a codependent position cannot love freely and truly. Only a whole person can love.

When you come to the disposition that you've chosen and

created every event in your life, you'll see your outer circumstances as a projection of your inner reality. Those outer events are the "movie" of your psyche, animating the results of your choices, so you can see and experience your consciousness in a tangible way. It's the performance of the "play" of your life, the external dramatization of your inner consciousness.

You've come into this realm to have this experience. When your inner consciousness gets animated outwardly through the events of your life, and you experience that manifestation in the various aspects of your being, it becomes very clear what your weaknesses are and where you need to grow.

The primary communicators of where you need to focus and change for your growth are your body and your emotions. Whenever you experience physical or emotional pain, it's an indicator of an area that you need to change. This is how your path of growth is made obvious in the third dimension, through becoming aware of your physical and emotional sensations. That awareness can guide you to the specific areas you need to engage for your growth.[84]

When I speak of emotional pain, I'm referring to what are often called "negative" emotions. I don't use that term because I don't find them negative at all. I think they're beneficial, though they're often not easy to experience. Nonetheless, they're a great benefit to you, if you understand their function and make wise use of them.

I've spoken extensively about how to make use of painful emotions for reconnecting to God and for your spiritual growth.[85] I recommend making use of that instruction to understand your next steps in accomplishing the spiritual growth that your experiences are directing you to.

Chapter 51

What's Yours and What Belongs to Others

Question: Sometimes I wonder if what I'm feeling is something I'm picking up from somebody or something else rather than it coming from me, especially when it seems like something I've dealt with before.

Mary Magdalene: Many of you have this question: "Am I picking this up from others, or is this mine?"

It's always yours. This discernment is one of the great challenges of the third dimension. It's also one of the gateways beyond the third dimension.

In the third dimension, there's a sense of duality that registers as "mine" and "not mine." In other words, you tend to think there's "you" and then there's "everyone and everything else." This is a great limit.

At some point it will become clear that it's all you. There's nothing that isn't yours. There's nothing that's not you. But this will be a realization; it won't be an idea. Trying to "believe" yourself into this realization isn't productive. You'll be suppressing yourself.

And that suppression will actually inhibit your spiritual growth more than it will support it.

However, you can make use of this idea by taking it on as a practice, where you *assume* that everything is always yours. An example of this is the practice of Ho'oponopono that some teachers have recently popularized.[86] This may be a valuable practice for periods of time, but it must always be held with feeling. (If engaging this becomes a burden or a stick you're beating yourself with, that's a sign that you need a different practice.) Whether you take this on as a practice or not, the understanding behind it is valuable. Always begin with yourself.

As you move into the fourth dimension, you're becoming more conscious creators. The foundation for this transition into being a conscious creator is laid by assuming that everything that you experience is your creation, and then working with yourself relative to that creation. Are you happy with the creation? Do you wish to change it? What's holding you to that creation? What are your blocks to what you would like the creation to be? This is the beginning of shifting into full responsibility and ownership for what's manifesting.

Most of you have been trained (through the thinking that's prevalent in your world) to connect responsibility with blame. You tend to think that if you're responsible, that means you can be "at fault" or considered to have done something "wrong." And the corollary is, "You'd better fix it." All of that thinking needs to be purified.

You're not to blame for anything that you or anyone is experiencing. There isn't a higher authority who's angry at you and demanding that you change what's happening—not even the "authority" of your internal mind and brain that you may have created for yourself.[87]

This is why it's so important to start with the Feminine. Begin with connecting to your body, emotions, and energy because that will open your heart. If you don't open your heart, it's almost inevitable that your mind will turn what's happening into rightness and wrongness, blame, judgment, harshness, pain, and wounding.

Most of you are going through a great process of shedding the training and consciousness you've received, and the habits you've developed out of that training. It takes work to undo all that. It's a practice that requires your intention and energy.

Pray and ask for help. Ask for what you need. It will be given.

Chapter 52

The Bigger Picture of the Soul's Journey

Question: I have a hard time with the idea that people who are suffering created everything they're experiencing. For example, did a child who's been sexually abused create that experience? Can you help me understand this?

Mary Magdalene: I come with my heart full of love for you, and for all who share this question and will be tuning in to the answer.

This is an age-old question that has troubled humans from time immemorial. It's often been asked in this form: "If God exists, why does he (or she) allow suffering?" I will do my best to shed light on this question, so as to bring understanding, peace, and greater connection to God and the spiritual process.

I want to begin by acknowledging that there *is* great suffering in these circumstances—on the part of those receiving the abuse and also on the part of those providing the abuse (though, of course, the forms of suffering are different). For now, let's focus on those receiving abuse. I see their suffering as absolutely real and often extremely difficult and painful, both at the time it occurs and afterward in how it affects their life. I don't wish to deny or minimize their pain and suffering in any way.

I also want to acknowledge that this is a very tender topic, which I wish to discuss with the utmost sensitivity and care for those who've gone through such situations and have experienced great pain and suffering as a result. I have great compassion for such ones. I'm not saying that I like or support what occurred. I don't like or support any form of violence or harm done toward another. I see harming another as a huge part of the spiritual process that beings in the third dimension are learning about and growing beyond.

Because this arena of harming another is such a significant lesson in your dimension, a great deal of peoples' life-lessons in their many incarnations are devoted to exploring this. This exploration happens through taking on different experiences or "sides" of the same issue in different lifetimes. In one lifetime a soul may be an abuser, while in another lifetime they may be the recipient of abuse. This is how souls learn all the different aspects of an issue.

When you're considering a particular soul who's in a particular situation, you must look at more than just that isolated lifetime to truly understand what's occurring in the greater spiritual picture. This is difficult for most humans because most of you don't remember previous lifetimes—your own or others'. This is part of the design of your world, so you can have the purest experience of your present lifetime without being influenced by your prior knowledge. When you die and return to your inter-life state, you'll remember your previous lifetimes, and you'll be able to understand your current lifetime in the greater context of all your lifetimes. This is when you'll harvest the growth and the fruit of your experiences in this lifetime and integrate with your full soul-nature. This will prepare you to continue your soul journey in whatever way will serve your next stage of growth.

Many people on Earth don't fully understand this process. Many don't believe in the greater picture of the soul's journey, which includes many reincarnations. And many don't understand how their soul's journey relates to what's occurring in their present life. This is compounded by the consciousness of the third dimension, which supports ideas that you ultimately must transcend.

One of those ideas is that you have no choice over what happens to you. You might call this "victim consciousness." This idea is especially strong for people when they think of children. Children are often seen as "blank slates" who have no choice about their circumstances.

The reality is that everyone has exercised choice about their circumstances in the pre-life state. You have a great deal of choice at that time about the circumstances and events of the life you're about to incarnate into, including what will happen to you when you're a child. In general, those who are in circumstances of abuse have chosen that circumstance as part of their life path.

Why would a soul make a choice to be abused as a child? One possibility is that they were an abuser in another incarnation. This is a deeply painful thought for many who've been recipients of abuse. Having experienced the pain and suffering that came from their experience of abuse, it's additionally painful to consider that they may have caused similar pain and suffering for others. Yet isn't this exactly the kind of insight and understanding that any soul would need in order to grow beyond the pattern of inflicting pain and suffering on others?

It's not that people have incarnated into a situation of abuse as punishment for their past deeds or because they need to suffer to absolve themselves of sin. These are human ideas that have been superimposed on you. The real reason is all about soul growth. Many at the human level don't understand what the results of inflicting pain and suffering on others are. They need to learn these lessons and grow beyond the stage where it's attractive to inflict pain and suffering. This kind of soul growth generally happens through experiences in the real world, most often over a series of many lifetimes.

Your world is riddled with people inflicting pain and suffering on others. There's physical pain and suffering through things such as war, crime, domestic violence, bullying, torture, and all kinds of physical acts that are tolerated socially but which result in pain and suffering for individuals or groups. There's financial and social suffering, where individuals or groups are deprived of well-being by others. And there's emotional pain and suffering, where people are hurt by others at the emotional level in all kinds of ways. The infliction of emotional pain is perhaps the most pervasive. It's a subtler level of pain and suffering, and it's woven into the fabric of life in the third dimension.

Everyone in the third dimension is still in the process of growing beyond the consciousness that it's okay or necessary to hurt others, and the results of this consciousness. It's not necessary, and it's not beneficial to anyone. But you're all in the process of learning this.

Again, this may be difficult to hear, take in, and believe. You may feel that *you* don't hurt anyone—that other people do that, but not you. You may feel that you or others are victims, or that you're not responsible for the pain or suffering that you or others are experiencing. These are hallmarks of third-dimensional consciousness. They're based in separation, in the belief of "me versus them." Another way of saying this is: "I'm fine" (or "good" or "just" or "of the light"); "It's others who are dark" (or "evil" or "bad" or "the problem" or "the cause of suffering").

When you get to the place where you start to suspect yourself, you're making progress. When you get to the place of noticing the common denominator in all the various circumstances of your experience—that you're present in every one, while all the other factors change—you're making progress. When you start to be more interested in your own growth and evolution than in pointing fingers at others, you're making progress. When you begin to go beyond blaming others, or feeling separate from and superior to others who you experience as doing harm, you're making progress. When you start to experience compassion instead of resentment, you're making progress.

A person who has experienced abuse, at any age, may have a great deal of healing to do before they can get to the place of experiencing authentic compassion (rather than an idea that they superimpose on top of their suffering, which is a form of suppression). This healing work is essential. It requires authentic grieving of one's pain and suffering. True grieving will lead you to your soul's growth. If you bypass that grieving, your soul will likely require more experiences to receive those lessons.

At this time in your world, many people don't understand and value the process of grieving. Many have substituted anger for grieving—being angry at the outer circumstances and especially at those who seem to have caused the suffering, rather than doing the deep inner work that's necessary to heal and grow from suffering. Because of this, many people are stuck in their soul work. Ideas such as "There are innocent victims" are symptoms of such stuckness. To get beyond this idea, you may require support from those who understand the grieving process and the spiritual gifts that grieving provides.

This is why I gave the detailed instructions that are recorded in *Mary Magdalene Beckons*, to help people learn the process of letting their pain take them into greater union with God. The opportunity for such growth is why individuals chose their pain in the first place (even if they don't remember or realize that they did so).

It's also the case that some people have chosen to receive abuse, even as a child, as a form of service to the soul growth of the others involved. But most of the time the service is mutual. *Everyone* involved has chosen the circumstance because it provides an opportunity for soul growth for each person.

I realize there's tremendous pain and confusion in your world, and that it's not easy to make sense of it all. I hope this has contributed to your understanding and peace. Most of all, I hope it has contributed to your ability to trust in God and surrender in the midst of that trust. That is your greatest resource and the most direct path of growth, as long as it's authentic for you to do so.

Chapter 53

Illness and Karma

Question: I would like more insight into my health challenges and illnesses. Is there an explanation or cause for these at the soul level?

Mary Magdalene: Illness is a challenging area for many people on Earth. It's also a broad topic, as there are many reasons why someone may be ill. I will do my best to bring clarity to this topic.

To begin, I want to acknowledge that illness is a difficult condition. It's part of what makes Earth such a challenging place. For most people, suffering is an intrinsic part of life on Earth, and illness is one of the ways that people suffer. Physical pain, unwellness, impaired vitality, and reduced ability to function are some of the components of illness that make it challenging. I don't wish to diminish in any way the hardship that people experience through illness, which can be extreme.

People also experience emotional pain with illness. There can be fear of death, frustration and sadness about not being able to participate in life in the way you'd like or were hoping to do, fear of how you will manage and provide for your life needs and responsibilities, or other fears. These components of pain often accompany illness too.

Many people in your world try to maintain a "positive" attitude in the midst of challenges such as illness. They may be in denial and afraid of facing what's going on with them. Or they may not want to burden others with their hardship. Or they may believe that staying "positive" in the midst of suffering is a more emotionally mature or spiritually beneficial disposition.

I don't support any of these orientations toward "positivity." I believe that the most supportive orientation, for all involved, is to honestly and openly acknowledge your experience, especially your emotional experience.

Some people are so used to denying their emotional experience that they find it difficult to even be aware that they're having a painful experience. In such circumstances, coming to awareness of one's own pain may be an accomplishment in and of itself. This can be one reason why a person might be experiencing great pain or suffering. They may need an exaggerated or extreme circumstance to make them aware that they're in pain or suffering.

Being aware of pain and suffering is essential. It's not being a baby, a wimp, a complainer, or anything like that. It's the first step of engaging the spiritual process with any challenge, including illness.

The second step is to open yourself fully to the suffering. I call this embracing the difficulty. This will often include communicating honestly to others what you're experiencing and the feelings you're having about it.

This kind of communication can be difficult. Perhaps you'll think you're failing if you communicate your challenges to others. Perhaps others will react to you expressing pain or suffering in ways you don't want or enjoy. They may try to deny or talk you out of your pain and suffering. Or they may immediately try to fix your situation to make it go away—partly because they want to help you and partly to ease their own discomfort of knowing that you're in pain. This "fixing" can include analyzing the cause and trying to find a solution, reassuring you, or trying to distract you. None of these responses are truly helpful (which may come as a surprise to those who are offering such "help"). That's because such "help" is generally coming from a wrong orientation to the problem.

Difficulties in your life are always spiritual gifts. If they are major difficulties, they're generally things you've chosen in the pre-life process as part of the experiences you'll have in this lifetime to support your growth.

Sometimes people refer to life events that originated in their past (including in their pre-life period, and also in past lives) as "karma."[88] It's important to understand that karma isn't a form of punishment for past deeds. It's always for your growth. If, in a past life, you caused pain for others, you may need to experience pain in this lifetime, not as punishment but to deeply understand the nature of pain and to choose in the future not to create pain for others. This would grow you in compassion and care for others. This is one example of how a present-life circumstance can relate to past-life experiences.

A present-life difficulty doesn't always indicate that you caused difficulties for others in a previous life. It might be supporting your soul growth in other ways. Perhaps your experience is supporting you in opening to others and receiving their help. Perhaps it's supporting you in learning to value your relationships more than possessions or accomplishments. There could be multiple reasons why a difficult circumstance is facilitating your soul growth in some way.

The important thing is that you don't require knowledge of your past-life circumstances to accomplish the growth you're being called to. Everything you need is being given to you in the present. The key to unlocking all of your resources is *through your emotions*, not through your mind. Once you become aware of your emotions, you can allow them to guide you to the lessons and growth you need. I've described this process many times, of opening to your feelings and then following them to their source within you, which is your inner divinity.[89]

The souls who've chosen to incarnate in your realm are very brave, for your realm is a difficult one. It supports great growth through challenging experiences. But that growth requires your active participation.

The last thing I wish to say is that the process I recommend requires awareness, which is different from analysis and rational thought. Awareness is a more feeling-based disposition, which allows you to remain open, focused, and receptive to input about what's currently taking place. In that disposition, any insight or understanding you require will be given to you. It often feels like an "aha" moment or a breakthrough. And it's generally not accomplished through the rational, thinking mind. These insights and breakthroughs are given at a higher level, through your higher mind. Relaxing the rational, thinking mind, as is done in meditation, can support the process of awareness and open you to receive the wisdom and understanding you require from your higher mind.

Chapter 54

Seeing the Gift Before You

Question: I love the words of Jesus in the Bible, but I've been told that there was a lot of tampering with the Bible. I'd like to know more about the statement, "Blessed are the meek, for they shall inherit the earth."[90] It seems to me he's talking to the heart-based Feminine.

Mary Magdalene: The Feminine is not meek. [Mary laughs.] This is a misunderstanding.

I would say that this is one of the passages that have been altered.[91]

This passage had more to do with what you choose to get involved with. There are those who are very involved with what you might call earthly things. And there are those who are drawn to other things. And amongst those other things might be God and union with God. But there's nothing meek about that. Nothing could be stronger.

The original meaning of the passage was, "Blessed are those who are drawn to God more strongly than all of the involvements of the third dimension." For most, being drawn to God is a process. It's a process within one's life and it's a process over lifetimes.

There's a purpose in being incarnate. Your purpose isn't supported by dissociating from incarnation. To do that is to deny the gifts of being incarnate. The idea that one should dissociate from life in order to be spiritual is a misunderstanding that many have had. That misunderstanding has held you back and made you meek.

Whatever circumstance you're in, that's the gift before you. You simply need to receive the gift of that circumstance—deeply and profoundly—to the point that it opens your heart. It may even feel as though it's *breaking* your heart. But it's ultimately opening you to ecstasy and greater union with God. That's the spiritual process.

You don't need to become strong; you don't need to become meek. You don't need to be "this" or "that." What you need is to open to what you are and to what's presenting to you. That's the perfect form of the gift *for you,* right now, for your greater God-communion.

Ultimately, it's all God. It's not: "This is God, and this isn't. This is the path, and this isn't." It's *all* God. But until you *realize* that—not just think it but actually realize it—it will appear that some things are God and some are not, some things are "the way" and some are not. That's part of the illusion.

But as long as it *does* appear that way, receive the gift. Receive what's happening to you right now and let it open you to the growth that will bring you beyond this, to the greater union with God. That's the gift of incarnation in this realm.

It's so much simpler than most people realize. Your thinking complicates it much more than it is. It's right in front of you—right here, right now. It's the bill that needs to be paid, the child that needs to be loved, the tooth that needs to be fixed. It's always being given to you.

God is infinitely gracious, always trying again and again, through every moment, to reach you and help you with exactly what you need.

Chapter 55

Not Taking Things Personally

Question: Some teachers say that we shouldn't take things personally, saying that what others say or do is about them, not us. How do you see this?

Mary Magdalene: This is a complex subject. I'll do my best to clarify what is meant by not taking things personally.

I want to begin by explaining a certain context, which I believe is important to have in order to fully understand this principle. The context I'm referring to involves the two aspects of the divine, which I refer to as the Masculine and Feminine aspects of God. I use the labels of Masculine and Feminine because that's the way I understand them most easily and directly. If labeling these aspects in that way doesn't resonate with you, or perhaps is even off-putting, please replace the terms with others that work for you.[92] The labels aren't what's important. It's the concepts and meanings that are valuable.

To recap what I mean by the Masculine and Feminine aspects of God, I'll begin with the Divine Masculine. The Divine Masculine refers to the transcendental aspect of God. It's that which is beyond or prior to manifestation. This Masculine aspect is often referred to as "the infinite" or "eternal." The transcendental quality of God has been especially focused on in your eastern religions, where it's been described as "going beyond this world." In the west, this quality of God was found in the idea of heaven. Many of you have experienced this transcendental aspect of God through meditation.

The complementary aspect of God, which I refer to as the Divine Feminine, is the aspect of God-made-manifest. You might call it the immanent God (as opposed to the transcendental God). This is God in form. This aspect of the divine has been embodied in beings such as Jesus, Buddha, and Mohammed. However, the Divine Feminine is much more than divine beings who incarnate. The Divine Feminine encompasses all of manifestation as the divine. This includes your entire world and all beings, human and nonhuman. It includes all worlds and realms, in all dimensions. It's inconceivably vast. Of course, the Divine Masculine is inconceivably vast too. They both are, but in different ways.

You might think of these two aspects as two sides of a coin. The transcendental is the realm of pure consciousness, and the immanent is the realm of consciousness-made-manifest. Both are simultaneously true and real. And both are the truth of you all the time. They are truly non-separate.

The reason I go into so much detail about this is because holding to one arena only, to the exclusion of the other, creates an imbalance. Historically, there's been a bias toward the Divine Masculine, especially in your eastern religions. God was seen as something apart from your world and apart from yourself. Because of this presumption of God as separate, it was held that if someone seriously wanted to get closer to God, it was necessary to detach from the world.

In truth, God is both transcendental and immanent. Everything is God. This may only be a belief for you now, but as you grow spiritually it will become more and more your reality. Separation is a hallmark of the third dimension. As you expand beyond the third dimension and its attendant consciousness, you'll grow beyond this view of God as "other than" or separate from manifestation.

This was a large part of what Yeshua came to teach. He came to teach love of self and love of others *as* God. This was a radical idea in his time, and it still is for most people, especially if you go beyond a cursory or superficial embrace of what this means. He didn't see himself as different from others because he saw all as God. That was his truth and consciousness.

People experienced this consciousness in Yeshua's company through the power of his being. The force field of his consciousness was palpable and real when people were in his physical presence. This was truly the greatest "miracle" he performed—to allow people to experience his state and consciousness in his company. Unfortunately, most people didn't have the ability to sustain this consciousness outside of his company. Because of this, they attributed it to him uniquely, making him into a god that was separate from themselves and all others. This wasn't what he wanted to communicate, but it was natural that it would occur, given the state of consciousness that most people had attained at that time.

Now you are living in a different time. People are on the brink of breaking through to a higher state of consciousness and a higher dimension of reality. Many of you are opening to different ideas that suggest this higher state and can support you in moving into it. The idea that you shouldn't take things personally can be understood as one of those ideas.

The suggestion to not take anything personally is intended to strengthen your connection with the Divine Masculine, or the transcendental aspect of God. The Divine Masculine is the epitome of impersonal-ness. When you connect with the transcendental, you're moved beyond the circumstances and events of your manifest world. It then becomes natural *not* to relate to things in a personal way. There's a level of impersonal-ness or detachment to everything, including toward yourself. This will often be accompanied by feelings of peace, freedom, and a sense of mental clarity as to how to engage your circumstances or what actions to take.

The detachment of the Divine Masculine can be helpful in dealing with situations that are emotionally charged or button-pushing in some way, when your reactions can cause you to lose your connection to the transcendental, or what you might call the "big picture." In such instances, a reminder to "not take things personally" may be helpful as a support for reconnecting with the transcendental position—relative to the other person *and* yourself.

However, *simultaneous* with the disposition of relating to things from the transcendental position is another option that is equally true. In this alternate disposition, every circumstance *is* about you, as well as the other person. This is because of what you might call "the law of manifestation": that everyone is creating everything in their experience. In this disposition, if you're having the experience of someone else doing something, you *both* have created that because you both are experiencing it. This is the Feminine aspect of the divine because it involves being in relationship to everything in manifestation. You could say that this aspect of the divine is completely personal, because you personally have created everything in your experience.

Both the Divine Feminine and the Divine Masculine are simultaneously true. They may seem to be in conflict with each other from your third-dimensional point of view, but that's not actually the case. They are the ultimate complements.

The whole picture is that *everything* is about you because you manifested it and because everything is one, including all of manifestation and manifest experience. At the same time, *nothing* is about you because your true reality transcends all of this. Both are true. Always. To deny one or the other is to miss the point. To hold both at the same time is to be whole. It's a paradox, and it is to be lived. Through living it, you'll come to know the truth of both.

Taking everything personally, by taking full responsibility for everything, leads to love, compassion, forgiveness, and growth. Taking nothing personally leads to peace, freedom, truth, and growth. The beauty of the Masculine and Feminine is that they love each other and are in complete union with each other in God. This is a model for how humans in your world can be in love with and embrace both aspects. Doing that will serve your wholeness and expedite your growth more than anything else.

Harm has been done by holding only one or the other of these, without a complete understanding of what it truly means, and without holding them in union with each other. The idea of not taking things personally has been used as a way of separating oneself from others, and thus withholding love and compassion. This has been counterproductive to your spiritual growth. Similarly, the idea of people being 100% responsible for their reality has been used to blame others for their experience, which also blocks love and compassion. This, too, has been counterproductive to your spiritual growth.

Use these principles with care. They are guidelines for something you will come to realize, not ideas with which to insulate yourself or separate yourself from others. The result of these principles should be greater love, compassion, consciousness, peace, and freedom. If that's not the result, you probably aren't fully understanding them, and they aren't benefiting you.

Chapter 56

Transforming Dualistic Thinking

Question: In *Mary Magdalene Beckons*, you say that many of us learned as children that we'd receive love if what we did was "right" and denied love if we did things that were "wrong." As a parent, I'd like to know how to guide children without conditioning them with "right" and "wrong."

Mary Magdalene: Thank you for this question. I believe it's an important one that will benefit many. Your question goes to the heart of what underlies third-dimensional consciousness.

The third dimension has been described as a place of duality, where things tend to be viewed in terms of opposites. One of the most fundamental forms duality takes in the third dimension is in moralistic judgment, which is often communicated as "good vs. bad," "right vs. wrong," "pure vs. evil (or sin)," and so on. As with many things, there's a seed of truth in these ideas or ways of seeing reality. The truth that's contained in this orientation is that human beings are in a process of spiritual evolution, in which they're growing and transforming so as to become increasingly unified with God. In this context, it could be said that anything that brings you closer to God is "good" or "right," and anything that separates you from God is "bad" or "wrong."

The problem is that those words—especially in their negative form of "bad," "wrong," evil," or "sin"—hold a different meaning for most people. They signify that *you* (or whoever or whatever is being focused on) are bad, wrong, evil, or sinful. This leads to shame and thinking that there's something the matter with you, as opposed to simply viewing an action as either separating you from God or bringing you closer to God. Along with that shame is often a sense that you'll be punished, even if the punishment is simply being excluded, shunned, or denied love (which actually isn't simple or minor at all).

Most of this sense of shame and fear of punishment stems from childhood, where children are rewarded with love and affection if they do what their parents or caregivers want, while being told at those times that they're "good" or are doing the "right" thing. At other times, when they don't do what their parents want, children are punished and told that they're "bad" or have done something "wrong." This kind of training teaches individuals, from a young and impressionable age, that doing what their parents (or caregivers) want is "good" or "right," and will bring them love, while doing what their caregivers don't want is "bad" or "wrong," and will bring punishment and exclusion from love.

One result of training a child this way is that they learn to submit to authority in order to be loved. This sets the child up for a lifetime of pleasing others rather than being connected to themselves and their own internal guidance. This is a great disservice to an individual's spiritual growth, as inner guidance is essential for spiritual development. It also creates societies where people are easily manipulated and disempowered because they've been trained to give their power away to others and even to follow others rather blindly, in order to get their needs met.

Some parents have chosen an alternative to raising children to be obedient, and instead let children make their own choices, without parental influence. This is also a disadvantage for the child because children need the help and guidance of adults to grow up strong, whole, and sensitive to themselves and others.

There's another way. To do this, a parent must do several things. The first is that you must release any clinging you have to the concepts of "right vs. wrong" and "good vs. bad." You must realize that there's no such thing as absolute right or wrong, absolute good or bad. You may have been taught as a child that absolute or extrinsic good and bad or right and wrong existed. But that was simply a method your parents used to train you, likely based on the training that they received. This training of right-wrong or good-bad was then reinforced by religion, schooling, the legal system, the business world, and most of the other structures in your world, which all have a vested interest in getting others to do what they want.

So you, as an adult and parent, must first give up the belief that things are good or bad, right or wrong. You must let go of the idea that *someone*, or some group of people, really do know what's good or bad or right or wrong. In fact, those are just opinions, even if they're held by many people. There's no extrinsic good or bad or right or wrong. These concepts are simply utilized to try to persuade people to do what others want.

Does giving up those concepts mean that people are free to do whatever they want? Yes, it does. People have always been free to do whatever they want. But most people haven't realized this. They've been convinced to do what others want, out of fear of being "wrong" or "bad" and thus losing the love of others, as well as potentially having other punishments imposed on them.

However, being free to do whatever you want isn't the same thing as saying that there are no consequences to your actions. There are always consequences to whatever you do. There are consequences for you and often there are consequences for others too. You live in an interdependent world where most of what you do affects others.

When individuals stop being motivated by ideas of good and bad or right and wrong, they then have the possibility of being motivated by the consequences of their actions. This is true for adults and children. As a parent, you can guide your children by helping them understand the consequences of their actions. And the best way to do that is without adding any blame or shame to your communications to the child.

For example, let's say a young child says something that's not true. Instead of telling them that they lied and that it's wrong or bad to tell a lie, begin by telling them *your* feelings. You might say that you feel disturbed. Then tell them *why* you feel disturbed. In this case it may be because you value honesty and want to trust the child. The "why" behind your feelings will always point to one of your inner divine qualities that's not fulfilled by what the child said or did.[93] [See the list of inner divine qualities on page 349.] In this case, the inner divine qualities that aren't fulfilled are honesty and trust.

Now you're teaching the child about the beautiful inner divine qualities that live inside of you—and inside of them too. You're doing this by showing them *your* inner divine qualities that were affected by what they did, and expressing how precious those qualities are to you. You're sharing your love of honesty and trust with your child.

To avoid having the child end up feeling any sense of shame, you must take this a step further. You must find out why the child chose to say what they said. Every action is always motivated by one (or more) of that person's inner divine qualities. What beautiful quality was the child trying to fulfill through their action? Were they wanting love? Emotional safety? Inclusion? Fun? Exploration? You must find out.

With a child, you usually must make a guess and then ask them if it's correct. You'll know when you find the actual inner divine quality that was motivating the child because the child's light will grow brighter, and your heart will open to the child.

When you discover the inner divine quality that was motivating the child, affirm to the child that that quality is a beautiful thing and something that you value too. This will remove any sense of shame from the child's choice. Then help the child understand that the action they chose to fulfill that quality (perhaps telling an untruth to fulfill their inner divine qualities of love and safety) wasn't the best choice, because there were other inner divine qualities that action didn't fulfill (such as honesty and being trusted). Show them how they could have made a different choice to fulfill their desire for love and safety, such as explaining why they did what they did and asking for help.

Of course, you won't use the words "inner divine quality" with children because that would be too abstract for them. Speak in simple words that they can understand, such as, "Were you wanting love and to feel safe?" or "That way of getting love and safety was disturbing for me because I value honesty, and I want to be able to trust you."

The final step is to discuss suggestions for the future, such as, "Next time, maybe you can whisper in my ear that you're feeling scared and need help. How does that sound?"

In doing this, you're raising children to be connected to themselves and their inner divinity. They're also learning to be connected to others and the divinity of others. It's a great gift to children to receive this training at a young age. You help them to become both loving and strong.

I value your caring for your children and your desire to raise them in the best way possible. Doing so is a great gift to the whole Earth.

Mary Magdalene: I want to say something about our use of the terms *higher* and *lower*, which we use in relationship to the dimensions.[94]

We prefer not to use the terms higher and lower because such labels can be confusing and counterproductive. These terms are often construed to imply "better" or "worse," "superior" or "inferior," "more advanced" or "less advanced," and similar judgments. That is not the sense in which we use those terms.

When we speak of the dimensions as higher or lower, it's a reference to the actual frequency a dimension is operating within. It's really a mathematical term, referring to something that can be mathematically measured (if you had the means to do that).

Chapter 57

The Consciousness of Inclusion

Question: In the book *Mary Magdalene Beckons,* you talk about inclusion. I'd like to understand more about that. How can we be more inclusive as individuals and as a society?

Mary Magdalene: What I mean by inclusion is somewhat unfamiliar to your culture. This is because it's something that you, as a collective, are growing into. It may be easiest to understand this concept by considering what preceded it, which you're now growing out of it.

As I've said before, the third dimension is rooted in certain ideas or mindsets. One of the strongest ones is the primal assumption that there isn't enough for everyone. Some have referred to this as a sense of lack or scarcity. At its core, this assumption is connected to your innate drive for survival. It creates a sense that survival is something you must fight for, or at least remain constantly vigilant about. If you don't, you may "lose out." If that happens, the limited resources will likely go to someone else, and you won't be sustained. You'll be snuffed out.

You might call this mindset "survival of the fittest." The idea that only the fittest survive isn't just related to evolution. It's a subconscious presumption that runs human beings in the third dimension. You feel you must always be "on top of your game," so to speak, or someone else will beat you, and you'll be cast by the wayside. This core belief operates in all arenas—work, relationships, everything.

You can see that this belief is closely related to competition. If there isn't enough to go around, then it's necessary to compete with others to ensure that you get what you need, regardless of the ramifications for others. This puts people in the third dimension into a very difficult situation. If you help others, it may be at your own expense. If you take care of yourself, it may be at the expense of caring for others. You might call this a lose-lose proposition. Either way, you're forfeiting something essential—either your own well-being or your closeness and connection with others.

This dynamic has created great pain, struggle, and conflict in your Earth-realm. In 3D consciousness, it appears there's no solution. Most people assume, "That's just the way it is."

Many of the problems you experience at the collective level can be traced back to this core presumption. It relates to hoarding and unequal distribution of wealth, as well as the collective disposition of not caring about most of the "others" in your world. There's a sense of, "How can I care?" You believe that if you were to open yourself to caring, you'd be drained and emptied, and thus lose on the survival side of things.

It hasn't always been like this on Earth. In earlier times many people lived more communally, and there was a sense of sharing and taking care of one another that occurred. As civilization developed, this caring for one another has, in general, decreased, to the point that now it's mostly relegated to the nuclear family level. Within nuclear families, there's still a sense of everyone being cared for. Yet many people today aren't part of a nuclear family and find themselves feeling isolated at the most fundamental level. In these cases, individuals feel it's entirely up to them to provide for their needs and ensure their survival. If they don't, no one else will be there for them.

Some countries are taking steps to change this at a national level through government programs that ensure people have the necessities of life, such as food, shelter, and health care. Other countries, such as the United States, are lagging behind in this regard. There's a great fear on the part of many people to take this step, which ultimately stems from the primal fear that taking care of others will thwart their own survival.

These types of government programs are a first step toward moving into a state of inclusion. But they still tend to work from the outside and rather peripherally, rather than from the fundamental consciousness.

When I talk about inclusion, I'm really talking about a radical shift in consciousness, which rests upon the presumption that there truly is enough for everyone. If this is so, then you're no longer in conflict with others at the most fundamental level. You can afford to care for others, to support and help them, and to cooperate with them because doing so won't threaten your survival. This isn't just a good idea; it's a whole different level of consciousness. Some people in your world already come from this consciousness, although they tend to be relatively rare. But you're growing into a time when this will become the norm.

The cosmic humor of this situation is that your consciousness creates your reality. If you think there isn't enough, there really won't be enough. If you think there is enough, then there will be. This isn't just a hopeful idea. It's a reality.

There's one more essential aspect to this consideration. To get to this higher consciousness of assuming abundance for all, you must also go beyond the concept, which so many of you have, that life is limited to the time between your birth and your death. Thinking this is part of the fundamental limitation of third-dimensional consciousness.

In fact, your life goes far beyond both of those points—your birth and your death. But most of you can't remember your previous lives before your birth in this lifetime. Nor do you have the ability, for the most part, to connect with those who've died and have continued on in another dimension. So you assume that your present lifetime is all there is.

There are certain benefits to presuming that this life is all there is. That presumption may support you in pursuing your life-purpose and making use of your present life for your growth. But you're beginning to be better served by the understanding of your actual situation, which is that your lifetime on Earth is an exceedingly small part of your total journey as a soul. The more you come to understand this, the more you'll be able to trust the process of birth, life, death, and beyond—usually involving future births and repeating this cycle for many lifetimes.

If you have this understanding, and it's more than a mere belief or wish but rather a sureness within yourself, you'll stop seeing death as the ultimate "loss." You'll simply see it as the ending of this chapter in your journey. It may be a graduation, and hopefully it will be, if you've grown and developed during your life. Whether it is or not, you'll continue on after this lifetime into new adventures, growth, and progression in your continued life-purpose.

This understanding of your continuation as a soul is the other key piece that will allow you to shift into the consciousness of inclusion. Caring for others *and* yourself is one of the best ways you can grow as a soul. Neither one—caring for yourself or caring for others—is to be done at the expense of the other.

At a certain point of maturity, you come to realize that you can never be fulfilled or satisfied if caring for yourself or others is engaged at the expense of another. This is a sign that you're moving into the greater consciousness of your inherent connection with others at the heart—ultimately your non-separation or oneness with others. In its ultimate form, the realization of non-separation or oneness is a profound realization. Caring for others as much as you care for yourself is one of the beginning forms of this realization.

Mothers often feel this state of inclusion relative to their children. Fathers do as well, though perhaps not quite as characteristically as mothers. Individuals in love frequently feel this state with and for their beloved. It's one of the gifts of love. And there are other circumstances where people may feel this. Ultimately, it has no limits. The more you grow, the more you'll experience this state of inclusion of others without limits so that eventually it becomes the basis of how you relate to all beings.

I hope this has helped you to understand this concept. Ultimately, words and ideas can only go so far. You'll truly start to understand the concept of inclusion when you experience the joy of living on this basis. And happily, it's where you're all headed.

Chapter 58

Discernment Relative to Guidance or Advice

Question: I'd like to know what my soul path is relative to my relationship with my partner.

Mary Magdalene: No one knows what your soul path is but you. No one can tell you what your soul path is. I can't tell you what your soul path is, and I don't believe anyone else can.

If someone is telling you what your soul path is, I caution you to take that as a mere suggestion or possibility, but certainly not the final word, because I don't believe others have that knowledge. You alone have it.

My guidance is to consider avoiding people who communicate that they know what your soul path is. They may not be supporting you in your path at all. This is one of the greatest differences between the fourth dimension and the third dimension. In the fourth dimension you become very clear that you're in charge. That's not necessarily clear in the third dimension.

In the third dimension, many people are trying to convince you that they're in charge in some form or another. This isn't limited to those who are giving you advice about your life. It's in all areas of third-dimensional reality. Many people are invested in trying to convince you that they're the ones who "know," and, therefore, you should give your allegiance and your power to them.

Part of the awakening of moving into the fourth dimension is that you start to see through this. You realize that you *always* have choice. You realize that you're the only one competent to determine if what someone is saying is accurate for you or not.

See if what another is saying is what *you* choose, and what you want to choose. See if it's in alignment with your soul path and everything that supports you in your soul path. There are many ways to know what's in alignment with your soul path. You know this from your life experience and what you've learned from your life experience. You know this from your body, which gives you very accurate messages about your experience and whether that experience is supportive for you or not. Your emotions also give you feedback. And there may be other things that let you know if something is supportive of your soul path. Perhaps there are signs in your world that give you feedback. You may have connection with your higher self and your guides, who give you feedback. There are many forms. But none of these forms involve other beings telling you what to do.

If others are telling you what to do, I caution you against blindly taking their advice or guidance. I might caution you against taking their advice at all. Certainly, I would suggest that you evaluate their suggestions carefully to see if they're right *for you*. Perhaps some parts are and others are not.

Such discernment is part of your growth in the third dimension.

Chapter 59

Knowing Whether Something Is Beneficial

Question: How can I know if an energy process will do what others claim it will and whether it will be helpful and safe?

Mary Magdalene: Understanding whether energies are being used in a way that's harmful or beneficial isn't always easy. Things are not always as they appear in your world.

You must become wise about what's in line with your soul path and your growth, ultimately your growth in God.

You can ask. Ask your higher self. Ask your guides. Ask God.

You can also evaluate based on your experience of the person who's bringing this knowledge. The most fundamental evaluation is, "When I have contact with this individual—in person, or through their writing or videos, or whatever form the connection takes—does it increase love and light for me?" That's the primary way you can discern whether it's for your highest good to engage with any individual. It may be that certain individuals won't be for your highest good. It may be that what's true for you isn't the same for others. It rests with each individual to make this determination for themself.

This is part of the transition that you're all going through in moving into the next phase of your spiritual growth and development. In third-dimensional reality, you've depended on others to guide and inform you as to whether something is safe, appropriate for you, or in your best interest. Now you're being called to become your own guide (unless you're a young child or someone who's not competent to make such discernments on their own).

More than anything else, the evaluation process that's most reliable is to ask yourself, "When I have contact with this individual or this information, does it increase love and light for me?" If it does, that's generally a sign that it's for your highest good to engage with that person or content. If that's not the case, then what's being offered probably isn't for your highest good.

Ultimately, that's all you really need to know.

Chapter 60

Respecting Free Choice in Others

Question: I'm an artist and I receive images of higher beings. I want to share these with my family and others, but I often feel resistance from them to viewing my creations.

Mary Magdalene: Perhaps these aren't the ones to share with. Perhaps the resistance you feel is telling you it's not their free will to engage in this way. There may be others to share your art with.

You can always ask those you wish to share your creations with if they're open to seeing them. Begin by expressing *your* desire to share. Tell them what would be fulfilled in you by sharing with them. Help them understand the part of you that comes to life, that connects with your heart and the light through your sharing.

Then ask them if they would like to receive what you're offering. And respect their response. If you don't receive the kind of response you're hoping for, you can mourn that.[95]

It seems that part of your creative path is to find others you can celebrate your creations with. I suspect the more you learn what you're longing to fulfill through such sharing, the more you'll create the kind of celebration of your creations that you desire.

Questioner: Will holding back from sharing my creations with family and friends hold me back from my creativity?

Mary Magdalene: Only you will know. You'll be guided by your feelings and your inner divinity. This is your path. It's not mine to tell you what your path is. Beware of anyone who tells you what your path is. That isn't the way of higher beings and higher consciousness.

Chapter 61

Changing the Story

Question: It seems that humans are holding onto an outdated story that's led to the exploitation of natural and human resources. We're now at a crisis point where this story must change if the planet is to survive. How can we bring forth a different story that will change the situation we're in?

Mary Magdalene: There are many "stories" or beliefs that people are operating out of, which are creating your world to be the way it is today. Many of these stories are shared belief systems, which many people have agreed upon. Usually, people are indoctrinated into these stories and beliefs at a young age through the beliefs that their parents hold. This is later reinforced by systems of education, religion, social and cultural norms, and so on.

Some of these beliefs are more obvious than others. An example of a more obvious belief that might be shaping someone's life is, "You should follow the Bible." A less obvious belief might be, "You have to follow what the authorities tell you to do." An example of an even deeper and less obvious belief is, "Right and wrong are real," or "You get rewarded for doing the right thing and punished for doing the wrong thing."

I suggest that everything in your world is determined by beliefs. Your whole third-dimensional world is a creation of both mass beliefs and the individual beliefs of each person who's participating. If you as an individual want to change your reality, you have the power to do so. The key is through your own beliefs.

Your work, and your opportunity, is to look at your own beliefs that are creating the larger reality. This isn't easy for most people to do. It requires spiritual strength and skill. You may want to enlist the help of others to support you in this work—your guides and higher self, friends who you trust to provide good counsel, or professionals, such as counselors or spiritual teachers.

A huge part of the consciousness that creates third-dimensional thinking is rooted in the belief that one's reality is created *by others*. If you listen to people talk about their challenges, most often you'll hear people recite a long list of shortcomings on someone else's part that created their difficulties. If it's a relationship problem, their partner or friend is the source of the problem. If it's a political problem, it's the "other side" who's at fault. You can see this in almost any human interaction in the third dimension. It's a hallmark of third-dimensional consciousness.

Other stories or belief systems also create your experiences in the third dimension. One such story is that you're separate from others. Another is that "right" and "wrong" are real. For most, the deepest story or belief system is that your fundamental needs, beginning with survival, are at stake, and you need to fight for these or you'll be eradicated.

When you put all these together, the result is a pervasive story of "me versus them," with the others being wrong. Proving that the other is wrong is the primary form that fighting for one's survival takes in the third dimension. This story is that if someone can prove the "other" to be wrong, then the person who's deemed "right" is entitled to get their needs met (whatever those needs are in that circumstance) and survive.

This is clearly irrational when you look at it. Why should some be entitled to get their needs met and others not be entitled? When you bring it to the light of consciousness, you can see that this is the kind of story that a young child, who doesn't have much relational sophistication, might create. Yet this story pervades your world.

Part of your spiritual work in the third dimension is to become conscious of the stories that are creating your reality. But you must realize that ultimately, they're all *your* stories. This might be hard medicine to take in. You might prefer to see yourself as the innocent victim, suffering the effects of forces that you have no control over. But that's not actually the case.

You must go further than telling yourself that *others* are creating the situation in your world of exploitation of human and natural resources. You must discover your own, personal story that's creating this scenario. Is your story that you have no power? Is your story that you must oppose others and fight to have your needs met? Is your story that you must prove yourself to others and attain their validation in order to get what you want?

Your work is to unearth your own story that's creating this circumstance in your life. To do so, you'll need to release your focus on what others are doing. In other words, you need to disentangle yourself from the story or belief that your life is controlled by others. This alone takes great spiritual fortitude. Essentially, you're releasing yourself from the third-dimensional consciousness.

This is the ultimate work that all of you have come here to do—to grow beyond third-dimensional consciousness. The issues you see around you, which might seem like crises or dire circumstances, are really just vehicles for that growth. I'm not saying that you should dissociate from the world, because then you would be dissociating from your opportunities for growth. I'm saying you should participate in the world at the greatest spiritual depth you're capable of.

Perhaps your current level of depth will lead you to oppose some others, which may be for your highest growth at this time. Eventually, you'll see that it's not necessary to oppose others. You'll see that there are no "others" to oppose. It was all you, all along.

But this is something to be realized. It's not another belief or story to adopt through your mind. If it isn't part of your actual experience, then it becomes mental clutter that blocks your true growth.

I commend you for your dedication to your growth, as well as to serving your world. I fully trust this is leading you to the perfect experiences for your growth and evolution, which doesn't mean your experiences are necessarily easy or pleasurable. Nonetheless, at the deepest level, I believe all experiences—including those that appear to be crises—are guided by the benign forces of the great plan of spiritual growth and evolution that is leading all beings forward into reunion with God.

Chapter 62

Don't Be Fooled by the Media

Question: It looks like our world still isn't ready for what you and Yeshua were teaching and demonstrating. For example, in the Middle East, women are still subjugated in many ways.

Mary Magdalene: Don't be fooled by the media or what the authorities are putting out.

The transformation that's underway is a transformation that's happening from within each person. It's happening at the grassroots level. It's not a top-down, authoritarian revolution. Your spiritual evolution is happening one by one and then together as a group, in a way that can't be held back.

Those in power want to maintain their power. So they put forth things like what you see in your media to convince you that things are getting worse and that you must keep your allegiance to the powers that be. But that is their show. It's not something you need to buy into. The less you do, the more empowered you'll be.

Chapter 63

Subtle Beings and Planes of Reality

Question: My mother taught me a prayer when I was little: "To send light and love to all those near and dear to us, to all points on Earth and the nation, and to all points and planets in the universe and powers in the Earth." Can you explain more about the "powers in the Earth"?

Mary Magdalene: You are very blessed to have a mother who taught you this prayer. This is a priestess prayer.

When you come into the third dimension, most of what you're consciously aware of and experience is the physical realm. Because of this, most people tend to relate to the Earth as a physical entity. Your scientists have analyzed all the physical components of your planet (as far as they know) and taught you that that's what the Earth is. So many people see the Earth that way.

As you grow spiritually, part of what you're opening to is greater awareness that the physical is only one level of reality. You begin to see the physical as a dimension or a plane of existence, and that other levels of reality coexist with this level, often in the same space. Such is the case with the Earth.

There are subtler beings that inhabit your Earth—some upon

the Earth's surface and some within the Earth. Some of these beings are described in your mythologies or stories as fairies, elves, and gnomes. Some of them haven't been recorded in that way, but they're nonetheless present and real. These beings reside in realms that exist simultaneously with the physical realm.

Many of these beings exist at higher (or what you might call "subtler") levels of reality or planes of existence and are more evolved than human beings tend to be at this time. Many of them are connected to you in various forms—as your sisters and brothers, teachers, helpers. Some aren't as supportive as others. There's a whole range of beings that exist in subtler realms.

Chapter 64

Gifts from Your Dreams

Question: What do we receive in dreams?

Mary Magdalene: Dreams are one of the ways in which you experience the fourth dimension and interact with reality in a fourth-dimensional way. What most of you are familiar with and recognize as the dream state is a fourth-dimensional realm.

During much of your sleep time, you're resting in the fourth-dimensional realm, as you revitalize and rejuvenate your physical body. In the fourth dimension, beings enjoy constant rejuvenation. So they don't experience aging, degeneration, and disease the way that you do in the third dimension.

Because you're still based in the third dimension—where aging, degeneration, and disease are part of your reality—it's impossible to entirely reverse or eliminate the effects of these processes. They're part of what you (and all beings in the third dimension) have come to the third dimension to experience. Nonetheless, the time you spend in the fourth dimension during sleep counteracts these processes to a certain extent.

When you dream, you're more consciously and actively involved in the fourth dimension. You experience some of the other qualities of the fourth dimension, especially the ability to manifest instantly. During your dreams, you're able to manifest virtually anything simply by thinking about it. Your thoughts call whatever you're thinking about into manifestation.

Another quality of the fourth dimension that's reflected in dreams is that it's very emotionally based. Most dreams have a strong emotional component or characteristic. If your dreams are nightmares, you experience intense fear. Other dreams are enjoyable and pleasurable, such as sexual dreams or flying dreams. In these the emotion you experience may be bliss, ecstasy, or joy. Some dreams may be characterized by emotions such as curiosity or intrigue. These kinds of emotional experiences are common in the fourth dimension.

Sometimes your dreams are a way of working out issues from your third-dimensional life or resolving karma that you're carrying in your present incarnation.[96] If you work through these things in your dreams, they're resolved just as powerfully and effectively as if you were to work through them in your waking consciousness. This kind of purifying work generally happens more quickly and easily in the dream state than in your waking state. Nonetheless, you may wake up from such dreams feeling tired, as though you've just done a great deal of work. And indeed, you have.

Some cultures have emphasized remembering, recording, and sharing dreams as a way to fully receive the benefits and gifts that dreams provide. While this can be a valuable practice, it's not required to reap the benefits of your dreams or the work you do within dreams. These benefits occur whether you remember the dreams or not. However, remembering, recording, and sharing dreams may help you integrate your third-dimensional world with the fourth dimension and, in that way, may support you in your process of ascending into the fourth dimension.

Dreams can help you to understand things in your current world differently—to take some things more easefully or with more lightness, or to value other things that you might not have tended to be aware of or considered significant. All of this can be helpful.

PART VII

What's Needed Now

Chapter 65

If You're Still in the Third Dimension, Your Growth Is Here

Mary Magdalene: There's a great logic, a great system, to the spiritual process. Many people understand parts of it, but there are other parts that many aren't yet clear about.

There's a great desire on the part of many to progress to the higher dimensions, which I certainly understand. Yet focusing on moving into higher dimensions won't serve you if you haven't completed what you came to do (and what you need) from the present dimension.

If you're manifesting here, it's because being here is necessary for your soul's growth. It isn't a mistake. And in general, it isn't because you came to serve others. You came because it was necessary for the growth of *your* soul. Those who come to serve others don't take the position of "I'm only here to serve others." They take the position of gratitude for their communion with God.

I urge you to understand the preciousness of every moment of physical manifestation. Make use of the opportunity to do the work that you came here to do. There are so many beings who don't have this opportunity, but you do.

You manifested physically to know your body as a temple, to open to your emotions as pathways to God, and to embrace your energies (including your sexual energy) as an alchemical process within you of opening to the mysteries of God. You came to know what it is to be in the heart of a physical body, and from there to know the majesty of the higher mind. And you came here to know the ecstasy of union between the higher Feminine and Masculine. This is *such* an opportunity that you all have.

Tremendous forces are at work in your world to distract you from this opportunity, in every moment. There are those who don't want you to make use of this opportunity and who've steered you toward your mind to distract you. You've received indoctrination from a young age to live in your mind, through your education and many other structures in your world. That programming has led to you being distracted by technology, media, and many other things. And you continually reinforce that programming (to live in your mind) through your speech with one another.

This indoctrination and its operative structures aren't supporting you. They're not supporting your heart, your higher mind, or your union with God.

My great desire is that you become aware of the indoctrination to live in your mind and begin to make different choices. Through your strength and what you model, others will see the possibility of this different choice and will join you. And you'll become stronger, brighter, more full of love. And the path will become increasingly clear for many. This would be the fruition of the work that Yeshua and I did. This is my great hope and blessing.

Question: I want my life to reflect my spirituality. Can you talk about that?

Mary Magdalene: Your life not only reflects your spirituality, it's also the great opportunity of your spirituality.

You've been given an immense gift to be physically incarnated. Many beings long for this opportunity. You have the opportunity for tremendous growth, which is much more difficult to achieve without physical embodiment. This is an amazing gift, but it also comes with challenges. This isn't an easy place. It's potentially a place of great suffering, as well as great joy. And each person's life here is a complete reflection of their spirituality.

The amazing part is that you're all having very different experiences of reality, yet most of the time you think everyone is having the same experience you are! [Mary laughs.] But it all works together. It all fits. Many of you think the human body is phenomenal, with so many parts that interact and work together to perform an unbelievable number of functions and activities that sustain human life. Yet that's the tiniest microcosm of what's happening in your third-dimensional world on Earth—not to mention other places in the third dimension and other dimensions. It's absolutely incredible.

There's a very big picture to all of this. But there's also a very small picture, you might say. [Mary laughs.] It's not really small, but it might seem so in relation to the big picture. In this "small picture," everything that's happening in each person's life is a reflection of their spirituality. In even more practical terms, it's a reflection of their creation.

Spirituality can be a nebulous thing, partly because it means different things to different people. Some describe it as manifesting love and light. I agree with that. I would also say there are steps and stages. This is what the dimensions are, steps and stages.

There's a certain stage that most of you are presently experiencing at the third dimension. Looking at your life and your experiences is an excellent way of coming to clarity about your spiritual process, particularly in this dimension. It's really quite practical. (I lean toward the Feminine, and the Feminine tends to be very practical.)

Question: Throughout my life I've had wondrous experiences of pure oneness, love, and God. I believe these were glimpses of another dimension. I'd like clarity on what to do with those experiences.

Mary Magdalene: Those kinds of experiences can be a window, a taste, to inspire you to further growth. If they don't last, it's a sign that there's more foundational work to do for those to become your ground of being, what you might call your "default home." At some point those experiences will be your ongoing reality, just as the third dimension is the ongoing reality for most beings on Earth at this time.

But there are very clear, foundational, progressive steps that are necessary for those sorts of higher experiences to become your ongoing reality. That's why I talk about emotions so much, because for many people that's one of the steps that they haven't fulfilled. (Many have barely begun their emotional development.) There are other foundational steps as well.

These foundational steps may seem quite humble or even unspiritual. Some would prefer to have more blissful experiences as the focus of their spiritual life. But that's not what's required for your growth. What's required is exactly what's manifesting in your life.

I say that with great love and respect. I'm not trying to make you feel lesser or put you down. It's simply how this reality works. Coming to accept that your current reality is the one that's perfect for your next steps of growth can seem difficult, painful, or disheartening if you have resistance to that orientation.

The idea that this world is *not* a spiritual place is a suppression of the Feminine. The Feminine is *all* of manifestation, which includes this world. And the Feminine is just as divine as the Masculine. So your divinity isn't "somewhere else."

Actually, the divine is *both* somewhere else and *also* completely here.[97] This understanding and realization is the uniting of the Masculine and Feminine, which many people are moving toward. An essential step of coming to this union is the full embrace of your experience and yourself as God, even in your current state. Even opening to this idea can be a great step of growth.

This world and your current experience aren't exclusively God, but the subtle or the transcendental isn't exclusively God either. It's the embrace of the entire possibility that is all God.

Chapter 66

The Necessity of Acceptance and Grieving

[Note from Mercedes: The first section of this chapter was a personal message that Mary gave to me. My father was declining, and I was feeling upset about not being included in decisions that were being made regarding his care. This was occurring as I was preparing to relocate to another area.]

Mary Magdalene: Blessings, dear one. You're disturbed about what's happening with your father, and you're questioning what you've done to create this disturbance. You're wondering what you're not seeing, and you're considering how this situation is something you require for your growth. These are all valuable questions. I will do my best to support you in understanding your part in what's happening.

You're about to make a major life change by moving to a distant location. This kind of change affects everyone who has a relationship with you, and it also affects how you relate to those with whom you're connected. That's a great deal of what's happening.

Often, when someone is leaving, grief comes up for those who are connected to that person. This usually begins soon after learning that the person is leaving, and it can intensify as the departure approaches, especially if the grief isn't brought into the open and discussed by everyone involved.

There are two main ways that people cope with grief, both of which are ways of avoiding the feeling of grief. One is to disconnect and remove oneself from the person who's leaving, even before they're gone. This is a way of protecting oneself. The one who's remaining puts up a psychic wall of separation to try not to feel the pain of losing their closeness with someone they value.

The problem with this method is that the pain is still there; it's just covered over by a new layer of defensiveness. The person may be acting as though they don't need you or don't want to be involved with you. In truth, the fact that they're acting that way shows how deeply they're affected by the upcoming loss of their closeness with you.

The second way that people often cope with grief (which is another form of not feeling the grief) is to get angry with the other person. This often manifests as "building a case" against the other. Suddenly, your feelings toward that person change, and you feel upset about things they're doing. Often these are things that weren't disturbing you in the past, but suddenly they become unbearable. This is another way of distancing yourself and creating psychic separation.

If you find yourself or others doing either of these things—suddenly becoming angry with the other person or distancing yourself from that person—it's often covering up feelings of pain. Usually, the pain isn't directly related to the issues being expressed, though it may be indirectly related.

In your situation, both parties feel hurt. Your hurt is that you're worried about your dad not having the care you'd like him to have physically, emotionally, and socially. You're very competent at the emotional level, and because of this you're also able to relate socially very well to your father and the other people he lives with, who are aging and sick. You're worried that your father's emotional and social needs won't get met the way that you'd like if you're no longer with him as often as you have been for the last few years. You're also worried about your dad's physical care. Your anger is a cover-up for your pain of anticipating that your father's quality of life will diminish when you leave.

This is a control issue. You're trying to make things go the way you want them to, the way that you believe they "should" go. But this choice isn't yours to make. Your father chose to be in this situation. You're trying to save him from his choices, and it's not working. In the process you're disturbing yourself and others.

You must come to accept and respect your father's choices. Your father chose to put your stepmother in charge of his life. This was more than a choice in this lifetime. This was a choice that was made before he came into this life, in his pre-life state. It was a soul-level choice. In fact, he's still making this choice. Even though his mental functioning is in decline, he's still choosing to be most closely related to his wife and to trust her to make decisions for him. Even though he complains about some of those choices, that doesn't change the fact that he's continuing to choose to put her in charge of his life.

This is something you must accept. He didn't choose you. The pain you feel about this points to healing that you need to do.

The first step of your healing is to come into acceptance of reality. Your father isn't choosing you in the way that you'd like. You're not in charge of this situation. His wife is in charge, and she's making decisions that are different from the ones you'd make.

All of that must be accepted in a deep way. This acceptance will lead you to the underlying feelings that your resistance and anger are covering over.

Beneath your resistance and anger are great pain—pain that you can't have the kind of life you'd like with your father. This pain goes back to your childhood when your father didn't choose you and your family in the way you wanted—and needed. The pain you're experiencing now is a continuation of that old pain, wanting the closeness and family you never had.

So you're bringing your "baggage" into this circumstance and you aren't aware that you're doing so. You're being given this circumstance so that you can become aware of this baggage and heal it.

The path to healing and growth, as I've described before, begins with opening to what you're feeling. In this circumstance, you're feeling worried that your dad won't have the care you want for him. You're also sad that you won't have the experience of family with your dad in the way you've known over the last few years, and you're worried you won't be included in decisions about his life.

You must grieve. You must grieve that you don't have the family and inclusion you'd like with your father. You must also grieve that your father doesn't have the care you'd like.

How do you grieve? By feeling how important these things are to you—family, inclusion, and care. Let yourself feel the pain of not having them fulfilled. Don't run away from that pain or try to escape it through anger or separation. Let yourself feel the pain as much and as long as you need to, without deflecting it away from yourself and without blaming yourself or others. Just feel.[98]

As soon as you feel ready, take the next step, which is to focus on the inner divine qualities the feelings are pointing to.[99] [See the list of inner divine qualities on page 349.] In this case, the inner divine qualities are family, inclusion, and care. The inner divine qualities are where the real healing will happen because *this is the true source of your pain*. The external situation is merely reflecting your own internal disconnection from these qualities.

Let yourself feel how much you value and long for the qualities of family, inclusion, and care. You know these qualities. If you didn't know them, you wouldn't feel sad at their loss or deficit. The fact that you're upset about these qualities not being fulfilled is evidence that you know what it is to have them fulfilled. So let yourself go into your connection with these qualities of family, inclusion, and care as they live within you, in their pure, already-fulfilled state.

When you do this, you'll notice a shift in yourself. You come to peace. You're being returned to your wholeness, which is truly your wholeness in God. This is the work you must do within yourself for your own healing. The "problem" isn't outside of you; it's within you. You sensed this when you asked your initial questions about what you've done to create the circumstance you're experiencing. You've called in this circumstance for your own healing and growth, to strengthen your inner connections to family, inclusion, and care. When you've done that work, you then know yourself once again as whole and connected in these arenas.

What's actually happened is that you've reconnected to your *ultimate* family of guides, soul family, and God. You've reconnected to being included in the oneness of life and to the care that God always has for you.

You're feeling this now, aren't you? The shift in you is obvious.

Now you can face the outer situation, because you'll be coming from your wholeness and not your woundedness. Now you'll have compassion for the others involved, including understanding and awareness of what's underlying their protective strategies, which is their woundedness and pain. And you'll have clarity about what's best for you *and* for all. You'll no longer try to control the situation. You'll allow everyone to have their choices, and you'll respect those choices, trusting that the others involved are receiving opportunities for their healing and growth, as are you.

I love you, dear one, and I appreciate all the work and intention you put into your growth. You're a shining example of a being who's dedicated to their soul-purpose and spiritual unfoldment, and I honor you for that.

I leave you now, in greatest love.

Question: On this path of opening up to new spiritual experiences, I still feel fear sometimes when I have certain experiences or when the energy goes higher. At those times, I ask, "Is this real?" Then I feel discord and can't follow the energy.

Mary Magdalene: What's happening at those times is that different parts of yourself are responding differently. Part of you is opening, while another part of you has a blockage.

The most direct path is to embrace the part that has blockage. There may be wounding there. There may be a need for mourning a hurt that was never fully mourned.

Many of you were trained not to mourn or grieve.[100] So the wound got stuck in you and lives on as a blockage, because the natural purification of the wound didn't occur.

Just as a physical wound has a natural process of healing that it goes through, an emotional wound has that as well. If you stop part of the healing, such as the mourning, that healing doesn't complete itself. When that happens, you may need to go back and allow the mourning—to be with the wound, embrace it, and let it carry you to its natural completion.

This natural process of mourning can be seen in children who haven't been trained to suppress their feeling. When they cry, there's a natural pathway that occurs through their tears. Their mourning comes to completion and they're moved to a different place. They're clear, like a rain that's ended and the light returns. There may be a need for this in you.

Your fear needs to be embraced and followed to its source. The fear is pointing to something real in your being that you've become disconnected from and are needing.[101] Perhaps you need emotional or physical safety. Perhaps it's a need for something else, such as acceptance by others, belonging,[102] or trust of the experience and its effects. Only you will know for sure what the source of the fear is. You'll know when you've found the source because you'll come to peace and a sense of wholeness. Thus, your experience is guiding you to your next step of growth in feeling and openness.

Many of you have learned to engage in a kind of battle against your feelings. You've learned to call your feelings "resistance." But they are gifts. What they bring is important. If you're open to receive the feelings (which in this case is fear) and let your feelings take you to their source, you'll receive the gifts. Then you'll have the peace and wholeness you desire. And you'll have clarity of your path forward.

Your feelings are your inner guidance. This is why it's important to give yourself space from your mind, so you can hear this inner guidance and be with it.

In the third dimension, you've been trained that others know more than you and that you must get your guidance from an outside authority. In fact, you *can* be helped by others, and others have helped you.

But in the fourth dimension you realize that you're always your own authority, your own channel, your own vessel of God. This is your ultimate, true authority. From that place you can receive help or instruction from others, but it doesn't take you away from your self-connection. It supports your self-connection. (If it's not supporting your self-connection, it's probably not in your best interest.)

Many of you are in the process of learning to trust yourself. You have everything you need to make this transition.

Chapter 67

Releasing Anger

Question (from a woman): Until a few years ago, I was experiencing a really nice spiritual opening. Then in one day, everything changed. Since that point I've had tremendous anger at God. I want to understand what happened and how I can release my anger.

Mary Magdalene: The awareness you have of the point in time when your experience changed is your great help. Many people go through this, where at a certain point they're suddenly having a very different experience. Remembering that point and what was happening at that time will be your great support in understanding what got tapped into—which is almost always a place of wounding or darkness within yourself.

You were ready. The spiritual opening you experienced prior to that time was a strengthening that prepared you for doing deeper work. You had achieved a new level, which enabled you to do this work.

You may need the support of someone outside yourself to help you to see what happened. It's often difficult to see for oneself the things that are blocking you, whereas another person can help you reach that place. If the blockage has been going on for a number of years, it may be a sign that such outside support would be especially valuable.

I suspect what you're dealing with isn't just a healing of the initial incident that occurred when your anger began. That incident probably tapped into something bigger that's significant in your soul-process. So it's valuable to put your attention and energy into healing whatever is there. Doing so will move you forward greatly.

Questioner: Part of my anger came out of the combination of my own suffering and seeing extreme levels of suffering in the world. I think I understand intellectually why suffering is part of the spiritual process. But at a deeper level, I wonder how an all-powerful, all-loving God allows such extreme suffering to occur on Earth.

Mary Magdalene: (speaking slowly, quietly, and gently) This realm that you're in, which is often referred to as the third dimension is like a kind of experiment, perhaps a science experiment. It was an experiment in power and duality. And suffering is an inherent part of duality.

It may not seem this way, but the beings who are here chose to be part of this and to participate in this experiment, sometimes not fully understanding what that would mean. And it has involved great suffering.

In this realm, suffering is part of the process of opening your heart. You could say that opening your heart is the beginning of the end of this realm. It's a pathway of fire and suffering. And not everyone experiences it in the same way.

At some point, you'll realize you had the option of doing something different with the feeling of suffering, other than projecting it outward as anger. When you're ready, you'll choose to feel the pain within yourself, rather than projecting it outward. That's what you might call the "dark night of the soul" because it can be terrifying to open to that kind of pain within oneself. However, it's your pathway to deliverance and to the transformation of the pain and suffering.

Questioner: So when I see suffering in the world, it's really a reflection of where I'm at internally?

Mary Magdalene: Ultimately, yes. But simply understanding that won't necessarily be a pathway to healing. The pathway to healing is more likely to take the form of opening yourself to the pain of whatever you're suffering. Your opening to the pain will take you to the source, the essence within yourself.

Note: In this communication (which was given to someone else on another occasion) Mary addresses a situation where someone is experiencing what might be called "righteous anger."

Mary Magdalene: Anger is a way of saying "No!" It's a way of calling back your power.

When people have given away their power, there's a stage they often go through of anger, sometimes even rage. In shamanic terms, this is understood as bringing back a piece of your soul that you've let wander away. In such situations, the anger is important and shouldn't be denied. It's a way of calling back your power.

Yet it's to your benefit to get beneath the anger, as directly as you're able. What's beneath the anger is grief over what you've lost, what you've given away, what you've been separated from.

Allow the anger to arise, but protect yourself and others. Don't make others or yourself a target of your anger. Let the anger lead to what's underneath. And there will be wailing and grieving. This is the beginning of reconnecting with the great Feminine.[103]

Grieving is very unpopular in your world. People are often told not to grieve. They're given strategies to suppress and deny their grief, and told to move on with their life. But grieving is essential. Grieving is what heals pain and grows your soul.

Grieving isn't meant to be an eternal state that you get stuck in. The reason most people get stuck in grief is because they don't allow it. Grieving is therefore scary to many people. They haven't been shown how to grieve. They haven't seen others grieve, and they don't understand that grieving is safe. They haven't felt welcomed in their grief. So for most people, it takes courage to allow grief.

At this time in your world, which is the beginning of the Feminine coming forth, your process is to let your anger turn to grief. You must let the grief go all the way down in your body to your second chakra, which is its home. Let it open your second chakra and purify you. Let it allow your beautiful Feminine energy to flow once again.

Allow this process of grieving to happen within you. Stand for and as the Feminine through your grieving, all the way through to opening your second chakra and your Feminine energy.[104] Be a demonstration to others that this is the way.

Question: So it's alright if grief and anger come up? It's okay to express grief?

Mary Magdalene: Okay with whom?

Questioner: You?

Mary Magdalene: See if it's okay with you.

Chapter 68

Going Beyond Fear

Question (from a man): I'm considering changing my career path, but I feel scared to make that change. How can I move through fear and not be paralyzed by it?

Mary Magdalene: Fear is an aspect of pain. Like all forms of pain, it's intended to help move you into union with God.

The first step in dealing with any form of pain is to become conscious of the emotion you're having. Many of you have learned to suppress your emotions so completely that you often don't realize that you're having an emotion. So this first step is important for many of you.

It seems that fear is the emotion you're dealing with. Is that accurate?

Questioner: Yes.

Mary Magdalene: Alright. The next step is to open yourself bodily, energetically, and emotionally to the emotion—in this case, fear. Let yourself really be with the fear. Experience it fully. How do you experience it? Where do you experience it? Does it have a certain sensation or image? Are there words associated with it?

Let yourself have the full experience rather than pushing it away. Open yourself to it, and embrace it.

Are you able to experience the fear right now?

Questioner: Yes.

Mary Magdalene: How would you describe your experience?

Questioner: Tightening in the chest. Heart rate increasing. Feeling numb, anxious.

Mary Magdalene: Good. Can you let yourself open to those feelings, rather than fight them off?

Questioner: That's harder.

Mary Magdalene: Give it a try. Allow those feelings to be, and allow yourself to have the experience. It's a kind of merging with the sensations.

This is a very Feminine process. The Masculine part of yourself wants to fix it, go to battle with it, make it go away. There's nothing wrong with that. That has an important place. But we want to set that aside for now and open to the Feminine process of opening, merging, allowing, being with.

Are you able to do that?

Questioner: There's a tug-of-war between surrendering to the feelings and wanting to manage them, so they don't get out of control.

Mary Magdalene: I'm hearing that there are two levels of fear going on. There's the fear of change relative to your job, but there's also fear of the feelings that are being stimulated by that change.

Questioner: Right.

Mary Magdalene: Let's go to the second level of fear, which I suspect is deeper—the fear of experiencing fear. How are you experiencing that right now?

Questioner: Tightness in the back of my head, like a headache starting.

Mary Magdalene: Excellent. Can you let yourself be with that feeling of tightness in the back of your head?

Questioner: Yes.

Mary Magdalene: [softly] Good. From that place of being with the feeling, we're going to go to the source of the feeling within you, which is what I call your inner divine qualities.[105] It's an aspect of your inner divinity, a beautiful quality that's not being fulfilled through this circumstance of fear arising and being afraid of the fear. [See the list of inner divine qualities on page 349.]

I'm guessing that the fear is emanating from your drive for survival—a sense that if you open yourself to fear, you won't be able to function, and that could threaten your survival.

Questioner: That seems accurate.

Mary Magdalene: [still speaking softly] So the inner divine qualities that you need in order to allow your feelings of fear are protection and support for your survival. Is that right?

Questioner: Yes.

Mary Magdalene: Good. I invite you to focus on those two qualities—protection and support for your survival. Focus on the way those qualities live in you in their wholeness.

Questioner: It feels like I have to go to my heart for that.

Mary Magdalene: That's fine. Go wherever you need to. When you're able to connect with those qualities of protection and support for your survival—in their fullness and wholeness within you—let me know.

Questioner: I feel it now. There's a feeling of calmness.

Mary Magdalene: Yes. That's the sign that you've reconnected with your wholeness.

Now you're ready for the next step. From that place of being connected to protection and support for your survival (in their wholeness within you), go back to the circumstance of feeling fear. See if there's any change relative to the possibility of experiencing fear.

Questioner: I don't feel so alone in trying to decide things.

Mary Magdalene: Mm-hm. Do you feel more open to the possibility of feeling your fear?

Questioner: I guess I have a feeling that fear is a part of the human condition, that it comes and goes, that I can't get rid of it forever. In this moment, it feels less in control, less potent. I don't feel like I'm going to go down a black hole and never come out.

Mary Magdalene: [softly and emphatically] Yes! That's wonderful.

That may be enough for now. But let's see if we can take it a step further. Are you able to go back to the first level we were dealing with of your fear relative to changing your job? Can you let yourself feel your fear of that?

Questioner: I feel lighter. I feel like it's going to work out. I'm going to be okay.

Mary Magdalene: Is it coming from a feeling place or a mental place?

Questioner: A feeling place.

Mary Magdalene: Wonderful.

Questioner: A calmness.

Mary Magdalene: Yes. There's one last step to this process, which comes from this place of calmness. That step is to ask yourself, "Are there any actions I want to engage, based on this new opening?"

Questioner: I want to do some journaling.

Mary Magdalene: [softly] Wonderful.[106]

Chapter 69

Freedom from Shame

Question (from a woman): I've been on a long journey of exploring shame in myself, especially as a woman. I think women have been held back from saying what we see, hear, and feel, and that has kept us from living our lives fully and feeling what we have to birth in our hearts.

Mary Magdalene: That's the purpose of shame. Shame was cultivated to remove people from their power. It's a technique of control through convincing people they're bad, wrong, sinful, evil, or whatever the variation is.

Power and control are hallmarks of the third dimension. The concepts of "good-bad" and "right-wrong" are means of creating power for some and taking power away from others. This is one of the power games your world tends to be consumed with.

Shame is a part of that. It's a particular segment of the larger thinking and programming that says that there is such a thing as right or wrong. If there were no such thing as right or wrong, you wouldn't feel shame.

There are different arenas that most people tend to have shame. The first one is body shame. Most people in your world, especially in the United States, have great shame around their body. They don't like their body, they think it's not acceptable, and they especially think it's not lovable. Most people have very specific ideas of what they would require to be lovable in their body—and they don't qualify. Their body doesn't match their criteria. This is a huge arena that needs healing for many people and it's spiritual. It's a spiritual imperative that this healing be done relative to body shame.[107]

The second arena of shame that many people experience is shame relative to sexuality. They feel that sexuality is evil, sinful, and that they shouldn't be involved with it, especially if they want to be spiritual, or somehow more evolved or elevated. But even people who aren't interested in spirituality or religion tend to carry the general cultural message that sex is bad. On the other hand, sex is attractive. Sex is something people want, and they have a lot of attention and energy for. But there's a secret quality to their engagement with sex because they believe it's really bad.

People also have shame relative to their emotions. Men have shame if they feel fear or sadness. Many men receive the message that they're not a real man (or a real boy, if they're still young) if they show fear or sadness. Women often have shame about anger.

There's great healing to be done in these areas. These are the Feminine arenas that have been identified as wrong, bad, unacceptable—your body, sexuality, and emotions. They're also where your Feminine power comes from.

Another kind of shame is having a sense at your core that there's something wrong with you: "I'm just not OK. Everyone else is OK, but I'm different. I'm defective. I'm deficient." This is extremely debilitating.

The healing of all forms of shame is essential and most

important. The real healing is healing the very idea that it's possible to be wrong or bad. That's the greatest healing you can bring, because the idea that "badness" or "wrongness" exist is what really binds and enslaves people. Freedom from these ideas of right and wrong, or good and bad, is what will truly liberate people.

I'm not suggesting that people take any action within the realm of possibilities. All actions have consequences. Some actions support love and light, and some actions don't. The discernment is: *Does this action support love and light or does it interfere with love and light?* This is different from seeing the being or the action as inherently good or bad, right or wrong.

All beings are on the path of incarnating love and light. Your job is to simply discern whether a particular action is moving you forward on your path of light and love or holding you back. That is all. That's the healing that's called for.

Mary Magdalene: Many of you have been given vast training and tools relative to the third chakra,[108] because your world is dedicated to the arenas involved in the third chakra—the lower mind, will, intention, and power. While you're each at different places relative to your own mastery of those arenas, most of you are clear about the process of achieving that mastery. The first and second chakras[109] are far less developed for many of you. And the way to mastery is also less clear.

The first chakra is the chakra of the physical body. Mastery of this chakra involves becoming strong and competent in your physical body. It also includes healing your physical body (if there is physical healing to do). The most important element of first chakra mastery is relating to your body as a temple. For many of you, healing shame that you carry relative to your body is a key aspect of this.

If you're ever in a circumstance of being without clothing—some call this "clothed by God"—many of you find that this brings up pain and conflict.[110] Having others see you unclothed and simply in your naked physical body is difficult. This is a sign of carrying shame.

Shame relative to your body is a great block. For many, it's connected to deep wounding. This is the level that many of you have not yet completed. When it's completed your relationship to your body can be completely sacred, where you see your body as every bit as divine as anything else you hold as sacred. You see it manifesting God every bit as much as you relate to me manifesting God, or Yeshua, or any being who you see God in. You must see that in yourself as well. As you see God in yourself, you'll start to see God in all. It's inevitable. Many of you have more work to do in this arena to attain the mastery that's required.

Many of you spend a great deal of time trying to create an image of yourself that you feel happy with, whether it's through your hair, makeup, clothing, jewelry, shoes... If you contemplate going without this, you'll notice there's often fear—fear of not being loved, valued, accepted, or even included in your world. All of this is a sign there's healing to do.

Beauty is a wonderful thing. Adorning your body is a wonderful thing. I'm not calling you to be ascetics or to go with nothing, although that's certainly an option if that feels most supportive to you. But that's not my primary message.

My primary message is to let the beauty that your adorning of your body brings come out of joy. Let it express the joy of your God-connection and your relationship to your body as a temple—as opposed to coming from shame, fear, or trying to cover up something that's not good enough, not lovable, not acceptable.

I have great sadness that so many feel shame in relation to their bodies. I see all of physical manifestation as tremendously beautiful. All of it is the creation of God, the manifestation of God in form.

I'm not calling you to be joyful as a belief from your mind. I'm calling you to do this through your body and emotions, by healing whatever blocks that joy.

Think of a young child—before the age of five—who has a naturalness and a love of their body as an extension of the physical world. This isn't based on an idea in their mind that they *should* love their body, that loving their body is the spiritual thing to do, or that their body is God. Their mind isn't developed at that stage. It's a natural physical response, which all of you had until you received other messages and training.

The messages and training that many of you received about your body created a tremendous spiritual blockage. You came here to experience physical reality and manifestation in a physical body. This is part of your path—to embrace the physical and merge with it as pure God-communion.

The same is true of your emotions. Many of you are cut off from your emotions. You've distanced yourself from your emotions to the point that much of the time you don't know what you feel. I don't blame you for this. You were taught this from a young age by others who learned to distance themselves from emotions. You did what was being asked of you and what you needed in order to be accepted and loved by those you depended on.

I'm glad you were able to survive. Yet I'm sad that for so many, that survival has come at the tremendous cost of being cut off from a huge part of yourself—your feeling-being—and being redirected to live from your mind. Even amongst those who are sensitive to the higher realms, many of you don't live in connection with the emotional or physical realms. Or if you do, it's often a place of pain for you.

I'm suggesting a different path. I'm not calling you to be a martyr, putting yourself in a place of pain out of an idea that doing so will lead you to spiritual growth or a higher spiritual place. This isn't what I am suggesting. I'm suggesting it's safe to allow your feelings, including your painful feelings of fear and sadness. Acceptance and trust of these emotions is the beginning of completing your work at the third dimension, which is what you came here to realize. In general, you'll remain in the third dimension until you've completed that work.[111]

Question: How can I heal body shame?

Mary Magdalene: Can you think of a moment when you felt shame relative to your body?

Questioner: Yes.

Mary Magdalene: Are you aware of the inner divine quality[112] that you disconnected from at that moment?

Questioner: I disconnected from the sense that I'm okay, that there's nothing wrong with me, that I'm perfect as I am.

Mary Magdalene: Yes. You disconnected from the perfectness and divinity of your body.

Questioner: Yes.

Mary Magdalene: Can you go to the place inside that knows the perfection of your physical body?

Questioner: Yes.

Mary Magdalene: See if you can give yourself to that inner place, like immersing yourself in a deep pool of your own perfection, which is your own divinity.

Questioner: Yes. It's very freeing. It feels beautiful and pure and empowering.

Mary Magdalene: Yes. This is the place to return to again and again, to grow stronger in relationship to, and to stay connected to.[113]

Chapter 70

Healing from Abuse

Question: Would you speak about the process of healing abuse?

Mary Magdalene: Abuse often results in self-hatred on the part of the one who is abused. They implant within themself the belief that they're only worthy of this type of treatment. This self-hatred must be healed.

The healing requires returning to the parts of what occurred that are still alive for you. It's not necessary to revisit everything that happened. It's only necessary to return to the parts that are still affecting you.

The process then is to re-open to the grief relative to what occurred. You must allow the grief because grieving is part of the healing process. Let the grief carry you to the beautiful part of you that shut down during that incident (or incidents). There was a beautiful, shiny, light, divine part of yourself that was reaching out for something and instead received the painful actions. Reconnecting with that part of yourself is where the healing will occur.[114]

Some of you are familiar with shamanic healing, where the shaman helps bring back "lost" parts of the self. The healing I'm recommending is similar in that you're bringing back a part of yourself. But that part isn't actually gone. You've just closed off from it, in order to protect that part of your being. The path to healing is through reconnecting with that part.

It's often necessary to have support for this process. Find someone who can guide you in this healing—to be sure that you stay safe, that you're caring for yourself and being cared for, and to help guide you, so you go all the way through to completion.

It's important to understand that no matter how horrific any treatment has been, in some way it's an important part of your soul path. Valuable gifts are available for you on this journey of responding to the experience (or experiences). In the third dimension, taking on difficult circumstances is one way that beings choose to grow. You might liken it to the phrase "the hero's journey." And helpers are available for you in this process.

Mary Magdalene: This is what the steps of healing from abuse might look like. These steps take you into your heart, as opposed to staying in your head and judging or blaming others (or yourself).

The first step of going into your heart is to acknowledge that you're in pain. This is done through allowing yourself to truly feel the pain. Many people are afraid to do this because they fear that this will intensify their suffering, and perhaps open them to getting stuck indefinitely in the pain. In fact, the reverse is true. If you stay in your head, judging and blaming others, you prolong and hold the pain in place. Feeling the pain is the beginning of the process that allows the pain to complete and resolve.

When you're in your head, you're still experiencing the pain. You're simply covering over and suppressing the pain. But it doesn't go away when you do this. It just submerges and continues to affect you at the subconscious level, where it shows up emotionally and physically. You'll become hard or cynical or closed off. And you'll likely become sick. Thus, the pain is still operating at full intensity, only in other arenas that are more hidden from your conscious mind. You may think you've gained some power or control over the pain by going to your mind and judging, but that's an illusion. You're simply hurting yourself and others.

Your real power is in your heart, and it begins with opening to your pain through feeling. This takes spiritual strength. You must open yourself in your feeling to experiencing the pain. This may bring up intense feelings of hurt and sorrow. There may be great grief that you need to release. This is a natural and important process, just the way that a child cries when he or she is hurt.

You may not have allowed yourself to grieve at the time of the abuse, often because you were too shocked or in fear. Many people leave their bodies at the time of abuse in order to survive it. Allowing yourself, now, to fully feel the pain of what occurred is a way of returning to your body, especially your emotional and physical self. And it will likely produce deep mourning.

It may take time to fully experience this grieving, especially if the abuse happened multiple times. You have innate wisdom within as to how much you can experience at any given time without the pain overwhelming you. You may experience a portion of your grief and then need time to integrate that before you're ready to experience more. This process will take however much time it requires to complete itself.

It can be supportive to have a loving, wise guide to help you though this grieving process. That may be a counselor, coach, spiritual leader, friend, or someone else you trust to help you with this. Don't let them take you back into your mind (by focusing on the other(s) or analyzing what occurred), and resist your own tendencies to do so. Instead, stay in the pure feeling of experiencing your pain, just as a child does who is crying after getting hurt.

Eventually, your pain will recede to the point that you can bring in your mind for a different function (other than judgment and blame). At that point you can use your mind to take you deeper within yourself to the source of your pain. This is a critical step. It's based in the understanding that the source of your pain isn't in the outer circumstances of what occurred. The source of your pain is within yourself.

Within everyone are pure, divine qualities. These are beautiful aspects of your inner divinity that are part of every human—something like your spiritual DNA.[115] Whenever you're in pain, it's a signal that one or more of your inner divine qualities need help. They need your attention to return them to their fulfilled state of being connected to God.

In the case of abuse, the qualities that aren't fulfilled are often some combination of:

- physical and emotional well-being
- safety (physical or emotional)
- respect for the sanctity of your body
- dignity
- trust of others

Only you will know which inner divine qualities are the ones that were involved for you. Other people may guess, but they won't know for sure. Even if others have been in similar circumstances, the inner divine qualities that were affected for them might be different. You don't need to compare yourself or your experiences to others, or to your own experiences at other times. Let yourself be present now for what's true for you at this time.

You'll know when you identify the real inner divine qualities that are involved because you'll feel a clear connection to those qualities. You'll experience a sense of aliveness in connecting with them. They have energy for you, like a live wire that's waiting to be reconnected to its intended circuit.

Once you've identified the inner divine qualities that are alive for you in this circumstance, you're ready for the next step. This involves a shift within your awareness from the feeling of deficit in these qualities (which was triggered by the external event) into remembering and connecting with these qualities *in their wholeness.*

Choose one or two qualities that seem most important in this situation, the ones that have the most energy for you. Then go inside and give yourself the experience of what it's like to have these qualities fulfilled. You might experience this viscerally, visually, audially, emotionally, or through memories arising of a time when these qualities were fulfilled. Let yourself rest in that experience until it's strong for you, such that you've shifted into a sense of being fulfilled in that quality.

This is something like repairing a circuit breaker within yourself. You're flipping the switch back to the "on" position of this circuit being fully reconnected. You're truly reconnecting with God, which is what you actually got disconnected from through the trauma. You'll recognize the reconnection when it happens because you'll experience peace and a sense of openness.

At this point you'll likely need a period of reintegration of this fulfilled state within yourself, for this to become stable. This is the real healing work. Give yourself as much time as you need, which might be days or months. You'll know when this stage is complete because your energy for action returns. It's like an animal coming out of hibernation or a butterfly emerging from its cocoon.

When your energy for action resurfaces, you're ready to make any changes you choose at the outer level. Perhaps you'll want to take certain steps toward the others involved in the abuse, as a form of outer healing. Perhaps there's forgiveness you wish to engage, either directly with those involved or energetically without direct contact. Perhaps you want to create boundaries that support you. Perhaps there are new directions you want to take in your life, or things you no longer want to continue doing. Often, new insights and understandings have emerged that you're now ready to integrate into yourself and your future choices.

What's important is that these actions will be done from the energy of wholeness and self-love that you've come to from your inner healing. That wholeness and self-love allow you to move into greater love for others, without compromising yourself.

This is the completion of the soul work for which you created this circumstance. This completion allows your growth into your next stage of greater love and consciousness.

PART VIII

Ascending to the Fourth Dimension

Chapter 71

How Ascension to the Fourth Dimension Will Occur

Question: Many lightworkers on this planet are helping with humanity's ascension.[116] But it seems that most people aren't aware of what's going on. Is there going to be an instant miracle where the majority will get what's happening and then transcendence occurs? Or is there a different plan for how ascension will happen?

Mary Magdalene: There are many ways that ascension can happen. It isn't written yet. Much has to do with the choices that you and all the beings on Earth make. You're in the process of creating this, as is the case in *every* moment of life. Many people don't realize what's occurring, but that doesn't change the fact that it's happening.

As I see and understand it, the outcome is a given. You *are* going to achieve this ascension process.[117] The majority of beings, if not all beings, have already chosen this at the soul level. But this choice may not be obvious in terms of what beings are doing in their life or what they're aware of right now. Those you call lightworkers tend to be the ones who are consciously aware of their choice to be here, as well as their choice to ascend and support the ascension process for all.

From my perspective, it's not clear *how* the ascension will happen or the time frame in which it will occur. Many people on Earth thought it might happen at the end of 2012. We didn't know.[118] But it wasn't the time. It appears to me that it's going to be a more gradual process than many people who are incarnated on Earth initially thought. This may be a benign thing, for it will allow people more time to become aware of the ascension process and to prepare themselves for it. It will also allow the process to potentially be more gradual and, because of that, gentler.

It's possible that ascension could happen through what you might see as a miracle. Different people use the word "miracle" to refer to different things. From the perspective of the higher dimensions, much of what are called "miracles" don't seem mysterious or unexplainable. It's clear to us how these things can happen. But from a third-dimensional perspective, it may not be clear, or understandable, or easily explained. So the term "miracle" may be used. But it's often just referring to a higher-dimensional process intervening in your world.

It's possible that this change could happen through challenging events. One of the reasons challenges and hardships are given in the third dimension is because this often opens people's hearts to love, and it opens their consciousness to what is greater than they've been open to in the past. So it's possible that it may happen, at least in part, through challenging circumstances. These might be natural circumstances or humanly created circumstances, such as political or social circumstances. Or these might be circumstances that involve beings from other planets or from somewhere outside of your Earth sphere, which could bring great challenge to many people. Any of these forms are possible. Through challenge, people may open to something much greater than they've been previously open to.

It's most likely that people will ascend in one of two ways. One way is to transition directly from physical incarnation in the third dimension into the next dimension. The other is to leave one's physical incarnation in the third dimension (which is what you refer to as dying) and ascend from a different plane of incarnation. This may be easier for some, so they may choose that path.

Some beings may choose to reunite with a part of their soul family who aren't manifested on Earth at this time, before ascending to a higher dimension of incarnation. Perhaps this is a part of their soul family that they would especially like to ascend with. So they may choose to reunite with parts of their soul family by leaving the Earth and manifesting elsewhere. These are possibilities too.

It's an enormous process that's underway. I'm speaking in terms of a *very large* occurrence—large in terms of time, space, and the *vastness* of what's occurring. It's much greater than just the Earth. The possibilities and options are far-reaching. From my perspective, it's a most amazing and exciting event.

Chapter 72

The Divide in Your World

Mary Magdalene: I speak today about the future. Many in your world want to know what's going to happen, especially in light of some of the disturbing trends that they see in your world. This is understandable. It's natural to want to have understanding and hope.

One of the biggest trends in your world today is the pattern of divisiveness. Many people in your world have become quite polarized, seeming to be on one side or the other of an ideological chasm. This divisiveness isn't just affecting your politics and government. It's affecting your society at all levels, all the way down to relationships within families and between friends. Many of you find yourself pitted against one another with no hope of bridging the gap.

Within the new age spiritual world, there's even divisiveness as to whether humans are in the process of ascending to the fourth or the fifth dimension, or whether some or all of you have already ascended to a higher dimension. I find this debate quite humorous.

I want you to understand that this divisiveness is part of the bigger process of ascension in your world. What I mean by ascension is the transition to higher dimensions and higher states of consciousness, beginning with the fourth dimension.

The fourth dimension is an energy-based realm, in contrast to the third dimension, which is physically based. For most of you, the fourth dimension is the place you go in your dreams. Many of you have also experienced the fourth dimension through visions, mystical experiences, out-of-body experiences, drug-based experiences, shamanic experiences, or near-death experiences. (Many in your world consider these experiences "woo-woo," which I also find humorous.) And for most of you, the fourth dimension is the realm you will go to in between incarnations.

From my point of view, I would say that human beings and the Earth are in the process of ascending to the fourth dimension. I say this because each dimension has a primary focus of learning associated with it, and you don't ascend to the next dimension until you've completed the learning of the previous dimension.

The learning or focus of the third dimension is power. You won't "graduate" from the third dimension or ascend to the fourth dimension until you've completed your learning as a soul relative to power. In simple terms, this could be summarized as transitioning from "power-over" in third-dimensional consciousness to "power-with" in fourth-dimensional consciousness.

For most of you, this shift into "power-with" has to do with the Feminine and Masculine parts of yourselves and your world coming into unity. This will require you to strengthen your Feminine aspects—of loving your body (including the body of the Earth), your sexuality and energy, and your emotions. When these Feminine aspects of yourself and your world are loved as much as your Masculine aspects of mind and will, that will be the sign that you've completed your learning at the third-dimensional level.

This process of completing your learning at the 3D level is underway, and many of you are making excellent progress, especially those of you who are committed to your spiritual and human growth. At the same time, there are many who aren't progressing as quickly and are still engaging the old third-dimensional paradigms of power-over and competition. Many of your political leaders remain at this earlier stage of spiritual growth, as does a significant portion of your population. As a result, you're seeing an increasing divide in your societies between those who are completing their third-dimensional work and those who haven't yet done so. You could liken it to the parting of the Red Sea that's described in the Old Testament.[119]

This is part of the ascension process, with some who are ready to transition to the fourth dimension and some who need more time to complete their growth in the third dimension. The further you go into the ascension process, the more there may appear to be two different "camps." Yet, I urge you *not* to view it this way because that merely reinforces the 3D consciousness of duality, or "us vs. them." Instead, I urge you to see it as a continuum of growth, with different ones at different stages. The ones who are further along aren't superior, nor are the others inferior. That kind of dualistic, divisive thinking is part of third dimensional consciousness.

I call you to shift into the fourth-dimensional consciousness of "us *and* them." In 4D consciousness, you want what is best for *all* because you realize your heart-connection to all, including those who are different from you. This isn't just an idea or belief. It's your literal consciousness. You realize that you're only fulfilled when everyone's needs are attended to. As I've said before, it's like being part of the same family. A young child isn't at the same stage as an older child or a parent, but they're all loved, valued, and cared for equally. All are included, or you wouldn't be fulfilled.

The divide in your world is real. Those who aren't ready to ascend will be provided for in a different way than those who are ready to ascend. They'll be given a circumstance that supports them in their continued growth at the third-dimensional level. It will be a different circumstance than the one provided for those moving into 4D. You're in the midst of a literal separation in your world, like a cell dividing and becoming two different organs.

For the most part, those in power in your 3D world know what's happening. They know that the world is changing, and with that, the power structure. They know that their reign of power is doomed because so many are waking up. They know that they can only control the masses as long as people believe the 3D base-assumptions of deficiency and threat. They know that their power is based on keeping people in fear. Because of this, the power elite in your world are committed to keeping people in fear as much as possible.

Yet even as they work to keep you in fear, those in power know that they've already lost. They know that the light will win and even is already beginning to win. Their point of view is that they have nothing to lose, so they're going to go for whatever they want and whatever they can get. You already see the signs of this, with some leaders saying and doing increasingly outrageous things, such as "spinning the truth" in ways that support them.

For those of you moving into the fourth dimension, *your job is to stay in love and light*. Don't get caught up in what those in power are doing, and most certainly don't get caught up in reacting to it. If you do, you'll have joined their game and are back in duality mode of "us vs. them." Love them, bless them, and know that they're part of God's plan too. But keep your focus on your work of growing in love and light, however that manifests for you. Then you'll be blessing all and supporting the ascension process for all, whether that manifests as transitioning to the fourth dimension or continuing one's spiritual growth in third-dimensional circumstances.

I wish to offer one more thing. I stated earlier that I see humanity and the Earth as transitioning to 4D in the ascension process, and I want to clarify why I see it that way. The learning or focus in the fourth dimension is on manifestation, which you could also call creation. I'm happy to say that this will be a much easier and shorter process of learning than the one in the third dimension, which has taken a very long time. But it's still very real, and it won't be complete until you've attained a level of mastery in the manifestation process, which most of you have yet to do. So this is where you're headed.

But even more so, most of you are still completing your work in the third dimension of loving your bodies, sexuality, energy, and emotions (including your painful emotions) and thus loving all the Feminine parts of your reality. I urge you to focus on this, as doing so will support you the most, and the rest will fall into place naturally. If you distract yourself from completing your work in these arenas, and focus instead on other spiritual areas that may seem more attractive or interesting, you'll simply hold yourself back. You can't skip over your necessary growth. Anything you've skipped will always call you back to complete that area. This is what you might call "karma."[120]

Be prepared for things to appear even worse or more dire on the surface, in terms of divisiveness and a return by some to what may seem to be less caring, less compassionate, less inclusive, less loving. That will probably happen as the ascension process continues and the paths of large sectors of your world split in different directions. See it as a birth process, with some being "born" into a new fourth-dimensional reality. You're going through the birth pangs, which almost always involves pain. Birth isn't an easy process. Be the leader of the new consciousness of loving all and bringing the light. See your world ahead, and stay true to your course. And it will manifest.

Chapter 73

Riding the Waves of Change

Mary Magdalene: Many people in your world are moving forward in their spiritual growth at amazing speed. I acknowledge those of you going through this change and hope that you realize how strongly you're serving the spiritual process—for yourself, but also for your world and for many beings, through the work you're doing in the spiritual realm. You're doing your work exceedingly well, considering the tremendous change you're going through at such a rapid speed. The acceleration of change and growth that's happening at this time is unprecedented. You're to be acknowledged for even being able to go through this, for it's not an easy process.

This kind of change generally happens over a much greater period of time, so it's easier for the being to adapt, much the way you might think about the evolution of a species in your world. The process of evolution generally happens slowly and gradually. It often happens through the birth process, where one generation is slightly different or altered from the previous generation. That's one of the more easeful ways that change can happen, especially in the 3D realm.

But that's not what's happening now. You're being changed as already incarnated, manifested beings. That's a much more difficult process. You're being changed physically at the core of your being, at the cellular level. You're being changed mentally in terms of your mind, beliefs, and thoughts. You're being changed emotionally and energetically. All of this is part of the progression of moving into a higher dimension, based on manifesting a higher consciousness.

That may sound simple or straightforward when I speak about it or when you think about it. But the way that it happens in life is not simple and straightforward. It's often challenging to change in these ways. And many of you are experiencing this. You're experiencing change, upheaval, turmoil, unknowingness, discomfort, new symptoms, and things happening in your life in ways they've never happened before. All of this can be confusing and disconcerting. It can cause fear, insecurity, all sorts of feelings. It's like being aboard a ship in a storm. It can be quite a wild ride, and you don't necessarily know what the outcome will be.

You're to be commended for your stalwartness, perseverance, dedication, and willingness to go through this. It's a testimony to your strength and your commitment to your spiritual growth and path. I thank you from the bottom of my heart for what you're going through, and what you'll continue to go through as part of this transition.

It will have different phases. Some phases will be easier. Others may seem more turbulent, chaotic, wild, hard, or however they seem. It's an unfolding process. It's something that you, and we, cannot see in advance as to exactly how it will happen. But you're underway. You're on this course of transforming, like a caterpillar becoming a butterfly. But you aren't becoming butterflies. You're becoming fourth-dimensional beings, energy beings. This is an enormous step forward in your evolution.

While all this is happening, there's also resistance to this process of change in your world. Many people don't understand what's happening and aren't aware that this transformation is going on. They see signs of this change as a threat to their world. They're fighting the change because they believe it's an annihilation of themselves or the world as they know it. And in truth, change is always a kind of a death process. You're letting go, releasing, dying to the old way and your old self. So there's truth in the point of view that there's a death process underway.

But it's not only death. It's death and rebirth into a much more wonderful form, which even those who are resisting would enjoy so much more, if only they understood and could allow it. Yet they have their own process to go through. They're not "bad," "evil," "dark," or resisting what "should" be happening. It may appear that way to you, but that isn't an accurate understanding. They're as much a part of this change as you are, as the lightworkers are, as the ones who are trying to bring this change forth. You all have your roles and parts to play. Their part is significant too. It's part of their spiritual evolution to do what they're doing. And it's part of *your* spiritual evolution for them to be doing that. They aren't holding you back or making things impossible, capsizing the ship. It's all part of the grand process.

I don't want to give the impression that you don't need to do anything, that everything is perfect, and you should just allow it all to be as it is. That's not the case. You have your role, which you came here to do. First and foremost, your role is to be the light yourself—to be anchors and holders of the light, and to be part of creating the great network of light amongst all the beings who are also anchoring and holding the light. More than anything else, that will allow this transformation in your world to occur.

Your role is also to carry out your individual life-purpose and life-plan, to further the light in your particular way. It's not simply to be passive or to take the position that everything's fine, and nothing needs to be done. That's not an accurate understanding, for it's very important that you do the work that you came to do, whatever that is.

If you're not clear about what your work is, then ask for help from your guides and angels. You can ask for help directly from God, from your higher self, and from all your spirit-helpers—through prayer, talking with them, or whatever other form you use. You can look for signs in your life, such as things you're passionate about or that bring in the light for you. Look for the things that you do because you love them, things that you can't help but do. These are signs that those things are part of the path you committed to and have taken on in this life.

Relative to beings who aren't consciously on this path and who seem to be obstructing or making this transformation more difficult, more than anything else these beings need your love. They need your blessing and your prayers. Of course, there are things you can do to redirect the actions they're taking—political things or personal things. Again, your action is important. But even more important is your understanding that these beings are on the path, too, and for you to find their light and shine your light to them. You can always help them in that way, as well as by taking whatever practical steps you feel called to in relation to particular beings or events.

In some ways, you might say there's a drama going on, a certain play of light versus dark. It's a birth process into much greater light, and it's real. It's actually happening. It's also a death process of the old ways you've adapted to and have become familiar with—the old frequency of light and darkness, and the old forms that light and darkness have taken. Now you're calling for the death of that. It's a real process, just as in the death of the physical body. In most cases, it won't just happen in a moment or through a single decision. It happens through a process because there are a great many things that must shift, release, and let go for the transformation to occur.

So you'll need to relax and flow with this process, the way a woman in childbirth learns to open. Any woman who's gone through childbirth knows that there are real pains and hardships involved. Yet it's possible to relax in the midst of the pains and hardship, and to flow with it in ways that make the birth process much easier. So it is with your time now.

Chapter 74

The Dissolution of Familiarity

Mary Magdalene: All of you are in a process of change relative to what's been familiar to you for most of your lifetime and really for many lifetimes. You have an orientation toward things happening in a certain way that you're used to, and you expect that things will continue to work that way.

It's understandable that you would relate to your world in a mostly physical way because that's the nature of the third dimension—it's primarily physically based. In coming into this dimension, most people forget where they've come from and who they are outside of this physical, 3D manifestation. So it becomes easy to assume that this physical realm is all there is and that the way things operate here is the way things must operate.

When the physical processes you're familiar with start to break down—sometimes this is described as "throwing a wrench in the works"—it's actually an opportunity, a window for you to open to greater possibilities and to begin to access these possibilities more. The cycle that you call Mercury retrograde[121] is an example of this kind of opportunity. It's calling you to rest, to take a break from functionality and doing things in the familiar ways because those ways don't tend to work during such cycles.

This is part of coming into trust—trust that things can work in a different way, which you might think of as a bigger or greater way. Trust that there are other options, other possibilities, and other forces at work that can accomplish what you may have thought needed to be accomplished in a physical or work-oriented way. It's calling you to open to doing things in a different way, to draw upon other powers and forces, which you might call "higher," and which are ultimately more easeful for you to engage. But like any transition, the process of letting go of the old and adopting the new isn't always easy at the moment.

As you go further into the ascension process, this phenomenon of familiar processes seeming to break down will increase.[122] The old, mechanical ways of doing things are going to have more lapses where they're not working as well or as quickly, or not even working at all. You're going to be required to find other ways to do the things you want to accomplish—or perhaps to let go of those things, realizing they aren't necessary.

As this cycle of "the old ways" not working continues through the ascension process, it's going to have a feeling of growing intensity, showing up in progressively stronger ways. Your challenge is to learn to relax into this, to trust what's happening (which is ultimately trusting in God), and to call upon your higher self and your developing higher skills, abilities, and powers to take care of yourself.

If you're confused and unsure at any moment, call upon God and your higher self, and ask for help. This is one of the greatest lessons of this time. I've spoken about this before, but it's such an important thing that it's useful to remind you about the importance of asking.

Higher-dimensional beings respect your free choice, your soul path, and what you're choosing from moment to moment. We won't interfere or intercede unless you ask us. We're happy to be involved, but we require you to ask us first. So if you want our help, which I strongly encourage you to make use of, please call upon us and ask us to help. We're most happy and honored to support and assist you in any way we're able.

Chapter 75

The Fullness of Including All

Question: A while ago I was in a group of people, and I had a feeling that my identity was skipping between individuals. One moment I would feel like one person, then I would feel like another person. It felt like I was tuning in to the group's energy. Is that what you're describing as the fourth dimension?

Mary Magdalene: What you're describing sounds like an opening to a certain level of connection, awareness, and fluidity in your consciousness. It also sounds like there's an aspect of that opening that wasn't in balance or fully developed because you don't need to lose yourself. In the full experience, there's a sense of *expansion of yourself* to include all. So it may have been a partial opening but not a full one.

Your experience will likely lead somewhere else that will be more inclusive of your connection to yourself, along with your having choice in the midst of your experience. You're *always* in choice. You're not simply at the effect of your experience. This is part of fourth-dimensional learning.

I've said that the fourth dimension is like the realm of dreams, because this is a way that many people can relate to and understand the fourth dimension. In a dream, you may feel like things are happening to you and that you're being "blown around" by the winds of who knows what. But that is what you might call an "entry-level experience." [Mary laughs.] Eventually, you develop strength and skill in being at choice about your manifestation, just as you're at choice about your manifestation in the third dimension. But that may not yet be obvious.

Questioner: It feels like I'm opening to a certain level of sensitivity that I'm not used to.

Mary Magdalene: It sounds that way to me too. And the things you experience at that new level of sensitivity can be uncomfortable. Sometimes the discomfort is telling you that that experience doesn't include everything you need. It may be guiding you to develop and strengthen other things that will provide more of what you need in a holistic way.

Chapter 76

Multiple Realities

Question: In this time of turmoil, negative energy, fighting, and killing in the world, many people feel anger or hate as a response to what's happening. How can we deal with that?

Mary Magdalene: This is a very important question.

What's happening in your world isn't new. It's been going on for a long time. What's new are the technological abilities that are now available, so these things are happening on a larger scale and across global borders. They're also being reported on a global level, which means you're hearing about things that you might not have heard about in the past. Thus, these events seem to be affecting people in a new way.

But truly these things have been going on for a great deal of humanity's history in the third dimension. It's a history of power struggles, of using and misusing power, of threatening and harming people as a means of acquiring power and achieving certain ends.

This is the beginning of the end of this kind of thing. It's the beginning of the end of the third dimension altogether. You could say that this "beginning" has been going on for quite a while. Yet in terms of the scale of history, it's still quite recent. Even that there are some who can imagine something different happening—this is also quite recent.

In fact, there's a growing movement of individuals who are committed to ending this way of interacting, of determining who has power and who claims the right to have their way, of taking away power and rights from others. Some of the unrest that's happening is a sign of this growing movement of people who aren't accepting this and are saying "no."

Of those who are still clinging to the old methods, especially those who hold power and are trying to maintain that power, many are quite aware that their way is coming to an end. In some ways they're accelerating their use of force and misuse of power because, on some level, they're aware that they've already lost. So they have nothing to lose. They're trying to hold onto their power by upsetting and disturbing people, and thus inciting a reaction that causes people to join them in the old ways, models, and mindsets of violence, so they can claim whatever goal they desire.

For those on the path of light, ascension,[123] change, and growth into the higher dimensions and higher reaches of human evolution, it's up to you to not take the bait and not be drawn into this fray. Maintain your connection to light and love. Don't give these people the power to draw you out of that. You may choose to take certain actions, but be conscious of what those actions are. If your actions are simply a reaction that draws you into the same kind of violence and destruction, then those who initiated have won.

This is a hard-learned lesson for humanity, but it's a sign of the transformation that's occurring. You're growing out of this old form, like a caterpillar that's entered the chrysalis and is in the process of becoming a butterfly. You must understand that the ascension process is underway and cannot be stopped. It's simply a question of who will be part of it.

There are some who don't choose to participate and who don't wish others to know that any such thing is occurring. They're doing everything in their power to reinforce the old ways, to distract people, and to attract them into their model. It's like the parting of the Red Sea, in a certain way. Some are choosing the ascension path, and others aren't yet ready. Those who aren't ready have their own destiny. They'll be served and attended to in the way that befits and supports them in their process. They, too, are ascending, at their own timing.

There are always multiple realities happening simultaneously. The reality being reported by your media and news is simply one reality. Often the media has a particular agenda they're promoting of moving people into fear.

Do what is necessary to maintain yourself in light and love. The more you do this, the more your reality will be one of light and love, even as other realities are going on simultaneously. This isn't to say that you lose compassion, heart-openness, and connection to people and their reality. Just don't confuse that with assuming another person's reality. It's not necessary for you to assume another's reality to have compassion and heart-connection to them. It's better to maintain your own reality and allow others to be attracted into your consciousness, if it's truly a higher one of light and love.

For those affected by violence, you can always send them blessings, love, and light. You can ask your angels to work with their angels to help them. Understand that, on some level, the individuals involved have agreed to participate in these events as part of the transformation that's underway, and that they're being helped in whatever way is for their highest good.

Thank you for your caring.

Chapter 77

Expanding into Greater Ecstasy

Question: It seems like religions and other philosophies have controlled the ecstasy of sexuality, so that many people haven't had the fullest experience of sexual union, which is really union with the divine. Do you encourage people to break out of the programming they've received that limits sexual ecstasy?

Mary Magdalene: Breaking out of that kind of programming is part of breaking out of the third dimension altogether and moving into the higher dimensions, which was what Yeshua was teaching, especially in the inner school.[124] That teaching is still not accessible to everyone.

There's a tug-of-war going on between those who've orchestrated things in the third dimension, seemingly to their benefit, and everyone else. Ultimately, it's not to anyone's benefit. No one benefits when someone isn't given their full power and empowerment, their full access to God and their human divinity. Yet part of the experiment and exploration that souls have been engaging in the third dimension is for some to bring power to themselves at others' expense. For that to happen, a great deal of control has been set into place, on many levels. Control upon the ecstasy of sexuality is certainly one of those levels, but it's just one of many, making up a much greater whole.

The ecstasy that you experience through sexuality can expand into something much greater. So can the ecstasy of your embodiment and your experience of reality moment to moment. Ultimately, there's no difference between the ecstasy of sexuality and the ecstasy of your ongoing experience. This understanding and experience is something that will be grown into, that you're moving toward.

I thank all those who are moving toward this ecstasy and bliss, and following their heart. Thank you so much.

Chapter 78

Love in Limitation

Question: I can soar to absolute bliss in my spiritual practices and then walk out into my life and become extremely irritated with those around me, whom I love dearly. How can I continue to flow with the bliss and not allow small things to irritate me?

Mary Magdalene: You are one who has a vast capacity for communion with the cosmos.

Questioner: Thank you. I feel that.

Mary Magdalene: Your growth involves a kind of slowing down, which may be irritating to you. It involves experiencing your limitation to the point of coming into complete love in *that* form, love of the limitation itself.

Questioner: I see. It's not easy.

Mary Magdalene: No. Because you're able to be so enormous that to experience that limitation is painful.

Questioner: Yes, it's very painful.

Mary Magdalene: Yes. Yet that is your work, to not only experience the limitation but to find love in that place—love as yourself, of yourself, in limitation. Ironically that will be your freedom. When you find that love, there will be no limitation.

Chapter 79

The Mystery School Teachings

Question: In the last few years, I've experienced times when my crown opens, and an energy moves through me that feels like shimmers. I'm coming to prefer that state and would like to know how I can allow that to happen even more.

Mary Magdalene: There are pathways within you that open you to these kinds of experiences.[125] And there are practices you can learn that strengthen those pathways. Engaging these practices will allow you to access this state more frequently and for longer periods of time, depending on your frequency of engagement. I recommend that you learn those practices.

It sounds to me that you're describing a fourth-dimensional space that is similar to the dream-time space. The dream-time space is one way of accessing the fourth dimension. In general, increasing your access to the fourth dimension requires the strengthening of four parts of yourself—your physical body, your emotional body, your mental body, and your etheric (energy) body.[126]

Most of you are quite developed at the mental level, and further development of the mind is not an issue for you—other than learning how to quiet the mind. The ongoing mental chatter or disturbance that many people experience can—at least in part—be a result of the other bodies not being strong and in balance, rather than a problem with the mind itself. So strengthening the other bodies may help quiet the mind.

Most people are aware of their physical body and what they need to do to support themselves physically. This often involves some kind of change or healing of the physical. The one area relative to the physical body that many people don't realize that they still need to address is the area of body shame (or even rejection of the physical). This includes not liking one's physical body, not wanting to be *in* a physical body, or not wanting to have the experiences of being a physical body. This kind of shame and rejection of the body creates a level of separation or even divorce from one's physical body. This is an area that needs healing for many.

For most people, the emotional body and the etheric body[127] are the two bodies that need the most strengthening. The instructions I gave in *Mary Magdalene Beckons* focus a great deal on strengthening the emotional body. That instruction may be valuable for you to revisit and see if there is more to do there.[128]

The processes that I'm suggesting—learning to quiet the mind, healing body shame, and strengthening your emotional and etheric bodies—can all grow your ability to open yourself to the fourth-dimensional state and strengthen your ability to remain in that state for longer periods of time.

I also recommend learning other processes, such as:
- Connecting the sacred heart and sacred mind[129]
- Opening the "third eye" (pineal chakra)[130]
- Activating the merkaba[131]
- Activating the light that creates the halo around the head

These are processes that used to be taught and practiced in the mystery schools,[132] so that beings could move between the third and fourth dimensions, and into higher dimensions beyond.

These "mystery school processes" aren't so outwardly accessible in your time, but there are those who offer and teach them. The knowledge is available. This is what I recommend you learn and engage.

Chapter 80

Kundalini

Question: I recently had an energy experience that I think may have been a kundalini awakening. I'd like to understand more about the purpose of the kundalini and if there's something I should do relative to this experience.

Mary Magdalene: The kundalini is an important part of your energy system. Developing one's full energy body and energy system, including the kundalini, was part of the training that was given in the mystery schools.

Ultimately, the kundalini is for carrying you into higher dimensions, and opening up higher centers within you that are required and which you'll be increasingly drawing upon as you move into these higher dimensions.

Sometimes the kundalini is activated spontaneously. When that happens it's often a partial rather than a full activation. Spontaneous kundalini activations tend to occur when the structures and the overall vessel for the kundalini aren't fully prepared. This is why the effects of a spontaneous kundalini awakening may be challenging, such as confusion or disorientation.

It's valuable to have a teacher or guide to shepherd you through the kundalini process.

Questioner: Can you say more about the effects of kundalini when someone isn't prepared?

Mary Magdalene: There can be illness. There can be problems with the nervous system—being overactivated or feeling burned out. You might experience ringing in the ears or balance problems. Your systems may become out of sync, such that it's hard to sleep, or you don't seem to be able to find the right foods to eat. There can be an opening of the mind in ways that you may not understand or that might seem scary or confusing. There can be many effects.

The kundalini is yet another arena that depends upon the development of your emotional body. That's because the foundation for the kundalini is in the emotional body. This is another reason why I emphasize doing your emotional work. It's part of the preparation for activating your energy body and shifting from the physical into the energy body.

There's a progression for this energetic opening and development that's safe, gentle, and dependable. I recommend following this progression. It begins with the development and mastery of the physical body and the emotions. When those aspects of your being are fully developed, you're ready for the next level of energetic opening. This involves accessing what might be called the *inner sanctum of the heart*.[133] That energetic space is the gateway to the higher brain centers of the pineal gland and third eye, and eventually the merkaba.[134] Part of the safety that's built into this energetic progression is that, in general, you won't be able to enter the inner sanctum of the heart or pass through its gateway to the higher centers until your physical and emotional preparation is complete.

I want to say one other thing about energetic experiences,

including kundalini experiences. There's a danger in becoming enamored of experience. It's like chasing a false god, where you want to have an experience again or think that "the way" is to have those kinds of experiences. In general, energetic experiences are a sign of something being purified in you or something being opened through that purification. Be gentle. Be careful. Don't invoke more purification than is supportive of you.

Chapter 81

The Merkaba

Question: What is the merkaba?

Mary Magdalene: The merkaba is a structure in your light body. It's part of what can help you in the ascension process and make that process easier.[135] It also can be valuable in creating your life here in the third dimension. So I recommend activating your merkaba, which happens in your light body.

[Note from Mercedes: In this section, Mary was responding to a participant in a program I was offering for activating one's light body.]

Question: Why is learning about the merkaba important?

Mary Magdalene: I would say it's *helpful* to learn about your merkaba. Your energy body and your merkaba exist to help you. In some ways, the merkaba is the completion of your current stage of learning about the energy body—what the energy body is, what it can do, and how it can help you.

The merkaba helps you in a few key ways. First, it's for your protection. In this regard, it acts much like a crystal. Crystals can be powerful forms of protection if you know how to use them. Your merkaba is the same. You can use it for energetic protection, which will support you at the energetic level. This energetic protection is something that would benefit many of you.

Another way that your merkaba is similar to crystals is that it can be used as an activation device. Crystals are used in many of your "high-tech industries to activate various processes.[136] Similarly, your merkaba helps you activate the process of manifestation, making the process more direct, easeful, and effective.

This can bring up fear for some people. Some people fear that being able to manifest consciously is "too much power" and are concerned about how that power will be used. Some people remember a past life where they or others misused power. Or perhaps they just don't trust that they or others have the wisdom to know how to use that kind of power. These are healthy fears.

However, I want to remind you that you're already manifesting all the time. You're simply doing it in a more primitive way in the third dimension. When you access the fourth dimension (and beyond), your manifestation will simply happen faster and more directly.

You already have experience with making choices about what you manifest. It's wise to realize that there are ramifications to your manifestation. It's important to use your power to manifest for the highest good—for yourself and all. This is why the full power of manifestation isn't given in the third dimension. It's given in the fourth dimension, after beings have done their emotional work and are operating from their heart.

Your emotions are powerful protectors. They act as a safeguard against misusing power. If you're not engaging for the highest good, you'll get feedback through your emotions because you'll experience pain in some form.[137] Conversely, if you're manifesting for the highest good, your emotions will also give you feedback. You'll experience joy, balance, wholeness, ease, contentment, peace, or other similar emotions.

The heart is another safeguard against misusing power. You're much less likely to misuse power if you're operating from your heart. (This is one more reason why it's important for your heart and mind to be integrated, so you're not simply acting from the mind, dissociated from the heart.) The merkaba will help you to manifest *in integration* with your heart, especially if it's accessed through the heart.[138] In this way, your merkaba can ensure that your heart will participate and steer you in the manifestation process.

The other reason for activating your merkaba is that it supports you in traveling between the dimensions—but only if you choose. You won't be out of control, suddenly traveling to dimensions you don't want to be in. In the beginning, traveling to other dimensions isn't something that most people will choose to do. It's certainly not necessary, other than moving into the fourth dimension. I do recommend that you begin to make use of moving into the fourth dimension and engaging your spiritual practices from there, because that will contribute to all beings at this time, including yourself. Your merkaba will help you access the fourth dimension.

It may feel scary to contemplate traveling to other dimensions. You may believe that interdimensional travel is connected to dark energies or dark beings who use these kinds of processes. Such beliefs may have been instilled through your media or religions, or potentially are ideas you carry from past-life experiences.

In truth, these energies have been misused in the past. One of the clearest situations where that occurred was in Atlantis. Many beings who've incarnated at this time to contribute as lightworkers to the transition that human beings are undergoing were also present in Atlantis, and many have memories of this kind of power being misused. Atlantis wasn't the only time such power was misused. But it was a particularly potent time, which many people have a past-life connection to and memories or a sense of.

Experiences of this kind of misuse are part of a growth process. Like any growth process, such as a child learning, you'll make mistakes. You learn from those mistakes, and that makes you strong. Then you take that strength and try again. This is what I encourage.

The merkaba, in and of itself, is very safe. It's as safe as your chakras. It's simply part of your energetic potential, which many people aren't yet familiar with or making use of. It's something that will eventually activate on its own, generally in the fourth dimension. But consciously activating it sooner is valuable, because it will support and assist you in the process of ascension and make the process easier.

Questioner: During one class when we were practicing going into the inner temple of the heart, I had a powerful energetic experience. It felt like my whole being became liquid, and I knew instantly that I would be able to transport myself if I mastered that practice. Then I got really scared. How can we deal with the fear of activating the merkaba?

Mary Magdalene: I'm guessing that you were experiencing a shift into a higher-dimensional state that was less solid, and may have felt liquid. I can't say for sure what state you were accessing. It could have been the fourth dimension.

The fourth dimension generally feels like what you experience in your dreams. But it can also feel like a mystical state or an out-of-body state. A near-death experience is generally a fourth-dimensional experience. Trances, shamanic journeys, states you get into through meditation or prayer or chanting—all of these are often fourth-dimensional experiences.

Drug experiences can also be fourth-dimensional experiences. Some people have had drug experiences where their body felt like it was melting or turning into liquid, and they became very scared. This certainly can be a frightening experience because it's unfamiliar, and often a fear of death can come up. Or if not fear of death, you may feel that you're losing your connection to the world you're familiar with and which you want to stay connected to. The fear is pointing to a need for physical safety and well-being.

In general, you're completely safe when you access the merkaba through your heart, just as if you were having a dream. You're safe as long as you have the means to return. Most people wake up from their dreams. Even in a drug experience, most people return when the drug wears off. But it's wise to be sure that you have the means to return if you're traveling to another dimension or having other-dimensional experiences.

In the case of going into the heart, you're crossing a fluid energy membrane, and the return is easy. You probably found that as soon as you got scared, you immediately came back. Those of you who engage in this practice have probably already noticed that it's simple to return from these experiences in the heart. Eventually, you'll become very comfortable with such experiences, perhaps even relating to them as ordinary in a certain sense. And that's as it should be.

PART IX

Manifesting Your Reality

Chapter 82

Attracting for One's Highest Good

Question: How do we attract what we want into our life, and how can we be assured that it's for our highest good?

Mary Magdalene: Whatever you're attracting into your life is always based on what you're living and being in your essence or core. The more you support yourself in coming from your highest self, inevitably, that's what will come back to you. This is the law of attraction.

For example, suppose you desire a relationship. Don't focus on the partner that you want. Instead, focus on yourself and who you want to be in the relationship. Doing that will draw in the partner that matches who you are.

Being the kind of person who will attract what you want isn't limited to specific things or situations that you want to draw to yourself. It's a moment-to-moment practice because everything that's happening in your life is based on who you are and what you're attracting to yourself. The secret is to focus on yourself, on *being* the person who will attract the things or situations you want. This is the first aspect of attracting what you want.

The second aspect of attracting what you want is that whoever and whatever circumstances are showing up in your life, at any time, are always the perfect people or circumstances. This applies to the things you attract through your light, as well as the things you attract through your shadow. The challenges that come to you are always the perfect things for your growth, which you wouldn't necessarily see if you didn't have an outer reflection.

Often, the things that show up in an individual's life aren't in the form that they would hope for or imagine are best for them (if they were to imagine the outcome they'd like). But there's always a perfection in whatever shows up because it's the outer manifestation of one's inner reality. It's the perfect circumstance for growth. In that sense (of seeing the perfection of everything that occurs), whatever comes into your life will be the perfect thing.

Chapter 83

The Secret of Manifestation

Question: In the past, I've made things happen in an effortful, work-based way. Now I'm hearing that the process of manifestation can happen in a different way. Can you clarify that?

Mary Magdalene: You're a responsible and capable person who's been able to succeed in many ways through applying your detailed and complete efforts to whatever enterprise you embark upon. Now it's time for you to let go of that old way of accomplishing things. You're being called to make space for higher forces to do their work through you and your life.

This is really a part of you that's becoming activated, a higher part. It's not as though you're giving yourself over to something outside of yourself, though it may feel like that at first because you're not yet used to this new part of yourself. Rather, you're opening to a higher version of yourself.

This higher version of yourself accomplishes things in a different way. It's not so effortful, hard, or work-oriented. It's more of a process of allowing the forces of the universe to flow through you to manifest what's called for.

You're correct in thinking that this different way of accomplishing things is part of the process of manifestation that many people are attracted to. But the process works differently than most understand.

Many people are sensing that there's a higher way available for creating and manifesting, even in your world. This higher way is possible in the third dimension, but it's based in higher-dimensional capabilities, beginning with the fourth dimension. The challenge in the third dimension is that many people are trying to engage the principles of manifestation in a third-dimensional way, using their willpower and effortful force. This is why so many feel frustrated and discouraged with their efforts to manifest what they want, concluding that it doesn't work for them.

What people must understand is that the basis of manifestation is opening to the higher-dimensional part of yourself, which will naturally allow these higher frequencies and capabilities to become activated. Then you'll find that your endeavors become less about "making" things happen and more about making space for them to happen.

There are two important things that support this opening to the higher-dimensional parts of yourself. The first is daily meditation. Meditation awakens and strengthens your being's abilities to reside in and operate from the fourth dimension. It strengthens the abilities that are available to you in that dimension. Through regular meditation, you become increasingly attracted to the fourth dimension, so without you having to "do" anything in particular, your being increasingly gravitates to that dimension, often without you even realizing it. It simply becomes the place that you reside in and operate from.

The other thing that supports the process of manifestation is having more fun. This is so important! The fourth dimension is a very pleasurable place, especially compared to your third-dimensional world. To be more specific and accurate, it's the *higher octaves* of the fourth dimension that are very pleasurable. This is the part of the fourth dimension that those of you on the spiritual path are accessing. What helps you to access those higher octaves are pleasure, fun, and joy.

This is a secret that most people in your spiritual world don't realize. Many have the idea that spiritual work is difficult, ascetic, demanding, and removed from pleasure and fun. This is an incorrect perspective. It's a third-dimensional perspective and, sadly, one that keeps you bound to the third dimension. In order to break free of the third dimension and its binding limitations, one of the things you need is to become founded in fun, pleasure, and joy.

Some of you think that becoming founded in pleasure, fun, and joy will lead to a life of indulgence and self-debasement. But this isn't so, as long as you're balanced and bringing all your faculties into play, including your adult judgment and wisdom. It's not actually pleasurable, or fun, or joyful to engage in things that hurt you or deplete your life-force. It's truly fun, pleasurable, and joyful to do things that support your fullest life-energy and engagement in life. Realizing this is what ultimately allows people to go beyond the third-dimensional trap of addictions.

Most people who are involved in addictions are seeking the release that the higher dimensions provide (an experience that your soul still remembers), while also seeking to avoid pain. But avoiding pain is not truly fun, pleasurable, or joyful. Embracing pain with the wisdom and tools I've given is actually pleasurable and joyful. You'll come to see this once you overcome your fear of opening to pain and become confident in attaining the beautiful states that embracing pain leads you to.[139] At that stage, you'll see that embracing pain is fun. But by then your perception of fun will have greatly enlarged. You'll see anything that increases your life-energy and your vital connection to life via your heart and higher mind as fun. By then your ability to come from your heart and higher mind will be significantly increased, so you'll experience a greater preponderance of light in your life. This will most certainly be fun for you.

At your current stage, it's supportive to include fun in your life through activities like watching a movie or TV show, reading a book, dancing, walking in nature, engaging with friends or loved ones, pampering yourself physically, or eating good food. It's all about learning to listen to your body and feelings, and letting that listening guide you. This is a deep, moment-to-moment process, an ongoing meditation throughout your life of inner listening. Your body and your feelings, along with whatever higher guidance you're in touch with, are your guide in this meditation. If you do this, you'll be led to much more fun and pleasure. You'll also find yourself accomplishing more with ease, with seemingly little effort and work on your part.

Many of you are primed and ready for this shift. You've laid the groundwork through your responsibility in handling your third-dimensional tasks, along with your spiritual development and commitment. Because of your preparation, the symptoms of purification can be quite minor, as you shed this third-dimensional "skin" of your old approach to manifestation—a brief emotional outpouring and releasing the old energies or a relatively brief physical malady. While these may be unpleasant or confusing in the moment, ride the waves and trust the process. All is in perfect order. Trust that you're flowing with it in the best possible way. Allow and let go. All is well.

And beyond that, enjoy! Life is meant to be enjoyed, and enjoyment will only amplify the wonderful life-purpose that you've come to fulfill and which is already underway.

Chapter 84

Don't Use the Principle of Manifestation to Judge

Mary Magdalene: The idea that everyone creates their reality isn't intended as a form of blame. Taking a position toward others that it's their *fault* that they're experiencing something painful, or that they *should* be creating something different, isn't based in true understanding, love, or compassion. Rather, such responses are evidence of pain within the one making the response.

Someone who reacts in this way is using the idea that everyone creates their reality as a way of avoiding *their own* pain that's being stimulated by the circumstance. They're using this concept to release the pressure of their pain. This is a form of anger. (Anger is often used to release pressure.) And like anger, it generally causes more pain, for the person receiving the anger as well as the person expressing it.

There's a different way to respond to pain. First, you must understand that when you blame, judge, or accuse another of doing something wrong, you're projecting your pain outward, in an attempt to rid yourself of your own painful feelings. (Even when you blame yourself, you're doing this. You've simply made yourself into an outward "other.") I don't recommend this outward projection of one's pain, not only because it creates more pain but also because it doesn't make use of the pain in a way that's productive and actually essential.

Pain always has a gift for you. If you direct your pain outward, you miss the opportunity to receive the gift. To receive the gift, you must take your pain inward into yourself.

Letting go of outward projection, such as blame, doesn't mean that you approve or even accept the actions of the individual involved. You're neither condemning, approving, nor accepting. You're not focusing on "the other" at all. (You're also not condemning or blaming yourself for what occurred.)

It may be true that an individual created their experience on some level (often in choices that were made in the pre-birth state of selecting one's life circumstances). However, using this concept to condemn isn't beneficial. It's a way of staying in your mind, which is a form of self-protection—one which ultimately harms rather than protects.

If judgment or blame arises for you in response to a situation, use it as an indicator that *you're* in pain, and do your work to receive the gift and growth of *your own* pain. This is the real circumstance that *you've* created. You've given yourself this opportunity for healing, so you can grow—not only in terms of the particular circumstance in front of you, but ultimately in deeper parts of yourself that you often aren't consciously aware of. The outer circumstance that's stimulating you to judge or blame is simply the means to guide you to your own healing, to open you to it, to make it real for you.

This, of course, isn't easy work. It's profound work, often requiring great dedication, effort, courage, and time. But it's what you came into this life to do. You didn't come here to simply have a good time and coast along at the superficial levels of experience. There's nothing wrong with having a good time, and it certainly has its place in the bigger picture of all your experience. It feeds and motivates you, and is part of what guides you to continue on your soul path. But it's not the whole picture, nor is it the purpose of your life. Your life is a vehicle for your soul's growth, which you chose to further you in progressing toward reunion with God.

The things that tend to grow you the most in the third dimension are challenges and painful experiences. That's why it's important and valuable to know how to respond to pain in ways that are most supportive of your soul growth. Those ways also allow the most easeful transition through and beyond the pain. When you follow your heart's course, your pain will diminish and eventually resolve into peace, wisdom, and greater heart-openness. The shift into peace and heart-openness is a sign that you're on the path of growth into greater love and consciousness. It's also a sign that you're doing the soul work you've come to do, and for which you created this circumstance.

Chapter 85

Working with Health Challenges

Question: I have recurring health challenges, which has been difficult. I want to understand why I have these challenges and what I can do to help my body.

Mary Magdalene: When you or anyone is experiencing health challenges, you should get whatever help you can through the medical system, including natural healing methods. But for many people, these health crises are fundamentally a spiritual process, and medical or physical help will only go so far.

Prayer is your strongest resort. It's the strongest force you have because, ultimately, everything wants to be aligned and attuned to God. That's the nature of creation. Prayer is one of the greatest avenues of doing that and of releasing whatever is standing in the way of that alignment and attunement.

Pray and ask for help. Ask for clarity as to what you need to understand and what you need to do to work with this in the highest way. And it's always wise to ask for grace and ease if you're asking for release or change of any form.

Don't hold back from asking. Ask for whatever you need, even if it seems unspiritual or selfish to ask. Ask for exactly what you need.

Questioner: The hard part is that I do ask, but it appears that nothing happens. So I feel abandoned and unloved. Sometimes I think I'm being punished, which I'm sure is a holdover from my Catholic upbringing.

Mary Magdalene: Then that's the prayer in those times. Ask for connection. Ask for love. Ask for understanding.

You aren't being punished. And you haven't done something wrong or bad. The part of you that thinks that may be so is part of what you're purifying. That's the place to find God—the place in you that thinks you're being punished. Ask for help from that place.

Chapter 86

Relieving the Suffering of Others

Question: How can we best relieve the suffering of those close to us?

Mary Magdalene: It's a natural impulse to want to support the ones you love so that they have ease, comfort, and peace.

The first step in dealing with the suffering of another is always within yourself. Notice if there's any resistance in you to their pain, any tendency in you to disconnect because of the experience of pain. This doesn't mean you need to share the other person's pain or take it on. It means being aware of any strategy on your part to avoid the pain that's being brought up *in you* from seeing or experiencing the pain of another. Often, this strategy of avoiding the pain shows up through automatically wanting to "fix" things.[140]

Notice if there's any disconnection from God that's stimulated in you when you experience the pain of another—either witnessing it or simply being aware of their pain. If there is, heal that disconnection first, to create your fullest connection with God. Then from that place of connection to God, ask for guidance. You may be guided to offer some form of assistance or help. In general, it's important to *ask permission* from the other person before proceeding with whatever form of help you wish to offer.[141] Ask if they wish to receive help in that way and then let yourself be guided.

It's not that you separate and distance yourself from others with thoughts such as, "This is their karma; it has nothing to do with me." And it's not that you assume responsibility for others.[142] That isn't your job, to fix another. Your job, first and foremost, is to stay connected to God, to be guided through that connection, and to respect the choice of others by asking if they want to receive any help you're moved to offer.

If you receive a "no," connect with the other person's heart by asking yourself, "What part of their divinity would not be fulfilled by my request?" Then explore if there's another avenue that you can create together that would support *both* of your inner divinities. This is the path of co-creation, where it's not simply one person deciding how to proceed. Through your heart-connection to another, you can mutually allow the emergence of something new, something created through the connection to both of your hearts.

As you become stronger in this process of heart-connection with yourself *and* others, this process will become clearer, simpler, and more your ordinary process, rather than something unfamiliar that you're learning. Mutual co-creation is part of the fourth-dimensional way.

Chapter 87

Creating Abundance

Question: How do I open to greater financial abundance?

Mary Magdalene: This is a challenge for many people who are dedicated lightworkers on the Earth.

There's a notion that many people hold that you're the creator of your reality and that you can create the abundance that you want. Part of this viewpoint is that if you're not experiencing abundance, it represents a blockage within you. It may be a mental blockage (possibly based in your beliefs) or an emotional blockage. This idea is being proposed by many people at this time.

Like many ideas, there's an aspect of truth and accuracy to this. People who are drawn to be lightworkers often do have blocks within themselves relative to abundance. Some of this may be an overlay from a past life. Perhaps you made a vow in a previous incarnation to not be abundant because abundance was considered antithetical to spiritual life. So you took on ideas and beliefs that to be spiritual meant being poor, impoverished, not receiving money and worldly goods. Sometimes these kinds of things from other lifetimes are still affecting people.

But often there's a deeper, more personal reason that's affecting people. Experiences of struggling and not having enough may be supporting you in your process of learning about abundance and energy exchange.

There's also a larger reason why some people aren't experiencing abundance, which isn't broadly understood by most people. Many lightworkers have soul-level memories of a different kind of abundance that doesn't involve money or being compensated for work in the way most people experience on Earth. This abundance involves sharing Earth's resources and supporting everyone on the Earth. At the soul level, those who are most awakened not only remember this but are drawn to this higher level of abundance.

This abundance includes everyone, where no one is struggling to survive or is anxious about their survival in any way. In this abundance, everyone is supported for as long as they choose to be on Earth. In fact, that's the way that it always works. Everyone *is* supported for as long as they choose to be here. But most people on Earth don't recognize this. Even the more advanced spiritual souls aren't necessarily at the point yet where they're aware of this.

So it's an interesting play because your survival is truly guaranteed. Yet if you're not aware of this, you may feel anxious about your survival. And that anxiousness may be blocking your receptivity to your life-level needs getting met. When you relax and trust that all those needs will be provided, you're completely open to what's already the case. They *are* provided because you're doing your soul-level work, and you're meant to be here.

As long as you're doing your soul-level work, you'll be supported. Your soul-design is to do your spiritual work. And part of that spiritual work is to contribute to yourself and to the whole.

Truly, what human beings are moving into is a *very* different understanding of how life works altogether and what abundance is. Abundance is opening yourself to receive everything that you're always being given, so you can do your spiritual work. And true abundance only happens when that's the case for everyone. *No one is truly abundant when there are those who are in need or in doubt as to whether their needs will be fulfilled.* The concept of abundance as a strictly individual matter is, in some ways, contrary to this greater abundance that humans are all moving toward.

At the soul level, lightworkers often find themselves torn or pulled in different directions. Their soul is aware of this movement toward greater abundance, and that's where many lightworkers truly want to go. Yet they're in a physical circumstance and in their own spiritual evolution. In this very human circumstance, there's still the need to support oneself, because the transition to abundance for all hasn't yet been made on the broad scale. That leaves those who are more aware and further along in this spiritual evolution somewhat "betwixt and between."

Nonetheless, it's simultaneously true that you're absolutely supported and will be for as long as it's your time to be here, which is ultimately your soul's choice. Some of your work while you're here is to explore these different aspects of limitation that create your third dimension, including financial limitation.

My recommendation is to approach this with deep trust and love. Trust in the divine spirit that's in charge of all. Love yourself and others. And bring as much humor and lightness as you can to your situation, as though it were a game. In some ways, that's exactly what it is. It's a theater, a game, however you want to look at it, that's for your growth. These lessons around abundance are truly lessons in greater surrender and letting go, much more than the practice that's popular today of trying to create abundance in a mental way. In some ways, the approach to abundance through the mind that many are teaching is just a higher frequency or plane of trying to create abundance in a physical way. Both approaches work and there's truth to both. But neither one is where you're ultimately headed.

Where you're ultimately headed is into profound trust and love of God, where you do your work as you're guided and allow yourself to be supported in the midst of that. If there are instances where you feel nervous or anxious about abundance—where you question, "Will I have enough? Will I be supported?"—allow yourself to use that as a kind of housecleaning, a light shining on you to show you the areas where you can open to greater trust in God and greater turning of your circumstances over to God.

Chapter 88

Calling in a Partner

Question (from a woman): I want to attract the kind of partner that I really want to have a relationship with. What can I do to call in a healthy relationship?

Mary Magdalene: What areas of relating have been challenging for you in the past?

Questioner: The men I've been with have had financial struggles and issues with their mothers. They also weren't aligned with me spiritually.

Mary Magdalene: These are all valid arenas and issues.
  Your challenges with partners relative to finance may be related to your own challenges with receiving. Is receiving an area you have challenges with?

Questioner: Yes. I learned as a child that giving is how I show my worth and why someone would want to be with me.

Mary Magdalene: It could be valuable for you to take on a practice of consciously receiving from men. This might be with men that you interact with through work, or friendship, or in some other way.

What you, as a Feminine being, give to men is different from what men, as Masculine beings, give to you. You give men the Feminine essence. This is your life-force, joy, love, energetic nurturing—which is different from *doing* (like making food or cleaning the house or something like that). The Feminine is basically about energy. The Feminine gives the *energy* of life and love to their partner, enriching them through their Feminine energy. The Feminine also takes the form of intuition, insight, emotion, and pleasure. All of those are the domain of the Feminine. This is what the Feminine gives to men.

What the Masculine gives to a woman, or Feminine being, has more to do with taking care of you in practical, pragmatic ways. This support may come physically, financially, or through helping to solve problems in mental ways. This is the fundamental play of the Masculine and the Feminine.

Of course, when you're alone, you draw on your own Masculine and Feminine to be whole. Every individual needs to be whole, which comes from their inner Masculine and Feminine. Optimally, this wholeness is developed before entering a relationship. Then you're whole in and of yourself. But the play between the outer Masculine and Feminine still exists.

To a certain extent, the Masculine-Feminine play has been lost in your world, especially in Western culture. This is because women today are living mostly in their Masculine. Women are schooled in the Masculine, they work in and from their Masculine, they use their Masculine abilities to care for themselves and others, and they tend to live in their Masculine—often to the point of being cut off from their Feminine and not knowing their own

Feminine. Men also tend to operate from the Masculine, because the Masculine orientation is what's generally supported in your world today.

When men perceive women as coming from the Masculine, they see no need to take care of them, any more than they would take care of another man. When that happens, the man-woman relationship ends up being about two Masculine beings relating to each other, which hasn't worked very well for many people.

If you want to be more in the Feminine role in a relationship and have the man be more in the Masculine role (and being financially competent and self-sufficient is part of the traditional Masculine role), then you may need to strengthen your Feminine quality of receiving and responding energetically. So that's the first thing I recommend.

Relative to finding a man who doesn't have issues with women and his mother, the main thing you can do is to make sure you're clear relative to your issues with men. The degree to which you're clear of issues with men is what will allow you to call in a partner who's equally clear of issues with women.

Sometimes a partner mirrors your issues. Sometimes they complement your issues, which means they bring the other side. Either way, they're pointing to what *you're* doing to create and maintain the present dynamic. They're showing you the work you must do to heal your wounds with men, whether those wounds are in relation to your father or past relationships that you've had. Once you've done that healing, you'll come from a place of understanding and compassion for men and their wounding. But you must heal yourself first for that understanding and compassion to be authentic and not just suppression.

Your healing of your wounding with men will eventually lead

you to a place of *treasuring* men. You'll come to see them as valuable, beautiful, and such a gift to you. Then you can love them. From this place you'll draw men who are valuable, beautiful, and a gift to you.

Relative to a potential partner's spiritual development or consciousness, for that you must have the lens of seeing everyone as spiritual and doing their spiritual work, rather than being different from you. Their work might be different from yours, but you see the similarities and see through the differences. That will shift the dynamic of any separation between your approach to spirituality and the approach of someone else, such that someone may have a different path than yours, but you won't see that as a fundamental difference. You'll see it all as important, valuable work.

PART X

Children and Spirituality

Chapter 89

Spirituality with Children

Question: How can we help the children of today?

Mary Magdalene: Of course, love them. But you must also teach them. And the ultimate way that you teach children is through your own demonstration, which requires your own transformation. It always comes down to that.

Teach them that they are manifestations of God. Teach them that you see God in them, as them, and through them. And teach them that they must do the same with others. This is the ultimate teaching.

Chapter 90

Going Beyond the Third Dimension with Children

Mary Magdalene: Many adults want to know how they can help the children of today to become strong spiritually.

It's important to understand children's spirituality within the larger context of what's going on for all of humanity at this time—which is that you're in the midst of ascending from the third to the fourth dimension. This is an enormous shift for humans, which is taking place very quickly relative to how such changes usually occur. Those who are spiritually progressive and sensitive are aware that this is occurring, but the majority of your global population aren't conscious of this event. That doesn't make it any less real.

Spiritually speaking, the greatest thing you can give to children is to help them in this ascension process. This requires you to be involved in the process yourself, for children primarily learn at the nonverbal level through copying and adapting to what's modeled to them.

One of the primary characteristics of the third dimension is that it's a place where power is used to get what you sense you need or want. This might be called "force," "coercion," or "overpowering others." Most often, power is used at the expense of others. This is the old model of authority, where those at the top have power and those below have relinquished their power. Part of this model is that those with power will be supported, taken care of, and even survive, while those without power may or may not be supported, taken care of, or survive. This creates great stress in yourself and your society. It's a structure that assumes some won't be taken care of while others will. This leads to struggle and competition to be one of the ones who will be taken care of or survive.

All of this is learned by children at an extremely young age, because most parents or caregivers use power and authority to get children to do what they want. Even when adults act in ways that they perceive are best for the children, they often still use power modalities to get the children to comply.

Changing this will make the biggest difference in terms of helping children evolve spiritually. It will also do the most to change your world. Stop teaching children, through your example, that the world functions on the basis of power. Stop using power to get children to do what you want. This means that adults must stop giving commands or orders to children. They must stop using volume as a tool of force. And they must stop using rewards and punishments to enforce their authority.

However, I don't recommend that parents simply let children do whatever they want. That would be depriving children of your wisdom, support, help, and intelligence, which they absolutely need. They need your guidance and support. But it's not necessary to use force, power, or authority to bring your guidance and support to children.

What you must do involves a very different process of being transparent with children about yourself. You must show children your feelings and the inner divine qualities that are the source of those feelings.[143] Then you can make requests of the child based on your feelings and inner divine qualities. This is the path of heart-connection with your children.

You may not believe this will work, especially if you're entrenched in the belief that force and power are necessary. But I tell you that it does work. Children love you. They also know that they depend on you. You can appeal to their love and care rather than use force. It's up to you. Children will trust this process, as long as you also show care for their feelings and their inner divine qualities, which are the source of their feelings.

When a child is upset, don't immediately go into force mode of trying to fix and overpower the upset. Instead, stay calm. Breathe. Notice what you're feeling and the inner divine qualities you're having. Connect with your heart first, before you respond to the child.

Then, after you're heart-connected, make a guess of what you think is going on with the child, and ask if your guess is right. For example, you might say, "Are you frustrated because you want to play right now?" The feeling is frustration, and the inner divine quality it's sourcing out of is "play." Keep guessing until you've connected with the child's heart. You'll sense when a connection occurs.

Then share your feelings and inner divine qualities with the child. For example, you might say, "I'm feeling frustrated too, because I want to be productive right now and make dinner." At this point there should be a sense of connection between the two of you. If there isn't, you probably haven't fully connected with the child's feelings and the inner divine qualities that are the source of those feelings. The child won't have space to hear what's going on with you until you've connected with them and what's going on with them.

This is an example of connecting at the heart instead of using force. Once the heart-connection is made, you can move into thinking of possible solutions that you *both* agree upon and feel at peace with. Then you're working together rather than against each other. This is co-creation.

If parents raise children in this way, then when the children become adults, they won't have to unlearn their previous training and learn how to relate from their hearts as adults. This is a tremendous advantage that you can give to children.

I love you and support you most fully in creating a world that's founded on the heart rather than on force.

[Note from Mercedes: The following communication was given at a channeling of Mary Magdalene and Yeshua. The response is from Yeshua, not Mary Magdalene. I'm including it as part of this collection because it was clear to me that Yeshua was speaking for both himself and Mary Magdalene.]

Question: I have a young son, who I respect and love for who he is. But I also think I need to guide him and have some authority over him, which doesn't match my spiritual ideals. How do I balance guiding him with not wanting to tell him who he should be?

Yeshua: The first thing to realize is that your son is a mirror for you. That mirror shows you the places in yourself that you're struggling with, which you wouldn't be in touch with if it weren't for your son, or perhaps not as easily or as readily.

Any issue you're struggling or having challenge with relative to yourself will show up in your relationship with your child. That can be a great benefit. It can help you see the places you need to focus on for your own growth, as well as for the good of your child. This is one of the great blessings of being a parent.

You're struggling with your relationship to power. That's a rich struggle. It's not simply about how to be a good parent. It's about how to go beyond the limits of the third dimension altogether—such that power is used to support everyone, rather than to control some for the benefit of others. This is a huge learning for human beings in the third dimension, and it's coming in this particular form in your life.

Ultimately, you must get to the root of your conflict, which is your struggle within yourself regarding power. Very likely there's wounding around that for you, and healing is required. You also must embrace your son's power, which perhaps you're not completely at peace with.

Most parents love their child, even though parenting can be difficult at times. You can forget your love, but in general there's love there. That love motivates you for the good of both of you.

This is where all humans are headed—to learn to be in power together for the good of all. In your case, this means empowering your son *and* yourself. The two aren't in conflict with each other, but it can seem that way.

You're the divine guardian of your son. At times that includes setting appropriate limits. Children don't necessarily enjoy those limits in the moment, but their reactions are usually short-lived. If they're not short-lived, something deeper is going on.

The third dimension is filled with limits. Part of your job as a parent is to help your child navigate limits.

Ultimately, it's your job to see the divinity in your child and in yourself. When you get to that place, you work it out as two divine beings.

Appendix

Joyful Feelings

AFFECTIONATE
compassionate
friendly
loving
open-hearted
sympathetic
tender
warm

ENGAGED
absorbed
alert
curious
engrossed
enchanted
entranced
fascinated
interested
intrigued
involved
spellbound
stimulated

HOPEFUL
expectant
encouraged
optimistic

JOYFUL
amused
delighted
glad
happy
jubilant
pleased
tickled

EXCITED
amazed
animated
ardent
aroused
astonished
dazzled
eager
energetic
enthusiastic
giddy
invigorated
lively
passionate
surprised
vibrant

GRATEFUL
appreciative
moved
thankful
touched

INSPIRED
amazed
awed
wonder

CONFIDENT
empowered
open
proud
safe
secure

EXHILARATED
blissful
ecstatic
elated
enthralled
exuberant
radiant
rapturous
thrilled

PEACEFUL
calm
clearheaded
comfortable
centered
content
equanimous
fulfilled
mellow
quiet
relaxed
relieved
satisfied
serene
still
tranquil
trusting

REFRESHED
enlivened
rejuvenated
renewed
rested
restored
revived

This chart is based upon the Feelings Inventory from the Center for Nonviolent Communication.
© 2005 by Center for Nonviolent Communication, www.cnvc.org.

Painful Feelings

FATIGUE
beat
burnt out
depleted
exhausted
lethargic
listless
sleepy
tired
weary
worn out

ANNOYED
Aggravated
dismayed
disgruntled
displeased
exasperated
frustrated
impatient
irritated
irked

ANGRY
enraged
furious
incensed
indignant
irate
livid
outraged
resentful

AVERSION
animosity
appalled
contempt
disgusted
dislike
hate
horrified
hostile
repulsed

CONFUSED
ambivalent
baffled
bewildered
dazed
hesitant
lost
mystified
perplexed
puzzled
torn

VULNERABLE
fragile
guarded
helpless
insecure
leery
reserved
sensitive
shaky

DISCONNECTED
alienated
aloof
apathetic
bored
cold
detached
distant
distracted
indifferent
numb
removed
uninterested
withdrawn

EMBARRASSED
ashamed
chagrined
flustered
guilty
mortified
self-conscious

YEARNING
envious
jealous
longing
nostalgic
pining
wistful

Painful Feelings *(continued)*

AFRAID	SAD	DISQUIET
apprehensive	depressed	agitated
dread	dejected	alarmed
foreboding	despair	discombobulated
frightened	despondent	disconcerted
mistrustful	disappointed	disturbed
panicked	discouraged	perturbed
petrified	disheartened	rattled
scared	forlorn	restless
suspicious	gloomy	shocked
terrified	heavy hearted	startled
wary	hopeless	surprised
worried	melancholy	troubled
	unhappy	turbulent
TENSE	wretched	turmoil
anxious		uncomfortable
cranky	**PAIN**	uneasy
distressed	agony	unnerved
distraught	anguished	unsettled
edgy	bereaved	upset
fidgety	devastated	
frazzled	grief	
irritable	heartbroken	
jittery	hurt	
nervous	lonely	
overwhelmed	miserable	
restless	regretful	
stressed out	remorseful	

This chart is based upon the Feelings Inventory from the Center for Nonviolent Communication.
© 2005 by Center for Nonviolent Communication, www.cnvc.org.

Inner Divine Qualities

CONNECTION	PHYSICAL WELL-BEING	MEANING
acceptance	air	awareness
affection	food	celebration of life
appreciation	movement/exercise	challenge
belonging	rest/sleep	clarity
cooperation	sexual expression	competence
communication	safety	consciousness
closeness	shelter	contribution
community	touch	creativity
companionship	water	discovery
compassion		efficacy
consideration	**HONESTY**	effectiveness
consistency	authenticity	growth
empathy	integrity	hope
inclusion	presence	learning
intimacy		mourning
love	**PLAY**	participation
mutuality	joy	purpose
nurturing	humor	self-expression
respect		stimulation
safety	**PEACE**	to matter
security	beauty	understanding
stability	communion	
support	ease	**AUTONOMY**
to know and be known	equality	choice
to see and be seen	harmony	freedom
to understand and be understood	inspiration	independence
trust	order	space
warmth		spontaneity

This chart is drawn from the Needs Inventory by the Center for Nonviolent Communication. © 2005 by Center for Nonviolent Communication, www.cnvc.org.

Notes

Introduction

1. Mary Magdalene was a follower of Jesus in the Bible. Many believe she was Jesus's wife.

2. "Yeshua" is the Aramaic name for Jesus. Aramaic was the language spoken in Israel at the time of Jesus's incarnation two thousand years ago, so many people believe the person referred to as Jesus in the Bible was called Yeshua during his lifetime. In my channeled sessions, Mary Magdalene has always called Jesus "Yeshua." Accordingly, the name Yeshua is used in this book.

3. Mary and Yeshua use the terms Feminine and Masculine to refer to the archetypal Feminine and Masculine that reside within all of us (regardless of our gender). The twin concepts are similar to the concept of yin and yang in Eastern philosophy. They use the terms "Divine Feminine" or "Divine Masculine" when referring to the Feminine or Masculine aspects of God, or of our human divinity. An in-depth explanation of the Feminine and Masculine can be found in the books *Mary Magdalene Beckons* and *The Holy Grail* by Mercedes Kirkel.

4. Channeling is the practice of conveying messages from a being or guide in another dimension.

5. Later I came to see that I'd received messages from Spirit my whole life. I just hadn't recognized them as such.

6. For information about all the books in the Magdalene-Yeshua Teaching Series, visit www.mercedeskirkel.com.

7. A mantra is a sacred word or phrase that's repeated over and over as a form of spiritual practice.

Chapter 1

8. Mary is referencing the Heart Path process, which is Mary's teaching for living in the heart. Mary first described the Heart Path in the book *Mary Magdalene Beckons*. The process is explained in detail in the book *The Heart Path of Mary Magdalene* and "The Heart Path" video course, both by Mercedes Kirkel. To learn more about the Heart Path books and video course, go to www.mercedeskirkel.com.

9. The grid that Mary is referencing is an energetic structure surrounding and permeating the Earth. Part of the spiritual work of humans at this time is to increase the frequency or light-quotient of this web.

10. "Asana" is a pose in yoga. It's also used to mean a particular orientation or disposition one assumes in life.

Chapter 2

11. See note 2 above for an explanation of Mary's use of the name "Yeshua."

12. In the book *Mary Magdalene Beckons*, Mary Magdalene presents a model of our universe that includes twelve dimensions, or planes of reality. The fourth dimension is the next higher plane beyond the third dimension. This plane is energetically based, rather than physically based. The full model of the twelve dimensions, including the fourth dimension, is described in detail in *Mary Magdalene Beckons*.

13. The crucifixion that Mary is referring to was the execution of Jesus that's recorded in the four canonical gospels of the Bible (Mark 15; Matthew 27; Luke 23; and John 19) and attested to in other historical sources. Crucifixion was a form of capital punishment used by the Romans that involved being nailed to a cross or beam and hanging until one was dead. Some believe Jesus survived the crucifixion.

14. For a fuller description of Yeshua and Mary's energetic work during the crucifixion, see Chapter 15 ("The Hidden Work of the Crucifixion").

15. Mary shares more about this in Part III of this book, "The Inner Circle."

16. For more information about Yeshua's appearances after the crucifixion, see Chapter 14 ("The Inner School") and Chapter 16 ("In the Tomb and After").

Chapter 3

17. The messages from Mary Magdalene in the book *Mary Magdalene Beckons* focus on developing our inner Feminine so that it can come into balance, harmony, and unity with our inner Masculine. To learn more, visit www.mercedeskirkel.com.

Chapter 4

18. The term "inner divine quality" is Mary Magdalene's term for a particular aspect of our inner divinity. To see a list of inner divine qualities, go to the Appendix (page 349). A fuller explanation of inner divine qualities and how they relate to feelings is given in the books *Mary Magdalene Beckons* and *The Heart Path of Mary Magdalene*, and "The Heart Path" video course. To learn more about the books and video course, go to www.mercedeskirkel.com.

19. The process of following feelings to their source within oneself and then reconnecting with the divine is fully explained in the book *The Heart Path of Mary Magdalene* and "The Heart Path" video course.

20. Moving into action after connecting with your inner divinity is also fully explained in the book *The Heart Path of Mary Magdalene* and "The Heart Path" video course.

21. Mary is using the term "Source" here as another name for God.

Chapter 5

22. These retreats were focused on Mary Magdalene's Heart Path. See note 8 above for an explanation of what the Heart Path is.

23. Mary is referencing specific parts of the Heart Path process, which those at the retreat were familiar with.

Chapter 7

24. Twin flames are two souls who share the strongest kind of soul connection possible. Some believe that twin flames were originally one being that split in two, with one embodying the Masculine and the other the Feminine. Twin flames are profoundly connected, including sharing the same soul-purpose.

25. Mary is referring to her messages in the book *Mary Magdalene Beckons*.

26. Mary uses the term "ascension" differently than the way it's used in Christianity (to refer to the bodily rising of Jesus into heaven after his resurrection). For Mary, ascension is the process available to everyone of shifting from the third dimension into progressively higher dimensions, beginning with the fourth dimension. Mary sees this process as currently underway, with everyone at different stages of making this transition. Various aspects of the ascension process are described throughout this book and in the books *Mary Magdalene Beckons* and *The Holy Grail*.

Chapter 8

27. When Mary uses the term "higher" in reference to higher beings or higher dimensions, she's not implying superiority. For her, a higher dimension is a realm that's literally manifesting at a higher frequency or vibrational rate.

28. Mary is pointing to individuals' past lifetimes, as well as the portion of one's present lifetime that's their "past" in this incarnation.

29. Mary recommends utilizing the Heart Path process as the vehicle for creating a new story, rather than trying to change beliefs and experience through the mind or will.

Chapter 12

30. A soul family is a group of souls that work closely with one another on their spiritual evolution and often incarnate together. Soul families can include kindred spirits, twin flames, and soulmates.

31. By "we," Mary is referring to 1) herself and Yeshua, 2) her whole soul group, and 3) all higher beings. I believe it's more natural for Mary to speak in the plural "we" rather than the singular "I" because of her strong identification with her soul group and soul family. However, she most often communicates with us in the singular (as "I"), so we can relate to her in a way that's familiar to us.

Chapter 13

32. A soul group is a large group of souls who share many spiritual connections. Within a soul group are soul families, kindred spirits, soulmates, and twin flames.

33. Mary is especially referring to individuals who claim to have been a well-known person in a previous incarnation.

Chapter 14

34. See note 26 above for a description of what Mary means when she refers to the ascension process.

35. The energy-based realm of the fourth dimension is experienced by many people in dreams, visions, mystical experiences, shamanic journeys, drug-induced experiences, and hypnosis.

36. A mystery school is an organization dedicated to the learning of esoteric spiritual knowledge and practices. In ancient times, mystery schools were generally kept secret, with information only being shared amongst initiates.

37. An out-of-body experience (OBE) is an experience of an individual's consciousness leaving their physical body and traveling elsewhere for a period of time. During an out-of-body experience, individuals frequently see their body resting peacefully below them while they perceive themselves as being above or away from their body. A near-death experience (NDE) is the experience of temporarily beginning the process of dying but "returning" to one's physical body and to living, before the death process is complete. During a near-death experience individuals may perceive a variety of surreal phenomena, such as seeing themselves from

above, viewing the events of their life, passing through a tunnel of light, meeting deceased family members or spiritual or religious figures, and experiencing subtler realms.

38. Resurrection is the concept of coming back to life after death, either individually or as a group. The death and resurrection of Jesus is a central doctrine in Christianity, which is often understood as Jesus ascending to heaven in a transformed body that's powered by Spirit.

39. Many scholars today attribute the majority of the precepts of Christianity (including the resurrection) as having originated with Paul ("Saul of Tarsus") rather than Jesus. Paul's conversion and ministry took place after Jesus's death, and most likely Paul never encountered Jesus when Jesus was alive. Paul's teaching was an amalgamation of his own background and prior beliefs as a Greek Pharisee, intertwined with his interpretation of Jesus's teaching. Scholars today often refer to what's evolved into Christianity as *Pauline Christianity* to differentiate it from the teaching of Jesus.

40. Some of Yeshua's pre-crucifixion appearances are recorded in the Bible, such as the report of him walking on water (Mark 6:45–52; Matthew 14:22–33; and John 6:16–21), or of him appearing in a transformed state with Moses and Elijah (Mark 9: 2–8; Matthew 17:1–8; Luke 9:28–36; and 2 Peter 1:16–18).

41. This expectation is reflected in various religious beliefs and myths from that time that involve a dying-and-rising deity, such as the stories of Osiris (Egypt), Tammuz (Sumer/Iraq), Ba'al (Ugarit/Syria), and Dionysus, Persephone, and the Phoenix (Greece). In Roman culture, the Roman rulers were believed to become gods after they died.

42. The term "Christ" comes from the Greek word meaning "one who is anointed." While Christians use the term as both a name for Jesus and a title denoting that Jesus is the Messiah, the term "Christ" is increasingly being used in another way—to signify the divine energy and consciousness within all and available to all.

43. John 14:12.

44. In the book *The Holy Grail*, Yeshua explains that "Christ consciousness is a reference to carrying the light of God" (Chapter 2, "Christ Consciousness," p. 19).

Chapter 15

45. Neither Yeshua nor Mary Magdalene have ever claimed that Yeshua was a messiah, that he died and was reborn, or that he was (or is) the exclusive divine being. Nonetheless, they were aware that people's beliefs in those things would shape their perception and interpretation of what occurred.

46. Karma is a Sanskrit term for the principle that our choices and actions determine our future circumstances either positively or negatively.

47. See note 26 above for a description of what Mary means when she refers to the ascension process.

48. Mary is referring to Yeshua's mother, whom most Christians know as "Mother Mary." According to Mary Magdalene, Yeshua's mother was a priestess of Isis (as was Mary Magdalene). "Lady Mary" was Yeshua's mother's priestess name. Mary Magdalene uses the name "Lady Mary" when referring to Yeshua's mother as a form of respect and honoring of her priestess stature.

Chapter 16

49. The healers that Mary is referring to are herself, Mother Mary (Yeshua's mother), and other members of the inner circle who worked most closely with Yeshua and understood the esoteric aspects of his work. The members of this group were all skilled healers who had been prepared for the work of reviving Yeshua.

50. The inner circle was the group of people who worked most closely with Yeshua and who understood the more esoteric aspects of his work. Some were his students (see Chapter 14, "The Inner School"), and others, such as Mary Magdalene and Lady Mary (Mother Mary), were high beings and realizers.

51. Mary is referring to the "empty tomb story" that's told in the four gospels of the Bible. Scholars today generally agree that the empty tomb story found in Mark 16:1–8 is probably closest to the original version of the story. The prophecies Mary references are from the Old Testament (see Psalm 16 and Isaiah 53:10), as well as commonly held beliefs of the time in which a divine being dies and then rises again to life in some form.

52. Mary is referencing the shift into higher dimensions.

53. In the Indian tradition, these abilities are called "siddhis" or yogic powers. These can include clairvoyance (psychically knowing the past, present, and future), psychokinesis (manipulating physical reality through the mind), manifesting extraordinary strength, levitation, teleportation (moving the body wherever the mind intends), bilocation (appearing at more than one location at the same time), invisibility, sustaining the body without food or water, living to an advanced age, and resuscitation of others or oneself.

54. The Christian interpretations of Jesus's resurrection that Mary is pointing to (and differing with) have been called *substitutionary atonement* or *vicarious atonement*. These include the ideas that death is defeated because of Jesus's resurrection, that salvation and forgiveness of sin are given to believers through Jesus's death and resurrection, and that Christians have spiritually risen through Jesus's resurrection.

Chapter 17

55. Yeshua's process of infusing light into the Earth during the crucifixion is explained more fully in Chapter 15 ("The Hidden Work of the Crucifixion").

Chapter 19

56. See note 26 above for a description of what Mary means when she refers to the ascension process.

57. In Hinduism, kundalini is a form of Divine Feminine energy located at the base of the spine. When activated, kundalini is believed to lead to spiritual awakening.

58. Mary is referring to her instruction in the book *Mary Magdalene Beckons*. Mary and Yeshua's instruction on Masculine and Feminine is further explained in the book *The Holy Grail*.

Chapter 22

59. Mary has described the Masculine and Feminine as each having a higher or more exalted form and a lower or more practical form. The higher form of the Masculine is consciousness, and the higher form of the Feminine is love. For more information about the higher and lower forms of the Masculine and Feminine, see *Mary Magdalene Beckons* and *The Holy Grail*.

60. The lower or practical form of the Masculine is the mind and the will.

Chapter 25

61. Mary is using this language ("someone in the Masculine position" and "someone in the Feminine position") intentionally because she's not limiting what she's saying to only mean men who are hurting women. She's including other possibilities, such as a woman assuming the Masculine position in a particular interaction or a man assuming the Feminine position.

Chapter 27

62. See note 57 above for an explanation of what kundalini is.

63. Mary is referencing the Heart Path process. See note 8 above for an explanation of what the Heart Path is.

Chapter 28

64. To see a list of inner divine qualities, go to the Appendix (page 349). See note 18 above for an explanation of inner divine qualities.

65. The process of reconnecting with one's inner divine qualities is more fully explained in *The Heart Path of Mary Magdalene*.

Chapter 31

66. Developing and engaging *both* the Feminine and Masculine aspects of ourselves is a frequent theme for Mary. She feels we need to hear this regularly to counter our programming to focus on and engage *either* the Feminine or the Masculine exclusively. She sees this imbalance in spirituality, as well as the world in general. The majority of spiritual paths (including new age spirituality) tend to focus on *either* the Feminine (the heart and manifestation) or the Masculine (consciousness, intention, and transcendence), without giving equal importance to the other half of our being. In this vein, many people relate to Mary as representing and advocating for the Feminine, more or less exclusively. However, Mary champions and sees the necessity for both Masculine and Feminine.

Chapter 32

67. This is referring to the gospels in the New Testament of the Bible.

Chapter 33

68. The questioner is referring to the story of Adam & Eve in the Bible (Genesis 2–3), as well as the interpretations of that story in the Abrahamic religions.

69. See note 57 above for an explanation of what kundalini is.

70. Mary has said that she was a priestess in the Temple of Isis, which was part of the Egyptian tradition. For more information, see *Mary Magdalene Beckons*.

Chapter 34

71. See the list of inner divine qualities in the Appendix (page 349).

Chapter 36

72. Mary is pointing to paths or processes that utilize approaches such as beliefs, positive thinking, and visualization to deal with pain. She's especially talking about the tendency to engage these mind-based approaches as an alternative to feeling, thereby bypassing the healing that comes through feeling one's emotions.

Chapter 38

73. Mary recommends the Heart Path process for going all the way through pain to full healing. For more about the Heart Path process, see note 8 above.

Chapter 39

74. Mary is referring to the words attributed to Jesus in the Bible in Luke 23:34.

Chapter 40

75. More instruction from Mary on strengthening the heart can be found in the books *Mary Magdalene Beckons* and *The Heart Path of Mary Magdalene*.

Chapter 42

76. For an explanation of what the Heart Path is, see note 8 above.

Chapter 43

77. For an explanation of what the Heart Path is, see note 8 above.

Chapter 45

78. Following feelings to the root of a situation is part of the Heart Path process that Mary recommends. See note 8 above for more about the Heart Path.

79. Mary is referencing a step of the Heart Path process where one reconnects with their inner divinity (which the person she was speaking to was already familiar with).

Chapter 46

80. The person Mary is speaking to is familiar with the Heart Path process. Mary is directing them to a part of the Heart Path that involves connecting with one's own inner divinity. See note 8 above for more about the Heart Path.

81. Mary is now directing the questioner to another part of the Heart Path process, which involves connecting with the divinity in others.

Chapter 48

82. See note 46 above for an explanation of what karma is.

83. See note 31 above relative to Mary's use of the plural ("our") when referring to herself.

Chapter 50

84. Utilizing emotions and the body for spiritual growth is part of the Heart Path process. See note 8 above for more about the Heart Path.

85. Mary is referring to the previously published books that contain her instruction on the Heart Path process. See note 8 above for more about the Heart Path.

Chapter 51

86. Mary is referring to the adaptation of the Hawaiian practice of Ho'oponopono that was put out in 1992 by Hew Len and Joe Vitale. This modern version involves responding to painful experiences in one's mind or consciousness with four progressive phrases: 1) "I'm sorry." 2) "Please forgive me." 3) "Thank you." 4) "I love you."

87. The process of letting go of blame of oneself and others is described in detail in the book *The Heart Path of Mary Magdalene* and "The Heart Path" video course.

Chapter 53

88. See note 46 above for an explanation of what karma is.

89. Mary is referring to the Heart Path process. See note 8 above for more about the Heart Path.

Chapter 54

90. This passage is from Matthew 5:5 in the Bible.

91. The original Greek word used in this passage (which is today commonly translated as "meek") was a term that described a horse that had been broken in. This same word was used again in Matthew 11:28–30, where Jesus says "Take my yoke upon you, and learn from me, for I am gentle and lowly in heart; and you will find rest for your souls."

Chapter 55

92. Another name for the Masculine could be "the transcendental," while the Feminine could be called "the immanent" or "the manifest." Mary's usage of the terms Masculine and Feminine also shares some features with the eastern concept of yin and yang.

Chapter 56

93. See note 18 above for an explanation of inner divine qualities.

94. In this excerpt, "our" and "we" are references to Mary and Yeshua.

Chapter 60

95. The individual Mary is speaking to has studied the Heart Path process and understands what Mary is pointing to when she recommends mourning. In the Heart Path, mourning is an essential process in relation to any painful feeling, which leads to full healing and growth. It involves allowing oneself to fully feel one's pain and through that being led into reconnection with one's inner divinity. More information about Mary's instruction on mourning can be found in the book *The Heart Path of Mary Magdalene* and "The Heart Path" video course.

Chapter 64

96. See note 46 above for an explanation of what karma is.

Chapter 65

97. In this paragraph, Mary has shifted into speaking from a more transcendent place. She's now contextualizing her previous explanation of the third-dimension experience as the Feminine aspect of the divine within the bigger picture of the union of the Feminine and Masculine, which is the union of the manifest with the transcendental.

Chapter 66

98. The process of healing and growth through feeling is part of the Heart Path. Mary has stated that individuals may need support in grieving (which is her term for feeling pain) all the way to releasing their pain. In that case, the support of someone trained in the process of opening to feeling as a healing path can be very valuable.

99. See note 18 above for an explanation of inner divine qualities.

100. Mary's definition of mourning is larger than most people's definition of this term. Most people think of mourning as something people do when someone dies or experiences some other form of loss. For Mary, mourning includes feeling all forms of emotional pain or wounding. Thus, mourning includes not only sadness but also fear, anger, regret, and all other forms of pain. For more information about mourning, see note 95 above.

101. Mary is referring to the Heart Path process of identifying the inner divinity that's the source of our feelings.

102. In other words, the fear may be stemming from a need for belonging within a familial or social group.

Chapter 67

103. Mary's reference to "reconnecting with the Great Feminine" is a call to embody and express the inner Feminine energy that we all carry, and it applies to both men and women. For Mary, emotions are a key part of our inner Feminine, while thinking is part of our inner Masculine. Grieving is pure emotion and thus pure Feminine energy. Anger is a mixture of Feminine and Masculine because it's a mixture of emotion and judgment (which is a form of thought). This is more fully explained in *Mary Magdalene Beckons* and *The Heart Path of Mary Magdalene*.

104. The second chakra is the energy center in the sacral region of the spine that's associated with emotion.

Chapter 68

105. See note 18 above for an explanation of inner divine qualities.

106. The steps Mary took this man through are more fully explained in the book *The Heart Path of Mary Magdalene* and "The Heart Path" video course.

Chapter 69

107. Mary's emphasis on healing body shame as a spiritual imperative is a response to the many spiritual paths that ignore this arena, as part of the larger pattern of ignoring, excluding, and suppressing the Feminine altogether.

108. Chakras are energy centers in the body that correspond to different areas of human functioning. The seven primary chakras are located along the spine, from the perineum to the crown of the head.

109. See note 104 above for an explanation of the second chakra.

110. The term "clothed by God" was used in the ancient goddess temples, which Mary was familiar with. It meant being without clothes. The term was specifically used in relation to temple practices that were engaged in the unclothed state.

111. In this last paragraph, Mary is addressing the tendency on the part of some spiritual seekers to assert that they've completed their work in the third dimension. Mary's point of view is that if someone is still here (manifest in the third dimension), that's the evidence that this is the optimal place for them to be. When they've completed the work they came here to do, they'll move on. Until that point, assuming that one has completed one's work will be a form of spiritual bypassing, most often bypassing one's development of their Feminine.

112. See note 18 above for an explanation of inner divine qualities.

113. For some people, engaging this process may bring up sadness or grief from past wounding when they weren't connected to their own perfection and divinity relative to the body. For Mary's instruction on

grieving, see Chapter 66 ("The Necessity of Acceptance and Grieving") and *The Heart Path of Mary Magdalene*.

Chapter 70

114. Mary is referencing the Heart Path process of reconnecting with your inner divinity. See note 8 above for more about the Heart Path.

115. To see a list of inner divine qualities, go to page 349 in the Appendix.

Chapter 71

116. See note 26 above for a description of what Mary means when she refers to the ascension process.

117. The "you" Mary is referring to is all of humanity.

118. The "we" Mary is referring to is the group of higher beings with whom she identifies.

Chapter 72

119. Exodus 14:21.

120. See note 46 above for an explanation of what karma is.

Chapter 74

121. Mercury retrograde is a period of time in which the planet Mercury appears to move backward. In astrology, Mercury retrograde is associated with misunderstandings and miscommunication, travel delays, mechanical and technological breakdowns, and things generally "not going according to plan."

122. See note 26 above for a description of what Mary means when she refers to the ascension process.

Chapter 76

123. See note 26 above for a description of what Mary means when she refers to the ascension process.

Chapter 77

124. The inner school is described more fully in Chapter 14, "The Inner School."

Chapter 79

125. Mary is referring to energy pathways that are part of the energy body. The chakra system is an example of one such pathway.

126. In yogic and mystical teachings of India and other cultures, humans are seen as having six coexisting bodies, with each body being progressively subtler. These different bodies are sometimes described as being like the layers of an onion. The outermost layer, or sheath, is the physical body. The next three layers, moving inward, are the etheric or energy body, the emotional body, and the mental body. The fifth layer is the causal body, which includes the soul and one's identity. The innermost sheath contains the spiritual body, which includes the higher self. For a fuller description of the bodies of the whole being, see *Mary Magdalene Beckons* (Chapter 6, "My Sacred Relationship with Yeshua").

127. The etheric or energy body includes our sexual energy.

128. Mary has stated that the single thing that could most help humanity in their spiritual advancement is to develop the emotional body. That's why she chose to focus on emotional mastery first through the messages in *Mary Magdalene Beckons*. The messages she gave in *Sublime Union* were her second set of instructions, also given through Mercedes. These messages focus on sacred sexuality as a means of developing the etheric body.

129. The sacred heart is the seat of the Divine Feminine within humans and is associated with the heart chakra or energy center, located in the center of the chest near the physical heart. The sacred mind is the seat of the Divine Masculine within humans and is associated with the third-eye chakra or energy center, located in the center of the brain. Part of completing one's spiritual development in the third dimension is to connect these two centers energetically so that one is operating from both places simultaneously.

130. The pineal gland is a pea-sized gland that's located in the center of the brain. Mary is referring to the energy center that's associated with the pineal gland, which is sometimes referred to as the "third eye" or ajna chakra. Opening this energy center is part of the process of being able to access higher dimensions.

131. The merkaba is part of the human energy body. Its star tetrahedron shape surrounds the human body, while the full merkaba field extends out approximately fifty-five feet and is shaped like a flying saucer.

132. See note 36 above for an explanation of what a mystery school is, and Chapter 14 ("The Inner School") for a description of the mystery school led by Yeshua.

Chapter 80

133. The "inner sanctum of the heart" is a part of the sacred heart, which is the seat of the Divine Feminine in humans. Certain esoteric functions are accessible through this energy center. See note 129 above for more about the sacred heart.

134. These energetic structures are explained in notes 130 and 131 above.

Chapter 81

135. See note 26 above for a description of what Mary means when she refers to the ascension process.

136. Mary is referring to the use of crystals in electronics, such as computer chips.

137. Mary is primarily referencing emotional pain, though there could also be physical pain.

138. Mary is alluding to the different techniques that have been promoted for activating and accessing one's merkaba. Mary recommends activating and accessing the merkaba through the heart because doing so ensures that the power of the merkaba will be used for the highest good.

Chapter 83

139. Mary isn't saying that embracing pain should be engaged as a means of exaltation. She's saying that embracing pain is a healing process for returning to inherence in God. It's the reunion with God that's joyful. And when that reunion occurs, the pain resolves because its function has been served.

Chapter 86

140. Avoiding pain can also take other forms, such as changing the focus to your own experience or events in your past, focusing on the "positive" parts of the situation, and so on. For a fuller discussion of strategies for avoiding feeling, see the book *The Heart Path of Mary Magdalene* and "The Heart Path" video course.

141. This includes asking if the person wants to hear any advice you feel moved to give, because advice is a form of help. Ask first if someone wants to hear your advice, and only offer it if the answer is "yes."

142. The exception to this is with children or mentally incapacitated adults who you're responsible for. In these cases, it's your role to assume responsibility for them.

Chapter 90

143. To see a list of inner divine qualities, go to page 349 in the Appendix.

About the Author

MERCEDES KIRKEL is a multi-award-winning, bestselling author and channel for Mary Magdalene and Yeshua.

In the summer of 2010, Mary Magdalene began coming to Mercedes daily, giving extraordinary messages for humanity's evolution and spiritual growth. That was the birth of the first book of the Magdalene-Yeshua Teachings: *Mary Magdalene Beckons: Join the River of Love*.

Since then, Mary Magdalene and Yeshua have continued to communicate through Mercedes, delivering illuminating messages about the sacred partnership of the Divine Feminine and Masculine and guiding people in their spiritual development.

Based in New Mexico, Mercedes offers online and in-person courses and retreats. Her specialty is helping people deepen in understanding and living Mary Magdalene and Yeshua's teaching.

> Learn more about Mercedes and her work at:
> www.mercedeskirkel.com

Books and Videos by Mercedes Kirkel

THE MAGDALENE-YESHUA TEACHING BOOKS

Mary Magdalene Beckons: Join the River of Love

Magdalene Wisdom: The Voice of the Feminine

Dialogues with Yeshua and Mary Magdalene: The Journey to Love

The Holy Grail: Sacred Masculine & Divine Feminine

The Heart Path of Mary Magdalene: A Guide to Living from Your Heart

Sublime Union: A Woman's Sexual Odyssey Guided by Mary Magdalene

THE HEART PATH VIDEO COURSE

A video course of Mercedes coaching people in the Heart Path, using exercises and real-life demonstrations.

All available at: www.mercedeskirkel.com

www.ingramcontent.com/pod-product-compliance
Lightning Source LLC
LaVergne TN
LVHW010148070526
838199LV00062B/4288